What people are saying about

Hearing the Cloud

Hearing the Cloud guides us through the soundscapes of contemporary neoliberal capitalism, from chillstep to nightcore, and recaptures the possibilities of collective listening embedded within these musical forms. Emile Frankel traces a pattern recognition of our moment, poised between dystopian nihilism and the receding possibilities of utopia. Against irony, fragmentation, and chaos, *Hearing the Cloud* helps us hear the material presence of sound in our lives and the whispers of a better future.
Benjamin Noys, author of *Malign Velocities: Accelerationism and Capitalism*

Hearing the Cloud

Hearing the Cloud

Emile Frankel

Winchester, UK
Washington, USA

JOHN HUNT PUBLISHING

First published by Zero Books, 2019
Zero Books is an imprint of John Hunt Publishing Ltd., No. 3 East St., Alresford,
Hampshire SO24 9EE, UK
office@jhpbooks.com
www.johnhuntpublishing.com
www.zero-books.net

For distributor details and how to order please visit the 'Ordering' section on our website.

Text copyright: Emile Frankel 2018

ISBN: 978 1 78535 838 8
978 1 78535 839 5 (ebook)
Library of Congress Control Number: 2018953732

A CIP catalogue record for this book is available from the British Library.

Design: Stuart Davies

UK: Printed and bound by CPI Group (UK) Ltd, Croydon, CR0 4YY
US: Printed and bound by Thomson-Shore, 7300 West Joy Road, Dexter, MI 48130

We operate a distinctive and ethical publishing philosophy in
all areas of our business, from our global network of authors to
production and worldwide distribution.

Contents

For Julie and Boris

Part 1

Mackerel Sky

Mackerel Sky Prologue

Be careful what you're saying. Every word you speak is a geological event at the level of palate tectonics. Not a speech-act, but a seismic reverberation.
Mark Fisher, White Magic

This book considers music's role in constructing the future. In philosophies of horror and philosophies of salvation, the future is often presented as a space which can be changed by simply speaking about it. That is, by making a sound about it. Science-fiction on the page and on the screen is accompanied by the dangerous and exciting thought that this imaginative vision could become reality. In contrast, abstract music is rarely described as having speculative potential. At the heart of my writing is a belief in one of the most frequently said, romantic and love-filled statements concerning the act of hearing: 'this music changed me'. Often taken as either a soppy fiction, or an unexplainable surface feeling, this claim — that a collection of sounds can evoke change — is regarded throughout this book as a fundamental and important truth of all listening, and a truth which places music at the level of other speculative mediums. From this position, I pivot my analysis around a series of important and overtly future-oriented albums, as well as a broader discussion of club culture, internet-born genre and the most basic act of hearing an online comment, post, live-stream, voice and utterance.

What music reverberates as, changes those who hear it. Constructing a future society is achieved through large policy decisions and revolution and resolute action, but it is also nurtured through small and lithe and mundane interaction. Meaningful, habitual scrolls over breakfast, moving lyrics from earbuds, royalty-free music behind a vlog and the structured noise of daily life become causally chained together. Meek and innocent and vehement and caring voices which might have once been lost to the world are newly amplified by wires. Platform technologies, social media and streaming economics promote a future becoming where individual and disparate sounds are swollen and snow-balled carriers for political change. Shared online listening converts 'this sound changed me', to 'this sound changed *us*', and this is an equally beautiful and terrifying thing.

In a wired culture where to speak, to type, is encouraged as an indelible right of the individual, the conflict between communality and neoliberal individualism brims within the work of exploited creators at odds with an age of machine voices, invented identities, auto-playing playlists and the cursed economics of like-based sharing. The following question becomes paramount: how do we imagine the future from within a market-driven present?

The tensions of shared yet isolated listening, algorithmic profiling and the influence of platforms like Spotify and YouTube become central to my discussion of this question. In turn, this book deals with the following:

A dialogue between the act of making new music and the technological, environmental and political crises of today.
An analysis of the way platform capitalism mediates patterns in composition.
A rejection of transgression and irony as methods of critique.
A treatment of the smallest building blocks of music as political actors, that is, a claim that the decision to choose one material, structure or sound, over another, is a political act.
A confrontation with dystopian aesthetics.
An antidote consisting of honesty, play and care.
A dedication to the world we leave in fiction's wake.

The artists I discuss in this book project their aural visions towards near and far futures. As in all good sci-fi, they do so as a passing of judgement upon today. Within the modes of listening their work encourages — to the rarefied album, to the darkened room sound system, to the twitchings of a browser window — I've found inspiration and warning in the sound of a whispered voice, in the sound of bodies typing comments in near-unison, and in the sounds of online abuse and ironic self-deprecation. All of this music is in part representative of a heightened feeling of a world in transition and crisis. Due to the semantic limits of sound, these futures are conveyed in broad material descriptions. In the progressive club space, a movement from the past 5 or so years has revived images of cyberpunk and tech-driven hyper-capitalist dystopias. Indicative of our present conditions — of whistleblowers stealing state secrets on the back of a Lady Gaga CD, of mass surveillance, of hidden and disguised user-agreements — the mechanisms of technology are felt to be already out of control and already dystopian. In aesthetic responses to this state of reality, music becomes an important space of fantasy and desire.

Worryingly, the image of a cyber-nightmare has become more than a dark aesthetic to be revelled in. It now informs a range of new right-wing political movements. Incited by Silicon Valley futurism, a dystopian imagination is argued to *encourage* rather than warn of the future it predicts. While one person's hell is another's utopia, I use the term 'dystopia' to describe that distinctly hyper-capitalist, unconditional accelerationist, Alt-Right, ANCAP (Anarchist Capitalist), Neoreactionary (NRx) future fantasised from within the mesh of these online movements. In all, I confront the desire for a technologically *re-enchanted* world. The mainstream revival of dystopian Hollywood and AAA cyberpunk videogames speaks to an alienated generation who find agency in imagining a chaotic and violent world where neoliberal heroics can be enacted through keyboards. These longings, dominated by the haunted reverie of

4

peak turn-of-the-century capitalism, describe dreams of a male body made sacred, the augmented made hallow and the CEO rendered god-like.

Presenting a dark future in sound is often intended as a critical warning. Some works to be discussed in this book conceive of themselves as mirrors to be held up to our detrital world. By contrast, I also detail music which offers itself as a playful compassion-filled alternative. As dystopia (and utopia) increasingly appear less as an abstract 'nowhere' and instead as a tomorrow already seen to be in creation, speculative art becomes more important than ever. In an effort to encourage and call for a positive praxis in music, when I write in criticism I also write to praise honest and caring future world-building — those imaginative sonic creations which aim to escape the dominant realism of capital-driven speculation. My method of analysis moves between examples from the fiction-making internet; the embracing yet isolating experience of lying on your bed home alone listening to music you adore; and a detailed theorising of the forces and affecting structures which found internet-mediated politics. Despite what at times can be an alienating method, I hope that I am generous in my explanations, and clear in their assumed consequences.

Finally, what we say about music taints it. Words form a vital and political and sly cartilage around sound. In the daily struggle against an urge to let music *just* speak for itself, I found myself writing from a position of fear. To speak is to take on a responsibility for every new word and its orbit. But to keep those thoughts writhing up there and remain silent, tongue-tied over wordless feelings sound inspires, is to shore up an ugly suspicion that music should remain locked in the prism of an unspeakable future. In what I hope is a tender and respectful overcoming of this fear, this book can be read as both a celebration of a recent history of experimental sound practice, and as an appeal for artists to take responsibility for the future their music depicts.

i) Enchanted Materials

\>Be me
\>soft soul
\>working part time job in data centre
\>cleaning cooling system all day for a week
\>mainly dust, old pipes a little mouldy
\>Not too hard, good pay.
\>day 4 lying below the servers
\>no one around, few with security clearance
\>No one to talk to
\>Begin to speak to myself
\>Singing in the dearth
\>the sound of the fans and liquid tubes begin to get to me
\>Go home sleep
\>All I can hear are fans
\>dream windy, I'm by the ocean
\>next day at work I'm underneath a stack
\>blue light
\>server farms are my audience
\>blowing out a little melody
\>liquid tubes spraying cooling gel
\>Hear footsteps give me fright
\>Sit-up quick cracking my head on a glass tube. Goo starts
leaking into a stack
\>99999999 Identities getting fucked by the gel streaming into
the machine
\>lucky for backups though
\>Crawl out covered in cooling slime
\>boss is standing there
\>Tears in his eyes
\>Mouth moving
\>'You did good anon'

Listening is the reception of the animated character of air. All animations are anonymous in of themselves. All animations can bring tears to the eye. The substance around us is displaced by the propulsion of sound destined to disappear almost as soon as it is birthed. Hearing relies on the gap created where that air once moved. The afterglow, or the *trace* of its momentary presence, is the space of our interaction, the earthliness it leaves, a lingering which continues its affects indefinitely. The speaking body — be it mechanical movements of a tweeter and cone, a larynx or a word on a surface read and spoken internally — provides this propulsion and displacement of the air and meta-substance around us. When it's quiet, understanding takes place.

Yet words stay, and mediums for replaying soundings exist. Press the curled arrow. Interacting with these traces of online sound brings forth a cycle of re-interpretation and speculation. Cycles of obsolescence and renewal. Send upwards a message to the Cloud and later call, and keep calling until you are graced with a trickle from its data-permafrost. What once hardened from ink or into petroleum veins on a disc, is now *untraceably* mutable: the self, the Soundcloud track, the album. New scepticism, or fear, or extreme nihilism grips our hearing and reading: quavers can move between listens, words, thoughts, sonifications and their exact temporal significance flicker. Reordering occurs silently in the background, and in the space between animations, the quietness necessary for understanding shrinks.

Central to my writing is the work of political theorist Jane Bennett. In *The Enchantment of Modern Life,* Bennett describes her unique materialist position, one which rests on a listening to, and experiencing of all those lesser talked of political and agentic forces which vibrate and wriggle energetically around us.

An enchanted materialism embraces the possibility that differential degrees of agency reside in the intentional self, the inherited temperament of a self, a play-drive, molecules at far-from-equilibrium states, nonhuman animals, social movements, political states, architectural forms, families and other corporate bodies, sound fields.[1]

In a realised Andrew Breitbart, Cambridge Analytica reality, where culture becomes data points from the criminal acquisition of private messages between friends, and where culture takes the lead in changing politics: words and sounds, not *just* as signifiers, but as forceful blocks of association (as Spinoza would have it), become radically important. Taking up Bennett's descriptions of enchantment, I not only consider the building blocks of sound as compelling political actors, but I treat the Cloud itself as a potent, energy giving and denying material. In the first half of this book, my aim is to start a much-needed conversation around the political implications of deliberately structuring music in a *specific* way. That is, the politics of choosing one sound over another, of choosing one compositional method over another. Here I find guidance in Bennett's descriptions of an enchanted, vibrating and animated world. Her philosophy confirms a long-held assumption that music should be treated not just as representational, but as something alive and full of agency.

At the same time, I consider the online forum 'green-text story' (with which I opened), and memes and internet culture at large, as a series of compact packages of affect and association with clear political repercussions. Green-text stories are prevalent in parts of the internet favouring new right-wing politics, and they function as poetic carriers and modifiers of online culture. Although they are treated almost always as fictional by the community, in their spread they remain powerful indicators of a politics intended to transgress norms and uphold traditional conceptions of masculinity through ironic self-debasement. Moving through time rapidly towards a speculated finish, often a story will have a twist at the end. They call to being a reality which is assumed to be kinked, misshapen in some way. They fit into a culture of conspiracy, and of a world which is almost *wished* into a fucked-up-being — a world wished to be as depraved as the anonymous user who self-deprecatingly accosts their own bodily conditions. Enchantment is two-faced. For Bennett it straddles 'delight and disturbance'. For me, it also stands in for a broader type of ugly thinking. I consider enchantment in line with magical thinking, and I argue that in all its beauty, magical thought also gives agency to those new and angry voices in the Alt-Right which have worked themselves up into a false sense of disenfranchisement. This twist at the end of a green-text story confirms a world view where the earth and the future itself, not you, are wrong. When I talk of the political implications of structuring music, I look at a track as a compact poetic carrier of culture, and I use differing conceptions of the future to try and make obvious the speculative ramifications for thinking more broadly through the double-edged blade of enchantment.

Like Bennett, I also talk of enchanted material because the alternative — the discouragement of fictions and the image of 'dead matter', 'dead sound', 'dead digital ruins from the early 2000s', 'dead Myspace and Geocities' — incites instead fantasies of 'consumption and conquest'.[2] When we decide to mine the earth for rare metals, when we decide to use music to soundtrack an online vlog, and when we decide to structure our compositions around feelings of turmoil — the treatment of sound, material, structure and the internet as *inanimate* denies a much-needed ethical consideration. Enchanted materialism not only levels the hierarchies between human and non-human, but it provokes moral and political contemplation in the basic act of making music. I want to make clear that the treatment of composition as something magical, enchanting and alive is all done in the service of encouraging the link between material and agency.

With this in mind, it is important to briefly discuss what I mean by that space known as the Cloud. Today in name alone, the Cloud functions almost interchangeably with 'the internet'. As a now indispensable utility for storing data remotely, and for accessing computing power invisibly, cloud services from Amazon and Google are the infrastructure which sustain the web. As a set of physical objects, that ephemeral non-space we call cloud-computing hides the truth of its existence: rows and rows of ionised shelves for spinning discs and solid-state drives, buried deep below the soil, providing computing power from the electrical runoff from the burning of the earth. In the linkage between hardware and software, the Cloud moves information, computes questions it is asked, and stabilises the fragmented spheres of online life. It is a machine in the most Marxian description: a housing of fervent interconnectedness, human life stored in objectified metal, and labour disguised behind a veil. For Marx, a machine is not simply a technical apparatus of iron and wood and gears and tooth-lined axes. It is the connection of metal, *and* a human labouring body, *and* the body which lashes relations of power through a clip-board-contract onto the labourer, *and* another human mind which provides the knowledge to piece together the metal and wood into a moving object.[3] In this sense, the machine, the Cloud, like an external organ of an assemblage of human brains and objectified knowledge, becomes more than a utility.

To enchant the world with words and sounds, we rely on cogent metaphors. Perhaps the Cloud is the most famous metaphor of the new century. In the late 90s when software patents began employing more and more protuberant lines and cloud-like illustrations, the idea that a network would be conceived of from within the earth was replaced with an important skyward allusion. To overcome that fearful consumer leap (having your information managed by an alien *other*) the simple act of *accessing something elsewhere* required the fluffiness, softness and safety of the sky. Elsewhere is imagined to be better than here; than now.

What's more, cloud watching has always been a metaphorical act. Searching for patterns above us is its own lost art. Today, for many of us, we have the luxury to just look at the sky and wonder: lying on the grass, peering up and finding a fluffiness which never *just* looks like a weather pattern. Shapes in the fluff: a loved-one's cadaveric face; a glimmering non-city; a *Farmville* Reward Crate; the shape of a beautiful stack of GTX 1080s in a crypto-mining rig. Lie on the grass and hold up your wrist to glimpse that sleek weather widget. Another scorcher! 45 degrees Celsius. Accuweather.com relies on cloud-computing to host its servers and troves of data. Yet in its ubiquity and accuracy as a weather tool, it undermines the origins of weather watching and the subtleties of looking to the sky and attempting to speculate. Through the cycles of storing and calling forth data, cloud services are not just profoundly future oriented, but they become the holding pen for oracular sets of data which support the implementation of new abuses of power. In this, the very utility takes on the mixed metaphor of atmospheric cloudiness. A weather widget in the palm further alienates us from that ancient parsing of the closeness of rain from patterns in the ultramarine. Invisible and external data services maintain and become the platform for further oppressions.

Like the sky, sound too has always been talked of in metaphor. The para-language of music has remained steadfast even after the great Enlightenment's de-mystification of sound as animated waves in the air. In what follows, *Hearing the Cloud* is thus also metaphorical. Often there isn't a sound to listen for. Hearing stands in for experiencing. The internal sound of experiencing. The living through of what is stored within those buried data-centres. And most importantly, this hearing is the experiencing of, and passing judgement upon a two-faced network: one which supports both the exquisite creation of new and profound art, while simultaneously maintaining the oppressive systems of today, and thus the slow cancellation of a post-capitalist tomorrow.

Many readings of Marx's 1857-58 *Grundrisse* locate hope in a future liberated by technology. Progress is seen as a liberating force to disrupt the foundations of capitalist social and productive labour. At a climatic point in his notebook, Marx even infers that machines will produce 'the material conditions to blow this foundation sky-high'.[4] However, from my vantage point writing in 2018, Marx in many ways appears to have been more accurate in metaphor than in physical truth. Our material conditions may indeed be found to have been blown skyward. Up there, the Cloud dictates more and more of the labour and material conditions of the earth. Yet sadly, at the heart of its economic exchanges remain modified versions of those first developed in nineteenth-century capitalism. The Cloud still positions us as born Robinson Crusoes: individual instances of 'Economic Man' operating in the market; death-bringers of our own existence.

While the foundations of our capitalist system are still maintained as a kind of brittle yet invisible mould, scientific progress has worked a few new things into the setting. Information as a commodity disrupts traditional labour-time, and machines, as non-human actors, live within other machines in these great underground data-centres. But most dramatically, the mainstream emergence of blockchain technologies also gives hope for a different set of economic interactions. Even the basic processes of cloud-computing are in the midst of an update. Companies like *Storj* draw new diagrams where dotted lines pass beneath the sky from user to user in an updated meshnet. Storage as a utility could soon be decentralised. Nevertheless, despite the efforts to work changes into the system, it remains to be seen whether new technologies and culture in the Cloud will continue to be governed by the same structures. Non-human to non-human interaction continues to bleed some and prosper others, and online culture grows and morphs plied by the interactions of invented identities, invented voices communicating endlessly in its comment sections. Perhaps for Marx, this would have been the most revolutionarily promising, and equally frightening attribute of the Cloud: a complete and pervasive future uncertainty. Crisis manifested in the new instability of truth.

Isolated and alone with your device, when a sound projects outward into the air, it's sucked up, not only by the ear, but by a quivering piece of machinery which feeds its captured waveform across continents and deep below the soil. The trace of its momentary presence attains new permanence, but the understanding we might have gained from it continually mutates through new mediums and forces of consumption. Listening changes. Reading a written vocalisation online changes. Understanding now lies in that memory of our first listen, and in that future point when we may finally click replay on the track, or refresh on the forum thread, and call it down anew.

A means or a medium, the trace is first and foremost our fragile link with the *certain place* where the sonorous *was* and the certain place whence it may be *brought forth* once again.[5]

In the Cloud, what once *was*, rarely is. An opaque revenant: the future coils around these traces, it distils them. Drink the solution and a relentless uncertainty takes hold. Magical thinking of all kinds sets in.

ii) Malediction

Can music be a curse?

What happens when we 'speak badly' of the future?
Do we commit the future to that which we say of it?
Does the future causally come into being through the act of talking about it?

Can fiction influence future-politics?
Can abstract expression be a form of concrete story-telling?
Does it matter if your artistic dystopia is ironic or sincere?
Does the future even care if we were once ironic or sincere?
Can ironic dystopias bring about actual dystopias?
By creating dystopian music are we uttering a 'malediction', a magical jinx?

Or, is it that speaking badly is a form of protection?
Or, is it that dystopian art is a reflection and a warning?
Or, is it that aesthetic honesty, play and compassion deny dystopia?

iii) Honesty

Music absorbs the atmosphere and materialism of the forces of wider society. In commercial visions of tomorrow, capital's unhinged desires are revealed, and consumer want is projected afar. In future-oriented music these desires and material obsessions instead become metaphors. Music without words functions as an alembic, as something that distils the vibe of wider culture and politics into a sonic material functioning in part as representation, and in part as an actual embodiment of these condensed tones. To perceive of recent online politics (in its enormity and flickering movements which bleed offline) we require the same listening mindset: a feeling-out of a wider and more ambiguous atmosphere, rather than an analysis of singular events. Music's interdisciplinary relations and affects cross spaces from gallery to club to cinema to private listening space. And it is in this private listening that I find the most significant reason to talk of future politics through music. Plugged into headphones at home or on the train, music becomes the base and the supplementing art of cloud-platforms. Content employs music. Music is streaming into oracular ears throughout all battery-powered and virtual space. And because music requires us to talk of it through comparison, it represents in a heightened and distilled state, those convoluted effects of future speculation.

In much of the music to be discussed, there is a condensed and prevailing 'darkness' within the aesthetic. In reaction to times of crisis; crisis filters into the work. A common future vision has become one in which humanity or the earth itself has descended into turmoil. Some future visions express crisis less as warning, and more as a state of being to be revelled in. Dystopian novels can often be accused of doing the same. Despite all of William Gibson's current and public left-wing politics, his fictional writing from the 80s has inspired in some, a deep *want* for that exact hyper-capitalist future he warned us of. In the same way, dystopian club music has its own problematic set of relations with the passing of time. Performed in venues built upon a legacy of dystopian desires and hedonistic nihilism, the club space has the aggressive ability to negate many outside politics of togetherness.

In contrast, utopianism is often seen as either naïve, or self-undermining. In *Radical Happiness*, Lynne Segal, quoting Fredric Jameson, explains: 'utopias have something to do with failure and tell us more about our own limits and weaknesses than they do about future societies'. Where I question dark and dystopian aesthetics, I don't encourage an all-encompassing cheeriness as a necessary alternative. But at the same time, I don't shy away from believing in the potential for a different kind of optimistic and vital future envisioning. Or perhaps the potential for a sonic utopianism. On this, Jameson describes what is often forgotten: the utopian work has value in 'its capacity to generate new ones'.[6]

When I question dystopian art, I question the politics which has inspired its creation. I lament the lack of honesty, care and most importantly, the lack of future imagination found in these works. Imagination can be a form of enchantment. To imagine a together future is to witness a disenchanted world, to be honest and descriptive of it, and then to perform the difficult task of exiting the present entirely. It is to show an outside. This is a form of magic. In the making fiction out of affect and atmosphere, music can imbue the future with new possibility. Despite my love of deconstructed club music, even my love of many dystopian albums which have touched me in different inexplicable ways, I try not to give up on this prior utopian thought.

Unlike sincerity, honesty is not the opposite of deceit or hypocrisy. One can be honest in one's hypocritical faults. It may also be possible to honestly believe in dystopia. Yet, to make an honest work of art requires a radical flattening of hierarchies between creator and listener. To be honest is to consider yourself as part of something shared and common. Honesty infers a morality. Honest humour is playful and joyous. It fights against the destructive tendencies of irony. Honesty is showing fear, when fearful. Dystopia cannot be revelled in, if one is fearful of it.

* * *

Depending on your circumstance, it can be either life-saving, or a worrying sign when clouds appear which look like a school of dotted fish. A 'mackerel sky' is one of the most noticeable and famous cloud formations because so many have historically survived upon its recognition. As the old saying goes, *mackerel sky, not 24 hours dry*. Rain will surely come.

Like cloud watching, Part 1 of this book looks at musical form and structure as an act of speculation. As the section title suggests, the hope or fear for the near future — rain or sun — is my entrance point for a discussion of those basic underlying forces which support and inspire musical speculation, and broader internet culture. Chapter 1, *Sweet Music*, considers the most prevalent online sounds, and the platform technologies which mediate their creation. Here, royalty-free music contextualises my diagnosis of internet culture. In *Enchantment can be Formalised* I discuss compositional methods which strive to encourage an unreal world. This chapter confronts magical thinking, the instrumentalisation of apophenia (the tendency to perceive meaningful patterns in random data), and machine-learning through a historical tracing of algorithmic music. Numbered reason, chaos and stochastic process are all discussed in turn. Chapter 3: *Revenant Speed: Spirits of the Singularity*, engages with 90s cyberculture and club music, Accelerationism and Silicon Valley Digitalism. This is a chapter tangled in the spiritual and double-edged thought which technology inspires within us. The conclusion to the chapter is called *Exit Music*, and within it I praise music which shows us an outside to our current predicaments.

Part 2: *Flooded World takes* the first half of this book as scaffolding, and considers a range of sonic materials, and their associated political ramifications. If Part 1 is a study of machinic and technological near-futures, Part 2 is an investigation into a future Earth, made either inhuman, alien or devoid of life. I discuss liquid and oil as a dominant sonic material in experimental electronic music. I look at child-like vocalisations in Nightcore, bodily fluids in transgressive music and the prevalence of chimeric bodies in these imaginaries. I conclude the book with an analysis of the struggle between irony, honesty, performative reflection and hammer-like criticism.

Present in these pages is both a labour of writing and a labour of listening. When this book isn't about music, it is about that more ambiguous quality of being: the ceaseless state of our listening bodies. As Seth Kim-Cohen exclaims, 'ears don't blink!'[7] When I'm online, when you're online, we are always listening. To hear the Cloud, and to make music which comments upon its technologies and potential futures is to labour with one's ears and eyes. Listening to the Cloud is an equally disturbing and heartening process.

I title this book as a small gesture towards those past musical writings made in allusion to forces of nature and technology: namely, David Toop's *Ocean of Noise*, and Kdwo Eshun's *More Brilliant than the Sun*. In this cannon, writers and musicians have tried to capture a period of contemporary music practice through a distinct immersion in the para-language of their present conditions. Theirs too is a labour I hope to build upon.

As is hopefully becoming clear, the basic processes of this book and my method rely on comparison. Throughout I call music many things: sweet, oily, abject, hollow, dark, light, dystopian, utopian, ethereal. The fact that music could be sweet, that music can be like an oil, that these sounds are like intricate machinery, or like the pus from a leaking wound — are all different evocations of my politics. What links them is the belief that sound shouldn't be understood as existing in an abstract place, or in a purely physical manner, a belief that in fact this is the most dangerous form of listening. Instead sound should be described by comparison, it should be connected to the world and to the politics of today.

Chapter 1

Sweet Music

All over the earth when it's dawn, flying creatures chirp sweetly in the branches. This sound of day-dwellers awaking is defined in many cultures as a distinctly sweet beauty. Bird vocalisations, and the sounds and products of the sky are joyous and hopeful. When it should be light but it is not — in an eclipse of the sun, or in the smog of a newly industrialised city — a lack of chirps informs an associated fear. This silent malaise of the biome above us, and its inverse, a healthy sky full of sounds, emphasises the psychopathological importance of sweetness. In certain musical histories, the human voice sounding like a bird, sounding sweet, has been the preeminent compliment. *Amazing grace, how sweet the sound. Beloved one; pleasing to the mind and senses; one in a sound or wholesome state; and, of water, fresh, not salt.*

Yet sweetness is also a hollow adjective. Sweet substances provide short-term satisfactions. During the forward assemblage of 70s capitalist mass-production, the chemically-processed food revolution claimed sweetness as the era's greatest product. The ability to turn the starched remains of a corn harvest into something disguised as edible, redefined the Western diet and narrowed it incredibly. Addictive, short burst energy content was a consumerist revelation — the affect and taste of molecular built-in-obsolescence. However, in recent years, and in part due to the new and expanding health-food market, sweetness has become characterised as a false seduction: a fattener and an ugly desire. The now common pairing with the adverb 'sickly' speaks to this. In what can be seen as a conflicting carrier of mood and neoliberal politics, I introduce sweetness to comment on the basic relationship between ideology and the equally conflicting forces of emotion and taste within abstract music. In concrete terms, I want to discuss the way the affect of a sound can be distorted by changing technologies, and instrumentalised by new economics of listening. And in more abstract terms, I write to describe the potential for music to affect us, and through this, the way it might help support or resist hegemony. In the space of a now thoroughly neoliberal internet, that link between mood and ideology becomes essential for understanding descriptions of the future.

When it's dark, my device lights up and softens everything. Long-looking at a rectangle of glass,

I search on YouTube: 'Sweet Music'.

A figure appears on screen. She's dressed in stripes.

Standing alone in her family's lounge-room she holds a plastic microphone in one hand. Her living space is intricately decorated and colour co-ordinated. Gold teddy-bears wearing matching t-shirts rest against a drape. What might appear as a crude green-screen — or transformative attempt to turn a space into the high production set of a pop music video — is instead lovingly hand made. Each item is placed carefully. A tablet rests in the corner displaying a giant rotating CD icon. And the curtain which surrounds the room — distancing it from daily life — is made from the same material as her dress: zebra print. Each camouflage the other with a black and white flourish.

She can almost disappear into the background.

Her name is 'Sweet Music Lady' and she uploads hundreds of videos a year singing covers of her favourite music, alone in her decorated living room.

This time she's performing 'Only Hope' by Mandy Moore. Digital strings from a royalty-free karaoke version accompany her surprisingly beautiful voice:

There's a song that's inside of my soul

It's the one that I've tried to write over and over again
I'm awake in the infinite cold
But you sing to me over and over again

So I lay my head back down
And I lift my hands
And I pray to be only yours
I pray to be only yours
I know now you're my only hope.

Sweet Music Lady's performance is deeply moving. After singing those final words the video cuts to a series of still images of her posing dramatically for the camera. Digital lights from an invisible paparazzi flash. Accompanying the pictures are the sounds of a fake audience screaming and applauding — chanting for an encore.

MUSIC gives me happiness. SINGING is my FASHION.

My passion in life is SINGING. Most members of my family love to sing too. I guess we started singing before we even learned to speak. I dream of recording my own CD. A grand dream; yes it is, that I would like to fulfil! I also want my own music room in my house where I can sing at the top of my voice.

IF you don't like me then don't watch my videos. I am what I am. I'm not changing for anyone. Like me dislike me that's your choice. I came to YOUTUBE to post my videos, if you can't say anything good then don't talk at all. If you don't like my videos it's ok no problem just leave my page...[1]

Ever since my closest friend, artist Alice dos Reis, showed me Sweet Music Lady's YouTube channel, I've associated this singing with that unknown yet assumed-to-be-present side of the internet where intimacy, sincerity and 'sweetness' occupies the space for an increasingly hollow web. Sweet Music Lady's 'Only Hope' karaoke cover has 38 views. Almost all of her videos slip into that expanding backwater of unwatched and *invisible* YouTube content. By online standards, 38 views may as well be unseen. Among the few unique spectators, human and bot, Sweet Music Lady's continual perseverance to share her voice to the empty echo chamber, year after year, strikes me as surprisingly utopian.

In Diedrich Diederichsen's essay *Music-Immateriality-Value*, he describes the act of creating a sounding for oneself as possibly the most utopian form of production:

> There are things that die as they are used, and their description is usually couched in utopian metaphors. A famous example is the life of birds, which…'neither sow nor reap nor gather into barns and yet are fed.' The same is true of the land of milk and honey, where things appear on the table, as they are needed, without any labor of storage or preparation… It is not we ourselves who produce all these things for our immediate use and consumption…but other instances and authorities of an enchanted world: the gods, a magic spell, or nature. Alongside this, music's basic situation becomes even more utopian. I pick up a musical instrument and produce a sequence of tones. These tones enchant my surroundings and me as I produce them. At some point I grow tired, the tones cease, and the enchantment passes. What I produced has vanished without a trace; it created no value – nor, however, did it depend on a providential nature and the miracles of the land…It was me. I myself, using my talents and abilities.[2]

Of course, Diederichsen's imagined scenario — a sequence of tones played for one's own ear — does leave a *trace*. After the animation of the air, the sounding continues to inform those who heard it throughout the infinite length of its new absence. Romantic as it is, what is produced has value not just in the moment of its hearing. In our post-NSA dataculture, a new aphorism and materialisation is often said: *what is once online may never die*. And the void which supplies the trace with its interpretative agency can be crossed by simply re-accessing the original media. When Sweet Music Lady sings to an inanimate room populated by children's toys and a standard definition webcam, the exchange value stays alive in that captured trace of her performance. In this case, her voice performs a contradictory exchange: on the one hand deeply utopian in its sincerity and openness to be shared (coin-free for the listener), and on the other, an act which has all its value situated in the amount of spread it achieves online. While many artists claim they make music only for themselves, yet secretly wish to be discovered, here this once-hidden desire is externalised in the very medium of YouTube. Behind the clicks which appear free in their transaction, the viewer exchanges their ability to listen to music and consume for their openness to be advertised through, to be character-profiled and to have their mood manipulated. For the artist, they exchange what could be a utopian act of sharing music worldwide without the expectation of a transaction (what could be sweet), for a hollowness which rests in the algorithm-supplied-chance that your video and music could be amplified virally.

Underlying every Sweet Music Lady video is the tacit assumption that Sweet Music Lady performs only to be heard and discovered. Here however, the un-spread, unseen video, an *Only Hope* karaoke cover, disguises the intention behind the music. What if a thing is made to be shared and viewed by the other; but is never found? Does this, in total isolation, imbue the art with a utopian value? Is this truly the sweetest act — sharing but never finding an ear to share to? Tech writer Kevin Kelly claims: 'To find something is the same as making it. To make something is the same as finding it.'[3] This resounds for interactions in the Cloud. You find an obscure YouTube channel and you feel as if you've made an 'object of art' for yourself. In its rarity, the media appears somewhere between reality and the virtual — its discovery is almost as embodied in the movements of the keyboard and mouse as it is in the screen and the geological location of the media itself. And it feels as if it is for you alone — that your virtual movements have dug it out of the earth.

In this chapter, that feeling facilitated by clever technology, of isolated personalised online discovery, becomes the mediator for an important set of dominant moods and affects. Like a perpetual archaeology of the self, the internet facilitates ideology through the ambient effects of browsing, scrolling, finding and experiencing in encouraged apolitical states of mind. What's more, in both the act of creating and uploading, and the act of viewing and searching, platforms like YouTube function as clear carriers for what could be considered an *everyday aesthetic speculation*. YouTube encourages (through categories, trending playlists and sponsored content) the creation of very-near-future-oriented work. As a music maker (with the unspoken assumption that you want your music to be found and spread) the platform's algorithmic influence on taste mediates your future creative decision-making processes. Aesthetics equate more than ever with a selfhood and identity defined by success (views) and aesthetics, as block expressions of economic speculation become clearly externalised in all once sweet acts. With the camera rolling, and in that moment of choosing to play a sounding for oneself, it is harder than ever to ignore that little trending flame icon in the sidebar.

Sweet Music Lady sings to a royalty-free modified version of *Only Hope*, in this, and through a discussion of the phenomenon of royalty-free music, I hope to provide a contextualisation for this book via a suitably fast-paced entrance into the dominant feelings of living through the Cloud. On the surface, royalty-free music fits into a communal world view of music as a universal, 'free' and shareable material. But underneath, its heightened commercialism and life-cycles tied to market forces makes this music an excellent carrier and expression of neoliberal ideology. While in ignorance, there is still a profound and beautiful honesty in this musical creation, I am conflicted by this honesty. Thus, in the always sincere, embracing and assiduous voice of Sweet Music Lady, I want to introduce a series of anomalous forces and structures which act within all my subsequent discussions of making and listening. In the politics of her expression, the online platforms we submit to live by held within her voice, and the spirit hidden within those spaces made near invisible in the Cloud, the fundamental question arises: how do we imagine a future in sound, when we listen from within the reality of a market-driven present?

i) Atmospheres for Content

Sianne Ngai's ground-breaking study of affect, *Ugly Feelings*, makes the important claim that tone can represent ideology. This often taken-for-granted assumption underlies most of the perceived relationships between art and political praxis, as well as between material and an intuited agency. When abstract art 'acts', it is understood to do so always through a representative relationship between work and world. But perhaps this relationship should be instead understood as an act of embodiment. Defining 'tone' in a literary work as an 'attitude', 'affective bearing' or 'orientation' the text conveys between its audience and the world, Ngai writes: 'to speak of tone is thus to generalize, totalize, and abstract the "world" of the literary object, in a way that seems particularly conductive to the analysis of ideology'.[4] Ngai makes an important connection: ideology, particularly that of neoliberalism, appears to us obscured and disguised, not simply as a straight-forward political doctrine relating to conservative or progressive views, but rather as a more generalised atmosphere which seeps into many facets of social life. Neoliberalism — that which promotes a privatised *limitless* body and self, and that which frequently decouples itself from political parties — is more than the sum of its distinct free-market policies. It functions as a tonal influencer, and as a collection of feelings which inspire our social interactions, consuming habits, dreams and desires.

Broadening Ngai's analysis of literature to function for all creative practice, tone can be conceived as that lingering imaginative landscape left in the wake of a seeing or hearing. That is, the tonal 'world' of a piece is found in the dense atmosphere or *vibe* we so experience: all the plethora of object to object relationships, and their lasting phenomena contained in our fading memory. A collection of tones forms a mood, and in music, mood is always experienced in excess of a series of individual rhythms and pitches. Mood is an atmosphere. Like ideology, which is itself a distilling of the vibe or atmosphere of wider socio-political actants, music can be conceived to affect us based on a condensing of these exact same forces. My metaphor of a material agency in music akin to the processes of an alchemical alembic could be said to also apply to politics. In both music and politics, the materially embodied representation of a set of real and serious daily conditions is found chemically distilled into the by-products of ideology and tone. From these same origins music becomes *more* than a representation of a politics, it instead begins to function as a space of ideological embodiment. Oppressions, violences, injustices, pleasures, excitements and longings compete within our reading of our own moods, the individual tones of wider society, and the sounds we listen to. In the present, they appear to us as a series of disparate events, but in the past and the future they become an obscuring mesh, one in need of analysis.

One of the primary qualities of listening to and hearing the Cloud is the continual living through and discovering of atmospheres of both real and hollow sweetness. The everyday content we interact with is full of music. The most common online sounds are found behind video memes, cute animal compilations, auto-playing advertisements and 'royalty-free' music for vlogs and live-streams. 'Content Creators' on YouTube, Twitch and popular Facebook groups plumb the internet and their lives for source material. This material — a joke, an image, a 140-character phrase — becomes an essential commodity. Creators struggle to rip the day-to-day existence of life out of the mundane and into something readily ingestible, uplifting or meaningful. And in a pessimistic reading of today, not much differentiates any personal interaction from content to be consumed. Following from a now cornerstone of media theory — 'the personal is geopolitical' — the personal is also content in its most volatile and tasty form. Consider a FB post between friends: material repackaged on Reddit to be laughed at. And consider your speaking voice in the home as salient content picked up by the always-on-microphone accessed by FB's Messenger app — ready to be analysed into tailor made advertisements. In the once anonymous crowd of a disaster, your body is now zoomed in and consumed on conspiracy forums: expressions, faces and limbs as content found in the flying bodies of humans moved and crushed through the force of a speeding vehicle. Sadly, this capitalist de/re-coding isn't anything new. The processes of repackaging alienated-life have simply accelerated since the era of the supermarket. Instead, my concern is the extended prevalence of music as an enhanced *supplier* of 'mood', placed behind all this repackaging. An atmosphere for content.

> Good content isn't 'viral' but psychopathological. Not an infection but a complex with roots in the viewer's soul.[5]

Content requires music. The value of good content is ruled by a doctrine of *vibe* and mood: *it's all about that sweet vibe*. The basic inter-media phenomenon of music and text or image is that music can enhance whatever it is placed beneath. Even joyous music placed underneath a devastatingly sorrowful video only serves to heighten the sorrow through its dissonant juxtaposition. Through this, music supplies mood. There is rarely a silence in the output of YouTube's most popular daily vloggers. Sound accompanies all mundane acts, and in the enormity and frequency of their uploaded quantity, new music is needed to fill the void. In my research, I believe that we are nearing a threshold where the majority of new music made today is not only anonymously released under pseudonym, but intentionally created to be used and spread 'royalty-free'.

* * *

Royalty-free music, as one of the Cloud's most hollow inventions, has flourished since the implementation of copyright protection algorithms. 'CONTENT ID', developed by YouTube in 2007, was one of the first large-scale attempts (independent of national government) to police the internet. It was remarkably successful, inspiring other websites to employ similar methods of machine-assisted silencing. In its wake, YouTube became a graveyard of muted infringing videos. Creators suddenly found their content vibe-less, and in the silence an entirely new economy emerged to replace what was once a space dominated by regular chart-topping pop music. This new economy functions on ad-revenue and platform subscription. Each play of a video, or stream of a song, earns the creator an exploitatively small amount of money. Instead of being traditionally sold, music created without copyright is instead spread widely in the hopes that through sheer volume of plays alone, it will earn the creator a basic income. What has ensued is the proliferation of anonymous musicians churning out music as quickly as possible, informed by the new conditions of streaming survival. The anonymity of the production process is essential to disassociate low-quality work from artistic legacy. In turn, the phenomenon grows through the availability of software purpose-built for speedy music making. It's not all bad though. By proxy, royalty-free music can support vulnerable creators in low-income countries, and through its speed and endless cycles of change we are graced with the sped-up emergence and death of new and unique musical structures, materials and the genres they support.

As the millennial equivalent of Muzak, today royalty-free music, in quantity, eclipses copyrighted music. In a network supported by hundreds-of-millions of subscribers, popular channels for royalty-free music include: 'NoCopyrightSounds', 'Audio-Library - No Copyright Music', 'Music for Creators', and one of the most prolific of all, 'Amazing Gaming Music'. In what appears at odds with traditional understandings of popular music markets, these channels actually de-emphasise the artist behind the song, choosing to largely ignore the financial potential once found in the platforming of an individual pop star. Spotify, Twitch, YouTube's 24-hour radio stations and auto-playing playlists intentionally hide information from listeners, relegating artist name, album and record label to obscured corners and functions of the interface. Here instead, a bizarrely meritocratic exchange occurs (one we should be wary of). When you submit music to a royalty-free channel, on the surface, identity and fame are secondary, all that is perceived to matter is the affect-inducing qualities of your music. Successful moods rule. Stimulating moods rule.

The word 'sweet' takes on another meaning: '*Sweet man, nice track dude.*' The lads of electronic dance music (EDM), Steve Aoki and Skrillex (who each have their own money-making royalty-free channels), have used their personal success to promote the new streaming world order. A new generation of bedroom music makers craft upbeat, speedy music of ebbs and tremors, of serotonin rushes and stagnations, marketed surprisingly towards the *background* rather than the foreground. Curated with specific moods in mind, categories like: bright, calm, happy, inspirational, funky, dramatic and sad, coexist with expansive and poly-vital sub-genres. Famous fusions of genre include: 'Glitch-Hop', 'Chillstep', 'Liquid Funk', 'Future Garage' and my favourite, 'Complextro'. The sweet track can be chill or lively, mysterious or sullen — almost like personality traits in Smurfs. Confusing subtitles like: 'Best Epic Relax Chillstep Music: Music for Studying', not only inform their neoliberal tinged purpose, but also speak to a disturbing reality where search engine 'like-button economics' mediate the direction of new creation. Trends and quick cycles of replication dominate expression. By far the most successful of these royalty-free genres is Chillstep. That which would normally be calming is newly instrumentalised to maintain focus with beat driven elements. I see it as the extrapolation of a Nootropics chemical enhancement culture: *the perfect stack of musical substances to make you relaxed but alert.*

Twitch (owned by Amazon) is the second most popular dedicated video streaming platform. Like YouTube, it is also illegal for content creators to play copyrighted music. As a solution, 'Twitch Music', co-run by Steve Aoki, not only employs an algorithm to identify and mute copyrighted music, but goes one step further. Disturbingly, the algorithm actually actively *collects* music which is identified as being copyright free. This music is then catalogued and made available for all streamers to access and include behind their content. Alarmingly, in machine-hearing and identification, a world emerges where even music made with non-consumerist intentions can be rigorously hunted out and assimilated into consumer culture. The music section of the website currently focuses on EDM, and it markets itself as an enticing space for new music makers. This genre emphasis places Twitch in a bizarrely powerful position to influence taste. As a platform famous for the live-streaming of videogames, the most popular gaming channels have historically and continue to be cyclical competitive ones. *Fortnite, PUB, Overwatch* and *Counterstrike* consist mostly of individuals fighting to the death (in what is called a *Battle Royale*) within a narrow and endlessly repeating series of battlegrounds. With streamers often broadcasting for an entire working day, music is given an even more important role in providing and maintaining mood in the monotony of the endlessly repeating game map. 'Best Epic Relax Chillstep Music for Streaming' and an emphasis in that grey energy genre, EDM, becomes somehow more understandable.

Charting these dominant, albeit stereotyped qualities, two moods stand out: chill and epic. After Ngai's *Ugly Feelings*, her follow-up book, *Our Aesthetic Categories: Zany, Cute, Interesting,* attempts to capture today's dominant affects and what they entail. However, I'd suggest two other categories: *chill* and *epic.* Videogames have long shared narratives inherited from the Hollywood Epic. Replete with heroes and villains, world-saving and world-destroying quests and journeys, AAA games are often pure expressions of neoliberal limitlessness. The Epic has always been profoundly masculine, and *chillness* partly comes from the laid-back and desirable chill *dude.* The Epic purports an ideology where the human can transcend body and world to either save or destroy. Evolved from its past inference of heroism in the grandest most prophetic sense, today, the adjective 'epic' simply denotes a vague positive attribute to any bland noun. 'Chillness' and 'epicness' both eschew political drives. They are atmospheres which homogenise tones into a kind of beige apolitical middle-ground. Here mood becomes disassociated from feeling, and instead chained to activity, not in a Heideggarian being-in-the-world sense, rather a *liveliness* measured in relation to cultural norms of success and participation. While Ngai argues that ugly feelings remain agentic, I'd say epicness and chillness, as affects, end up flattening all they subsume — instead *denying* agency. In fact, what appear as opposites, chillness can also apparently be epic. Listen to this 'Epic Chillstep 2015 Collection [2 Hours]'[6] video and you'll experience the commingling of equally ambivalent tones.

What is occurring is a cyclical phenomenon of creation, listening, re-creation and homogenisation. Platforms like Twitch and YouTube interconnect music makers with consumers. Listen to some 'Glitch-Hop' online, and you are often immediately recommended a video tutorial teaching you how to make the exact style of music you were just listening to. The new ease and accessibility of music software like Ableton, commingles with the economic incentives to create music tutorial videos for ad-revenue. One can easily find hundreds of tutorials on YouTube for almost all of these sub-genres. Thus, the sonic intricacies of the music become explainable, and easily replicable. Original techniques of style are no longer kept secret and hoarded, instead, originality in technique translates to a profitable new tutorial video. Music making, and its required knowledge, should be egalitarian, but these market-mediated cycles promote a flattening of style. The creative knowledge required to make a unique genre of music is only shared when blocks of musical material have proved to be popular. Through this cyclical pairing off, the recommended video algorithm influences the act of creation. You begin to hear the medium. This direct link between creator and a potential future-creator not only promotes the categorisation of sub-genre and classification, but it dramatically regulates our listening environment. These categories of variance inform a homogenised music making process, where taste becomes data points, and the elements of music (texture, harmony, melody and rhythm) become *sweet* rhythmic groupings, *sweet* tones, chill or epic harmonies.

Within each of the plethora of genres found on royalty-free channels, the music is therefore very similar. Aside from consisting of structural and material additive fusions of each other, most genres become mediated in near identical ways by the trends of broader ever-changing tastes (and the constricted knowledge shared in tutorial videos). In subsequent chapters, I will give a detailed analysis of some of these dominant compositional structures. To signpost them here, a few sonic materials have become commonplace: a reliance on solid and attention-grabbing lead synth; a side-chaining of beats and other musical elements to create clear edges in the spectrum with defined musical and textural borders; and a compressed dynamic range in support of an ever-present tactility. This is music which speaks to the same distortion-free 60 frames per second smoothness of the games it accompanies. A sonic imaginary dominated by both bubble-gum environments and demonic fantasy inspires metal-guitar-esque stadium lead electro, arch narratives and golden mean climaxes. The soundtracks of videogames have historically had a profound influence on outside genres of music. However today, the mood of royalty-free music actually reverses the direction of influence, turning its energy and character back upon the creation of future games. A masculine, energy dependent culture promotes sweet music in support of an increasingly tiring day-to-day existence where alertness and energy are blessed.

The simple concept of an auto-playing playlist of music promotes quantity over quality. It's in the word 'auto': once it starts it doesn't stop. When using a free Spotify account with Google Home, I was alarmed to find that I couldn't even choose an exact song to listen to — the only agency I possessed was to choose a mood or style. And the playlist ticked on. Here the economics of creation — speed and quantity — favour music which can be algorithmically reconfigured again and again based on the same compositional material. Identical beats or melodies can exist anew when combined at different tempos or with different components. This is additive composition. A chill melody and beat becomes epic when sped-up. With one quick change of parameter the creator has two money earning tracks. In fact, simply jam two different pieces together and you have a new 'Complextro' song. What's more, in these cycles of economic incentivised homogenisation, algorithmic replication becomes much easier to implement. Today advancements in algorithmic creation are slowly removing the unique steps for 'original' composition. As I write, we are at the stage where an algorithm can construct an entire (albeit pretty low-quality) finished song. The big players have reacted to these new conditions, and there are industry rumours that Spotify pads out its own playlists with copyright free music it has either commissioned, or algorithmically generated itself. With the dawn of machine-learning, this process becomes even more disturbing. The algorithm eventually will begin to enter loops of self-reference.

The paradox is that royalty-free music has compositional borders which are very clear, yet at the same time tonally ambiguous. The economics of fitting into sellable mood categories is responsible for this ambiguity. A fast-upbeat track in a minor key can be marketed and spread not just as the mood supplier of 'exciting', 'adventurous' and 'cinematic', but also as 'sorrowful', 'inspirational' and 'dramatic'. Slow beat-less music is financially limiting. More categories exist for upbeat moods. Harmony in sound becomes mediated by a culture of 'activity' and 'movement' that now forgoes romantic conceptions of poignancy in emotion. From this culture dominated by epic and chill, the future, as presented in mainstream cinema and music, comes to us as a space of ambiguous tones. The agency perceived to either be gained or denied in such a future vision is forcefully defined through its relationship to neoliberal ideals of action and self-governance. Action is cinematic; future speculation in sound is *made* cinematic. Through political ambiguity, music created for a culture of heroes and villains encourages mainstream images for the future to be thought out in similar crude dualisms of good and evil. And as consumers we begin trust market slogans like Google's motto: 'don't be evil'.

The contradictions in royalty-free music deepen. Categorisation via algorithmic taste should in theory encourage music to exhibit easily differentiated and organised qualities. But instead, the economics of the auto-playing playlist require differing genres to bleed seamlessly into one another. Tonally interstitial tracks maintain the continuity of listening attention. Broader trends begin to separate music into messy sides. Like politics, future speculation begins to be presented in diametrically opposed ways — as hollow ambiguous dystopias and hollow ambiguous utopias.

In later chapters of this book I will discuss the low rumble of bass in Hollywood sci-fi future visions as an equally apolitical sound. Additionally, that compressed flatness in both mood and material of hyper-commercial music for gamers will be taken up in depth through a discussion of the label PC Music. Despite the damaging means of their construction, I legitimately love some of these new and inventive royalty-free genres. So I describe this music not to pass judgement on its quality, but instead to help contextualise the forces acting on the individual artists and albums I will discuss throughout the rest of this book. What follows are artistic languages which react to these new atmospheres of speedy, epic and chill moods. And importantly, to use sound as a supplier of mood in service of the construction of the future, I signpost here the potential for misuse, as sound and music become tainted by the movements of lithe and invisible ideology.

ii) Silent Vector-Graph of the Somatic Gamer

I have so far described an experience of the internet as noisy and full of Background Music. However, if we were to really map the intricacies of the Cloud we would see it as paradoxically flat and silent. Within our social networks and the cloud-platforms upon which they rest, we are bombarded by content of all soundings. Yet, between these circles in which we may move, lies an enormous void. Much has been written about the algorithmic separation of active voters in the 2016 American election. In this separation we call out and keep calling out to people who read the air in the exact same way as we do. Dialectical politics is prevented by an algorithm which only feeds us the content we already agree with (or are close to agreeing with). The most destructive ramification of this technology is that there is no longer one atmosphere, but many fragmented self-gratifying globules of sociality. And importantly, between the imagined vector-graph of social interaction is only a sliver of crossover.

In sound, this silent middle within the vector-graph of communication can be reconsidered in regards to private and collective listening practice. The majority of music is now, for the first time, listened to in private space as opposed to in public. Since the invention of the Walkman and other technologies of private listening, our basic modes of listening have dramatically changed. Besides other collective forms of listening throughout history, such as in a festival dance, the town-square, the concert hall or in front of the kitchen radio, perhaps the most pertinent change has occurred in the factory and the workplace. From a history of Background Music in factories which once functioned as the facilitator for a collective listening practice (a shared sound tasked with orienting workers towards the creation of capital), today, factory workers (when allowed to) listen privately to their own individualised music. In these cases, productivity no longer relies on a shared communality. Instead, music has become tasked with a new and hitherto unseen role — to improve the privatised and isolated self.

There is something undeniably beautiful in the distant sound of music leaking from a pair of low-quality earbuds, plugged into a nodding head, listening in the solitude of a lonely bedroom. And it is a sad beauty at that, because this occurs in a new type of solitude defined by the silence of those around us; those who listen to the same things as we do, yet rarely, if ever, form personal connections with us. Shared yet private listening. Silent yet overwhelmingly interconnected communication. The 'lurker' on a forum finds a home through their silent appreciation and one-directional empathy towards the other speaking members of the community. A vlogger speaks to a mass which responds mostly with an echo, still the person behind the camera knows they are listening and partaking in a shared imagined act of togetherness. The Cloud among other things is a home. It is a community. It can be a space of togetherness. However, private yet shared listening goes wrong when it becomes a form of sonic neoliberal biopolitics.

The liberal ideals of self-determination and radical autonomy provided the ideological groundwork for the birth of the early internet — a network which would increasingly disguise the rabid privatisation of the self behind ideals of collectivism and connectedness. What was once considered Background Music would of course react. In the same decades which marked the disappearance of Muzak from the West, neoliberal capitalism began to encourage a different conceptualisation of the self. Paul Roquet charts this change of culture in *Ambient Media / Japanese Atmospheres of the Self*. Drawing on the work of Nikolas Rose, who writes within a Foucauldian tradition, this movement can be contextualised as a once inner 'psychological understanding of the self' becoming an outward facing 'somatic self'.[7] Rose charts the disturbing change from a selfhood which was once understood by its interiority and unconsciousness, to neoliberalism's externalised notion of identity. In this externalisation, the self is perceived to be limitless, physically malleable at any level, and devoid of any Cartesian mind-body split. Rose refers in part to Somatic Cells in biology, any cell which is not a sex or stem-cell, and to somatic practice in psychology, an entirely body focused therapy. *Soma* — Somatic practice (the body itself as perceived from within) — is symptomatic of the physical pressures of neoliberal capitalism. Those same pressures which made chemical changes to the taste of edible substances in food, and those which drove developments miniaturising the speaker-cone to become small enough to fit inside the cavity of an ear, coincided with an increased pressure to exert dominance over the processes of the body and brain. Here, interiority and all it entailed (unconscious desire, emotional instability) became re-conceived as myth-like. From the smallest components of a cell to the neural-networks of the brain, dominion over the physical body (a biological market-driven and disenchanted understanding of the brain) produces a self which can supposedly be entirely built-up from a tabula rasa — the biopolitical American Dream.

Today's biopolitics enact an ever-accelerating quest to be the optimal agent in consumer society: *micro-dose LSD to improve creative risk-management in investment banking; buy experimental Nootropic substances on the darkweb to 'overclock your brain' for your High-School exams; do yoga or lift weights to cure any supposed mental illness*. And of course, the pressure to be this 'optimal agent' also plays out in the negative. Biopolitics chemically denies and restricts those who desire to be outside of imposed gender norms. The privatisation of the self, understood as the ideology of a limitless body and mind, has birthed an instrumentalised listening practice. Technology has distanced music from a once inseparable collectivism held in the act of creating sound together. Technology has separated us from utopian modes of production. Music's exchange and value has thus shifted from a tapping into the interiority of our once *limited* selves, to become a tapping into our *potential* selves. All music now incurs the added possibility to be heard and *asked* to transform any space and any mindset. Lifehacker.com, theartofmanliness.com suggest: *pro-tip: playing music while you are working on something boring does wonders — you know... whatever it is you're doing, mundane etc. listen to that pump up Tuuuune!! Personally, before my first date with a sexy lady I LOVE to listen to my workout playlist — speed and sensuality, seductive beats, that's what YOU become, you are the beat, you are that handsome melody.*

On YouTube, 2017 and 2018's most popular daily vloggers are the infamous Disney Channel, teenage Paul brothers. Each daily video by Jake Paul begins something like this: '*Good-mooooorrning*

Jake Paulers, we are Team 10! *Camera zooms in and out as Jake Paul punches the air in front of him*

Jake stamps his feet side to side, causing the camera to shake as if in an earthquake

I'M Jake Paul...and YOU are the Jake Paulers...what's uuuuuppppp!!!'[8]

In the crescendo and upward scale of Jake yelling 'up' I realise something: I'm no longer just a private individual, I'm a Jake Pauler. These soundings simultaneously promote the importance of an American-Dream kind of individuality, while at the same time manufacturing collectivity, and the transformation of us viewers into a privatised consumer of Jake himself — linked to all other viewers — a devotee of Jake. In contrast to Fordist collectivity, in the vlog space, I'm linked to the other through consumption, not creation. The popularity of many daily vlogs stems from an assumption that by viewing a person who has a polished lifestyle, their success will somehow rub off on you. Trickle-down economics of the self. Within each video you'll supposedly discover the minute keys to success. You'll see the workout routine, the instagramable breakfast, their energy will imbue you with the power to take control of your own existence. Here the consumption of the other is directly funnelled into the false-premise that it helps *create* you. Music plays an essential and horrifying role. Throughout these exceptionally mundane vlogs, music amplifies the core tone of each scene. When language runs out, when the day-to-day life of an individual so much as borders on the mundane, music is introduced to lift it — to take something without mood and force it to 'matter' to us.

In the rival sphere of Amazon's streaming service, one user has emerged as the self-proclaimed 'face of Twitch'. His name is *Dr Disrespect*. Retro 'synth-wave' music serves as the introduction to his live-streams. He wears an 80s military vest, mirrored sunglasses and a giant handlebar moustache. Above the video the words *Speed, Momentum, Violence* are engraved into the screen. Three words to sound his and all his devotees' mantra. When he reads these words (during victories in a game) he puts a delay and distortion effect on his voice. *Vio-vio-vio-lence, Spe-ed-ed-ed* and by the time he screams 'momentum' the sound is bouncing around him furiously. As a form of financial manipulation, viewers are encouraged to donate larger and larger amounts of money to reach the top of the competitive and always visible donation chart. In one live-stream I watched, a kid donated ten dollars to Dr Disrespect along with the message: *'Doc, you got me through the passing of my Grandma, and the bullying of a new school.'* Dr Disrespect responds to this donation with his standard catchphrase: *'Another Champion, Primed Out of Their Mind,'* and then follows up by saying, *'thanks for the donation but I don't wanna hear about your grandma or any of this morbid shit.'* [9]

Portable-personal sonic inventions place the distinct responsibility and decision-making emphasis of what to listen to with the individual alone. Music fed directly into the ear can overpower all other ambiences. With the market-driven transference from a selfhood and mood which was once influenced by shared listening in public space, to a new era of private listening in private space, music (embedded in online media) has gained the heightened responsibility of nearly defining *who* a person *is* and can *be*.

Royalty-free music is being made and used to achieve the similar mood control of sound which was once intended purely for advertising. And most importantly, all of this content *isn't* advertising — it's the stuff the ads were once meant to promote. The total effacing of lines between content and advertising is propagated through the disguised exchange values of YouTube and streaming platforms, as are those marks between a once utopian sharing of music, to today's forces of instrumentalised listening. The result is an online experience where even the most basic meaning in life is something we can supposedly gain via the direct consumption of content. Watch a few videos of people doing meaningful things and you too can attain meaning. Listen to a few *powerful* tracks of music and you too can become powerful, violent, fast and momentum driven.

To clarify, much of private listening obviously still occurs purely in appreciation of musical value. Listening for pleasure will always exist, enacted to cognitively and emotionally admire musical construction, form and the manipulation of sonic attributes. However, under neoliberalism, music for private space also gains an *added* functionality, and this is the key differentiation to make. The somatic self requires music to have a physicalised use value. It requires music to improve space, content and the body. In the chapters that follow, the tensions between private and collective listening are not always visible, but I think that it is important to keep these tensions in mind throughout my discussions of the dance floor, of the lonely bedroom teen, or the rarefied concert-hall setting. Even imaginative musics, playful and joyous ones, are forced to submit to the potential of political misinterpretation, and a possible misuse of their intended construction. Yet at the same time, the wriggling contradiction of our new private online listening conditions is that they are *still shared*. We can enact digital togetherness privately. In the same way, those musics promoting togetherness might employ collective listening and hearing among other bodies, in the same space, as an evocation of a distinctly different labour, and perhaps as a tapping into the potential for enhanced political activism.

Musicologist Brandon LaBelle's book *Sonic Agency* claims that political resistance is an innate potential and quality within the making of and listening to music. Darting between a number of sonic masterpieces, and the sensorial lessons to be gained from them, LaBelle repeats his own mantra: 'This is what captures my imagination: *the hearing that is the basis for an insurrectionary activity, a coming community.*'[10] For LaBelle, hearing always offers a communality in its function as a shared sensibility. Music's ability to give agency to the less-observed, the once-invisible and the abstract enables it to enchant those efforts of resistance which require us to think through our relationship to the non-human and 'invisible' long-term forces like climate change. The future, particularly as expressed in utopian thought, easily slips away from us as an invisible, almost inconceivable nowhere. I agree with LaBelle, that in sound and its 'communality in shared sensibility without shared vision', we find a medium for insurrection, for helping imagine the once unimaginable, for bringing disparate communities of people together. Unfortunately, working in opposition to this communality is the privatisation of our senses. Royalty-free music, and the privatised selfhood expressed in the daily vlog, obscures communality through its exacerbation of, and making sacred of, the individual. Sweetness becomes invisible within the flood of other sounds. Those 38 views of a karaoke cover become a rare object of resistance within that always expanding space of the Cloud, unseen and unheard.

If music can function as an embodiment of ideology, then it can also function to make politics visible, to shine light on those difficult to *see* qualities of neoliberal influence. Through this, perhaps the privatisation of our senses can be turned on its head, made into an expression of resistance through the making visible of that lithe atmosphere and set of feelings it hauntingly inspires in us. In later chapters I will consider this 'exacerbation of a commercial aesthetic' as a form of insurrectionary behaviour. More importantly, royalty-free music, like neoliberalism, is one of the few ambiences which crosses gaps between the algorithmically separated political spheres of left and right. We almost all hear royalty-free music daily. It plays out in our own echo-chambers and political spheres. And significantly, the very *same* music plays out to those we disagree with, it plays out despite our divisions. Can it be co-opted, can we reclaim its sweetness, *a becoming togetherness*?

iii) Listening to the Weather

Japanese director Shunji Iwai's exquisite film *All About Lily Chou Chou (Rirī Shushu no Subete)* can be read as an excellent study into the contradictions of shared yet private listening. Set between digital and real life, the film follows the struggles of two pre-teen boys linked through their love for the fictional pop singer Lily Chou Chou. In real life, one boy bullies the other violently, but online they share an anonymous friendship through a forum dedicated to the magic of Lily's music. In the lineage of nihilistic coming-of-age novels like Mishima's *The Sailor Who Fell From Grace with the Sea (Gogo no Eiko)*, *All About Lily Chou Chou* charts the brutal realisations of one boy, Hoshino, whose near-death drowning twists him towards a life of extreme violence and self-consuming nihilism. Here, a total disregard for life fuses (as in Mishima's philosophy) the traditional narrative 'all men must strive for' — glory and honour — with the seductions of a total nihilistic existence. Iwai's film is famous for its incredible text-only scenes depicted in the black of the early Bulletin-Board-Internet, and for its exploration of the terrifying and paradoxical isolation of online-connectedness. At key moments throughout, Iwai captures the abusive antagonist, Hoshino, standing alone in a field of green rice listening to his Walkman. Private listening is shown to be the melting pot of self-identity: the Walkman's ambience allows a boy to escape a violent disconnect between their real-world and online selves. Hoshino, who IRL blackmails young girls into sex work, lives a second existence online under the alter-ego 'Blue Cat'. On the forum dedicated to Lily Chou Chou, Blue Cat comforts his fellow classmate's suicidal tendencies, and eloquently discusses the power music has to change one's life for good. The invented online lives of others are portrayed as having sometimes more power than 'real' voices and physical bodies. Seeing this as a landmark early warning of the simultaneous violence and beauty of online life, *All About Lily Chou Chou* has remarkable purchase in today's political climate.

In Iwai's fictional Bulletin Board, the children who use the forum debate which one of Lily Chou Chou's songs evoke the greatest feeling of the *ether*. Ether, and the act of hearing it, becomes a key metaphor for sound. The notion of ethereality — reality experienced in an upper or heightened strand of space — has historically always attached itself to the processes of music. *Music takes me above and beyond my current surroundings, it lifts me up like a feather*. The atmosphere of the early internet, and the cloud-computing of today, can also be said to be made of ether: a material superstitiously believed to populate the sky. And in many music cultures the celestial or ethereal sound has been, like sweetness — longed for. In the ontogenesis of ethereality we encounter some of the greatest underlying fictions of music — that it is *alive* — that it is around us metaphysically — that it is transportive — that it can die — that it is mood enhancing.[11] The historical notion that music can improve productivity in a factory relies on these unprovable post-truths of sound. The factory might see an 11 percent increase in worker speed, but no one knows exactly *why* music has encouraged those exploited workers to labour harder and faster. We can guess of course, but science and empiricism can't *yet* externalise the exact effects music has on the internal self. The notion that the neoliberal somatic self can also be improved by music, meditation, silence, noise, whatever the correlation, relies on a future-truth of listening assumed to eventually reveal itself when science finally maps out the mind. For now, efforts to instrumentalise listening, or to simply hear and make music in ways that are entirely physically reductive and mathematically explained ('*I just make dance music — the movement of the beat is the only thing that exists for real*') ignore the post-truth fiction that music *can* think and is *alive* and cognitively life-giving. On Lily Chou Chou's forum, one anonymous child types: 'For me, only Lily is real. For me, only the Ether is proof that I am alive.' In some ways, the ether appears to these characters as a kind of enchanting vitality which surrounds them all the time. Lily's voice taps into this energy — a latent force which calls to being contrasting atmospheres symbolic of both great isolation and also great togetherness. And in this regard, *All About Lily Chou Chou* pointedly captures the contradictory nature of private listening and individuality: through sharing, tensions of the self (be that nihilism or the destructive penchants of neoliberal encouraged limitlessness) can be overcome through digital togetherness.

In Iwai's narrative we find a passionate dedication to the power of two or more radical individuals coming together, despite separations, through the sharing of sound.

* * *

To support my allusion to patterns in the sky, to the *ether* and to that floaty feeling of *sweetness*, I found parallels in the work of philosopher Watsuji Tetsurō, who was responsible for the concept of 'listening to the weather'. In *Climate and Culture*, Watsuji broadens Heidegger's *Stimmung* into a metaphorically rich blend of atmospheric weather, mood, family, communication technology and community. Like *Stimmung*, Watsuji argues the 'climate' is the medium which allows us to understand our existence and being-in of the world. Japanese-ness, and more fundamentally, the self, is supposedly found in the atmosphere, and in the actual weathers of a nation. 'We discover ourselves, that is, in the atmosphere.'[12] From 'Monsoon' to 'Meadow' to 'Desert', the biomes of a country, its sky, its rain or sun or wind, supposedly support and define our understanding of selfhood.

In *Japanese Atmospheres of the Self,* Paul Roquet draws on important critiques of Watsuji, such as Yamamoto Schichihei's *'Kuki' no kenkyū* (Research on 'air'), to describe the legacy of a nationalistic philosophy which ascribes atmosphere the power to define selfhood.

...atmospheric essentialism meshed with a larger cultural emphasis on 'reading the air' (*kūki o yomu*) to determine correct behaviour. Reading the air was espoused as essential to maintaining a harmonious social mood...The social imperative to attune to the 'air of place' (*ba no kūki*) has remained prominent in recent decades. A person who misses implicit social cues and expectations is now often labelled someone who 'cannot read the air' (*kūki ga yomenai*). The phrase experienced a surge of popularity early in the twenty-first century with the abbreviated version of the term, KY, nominated as one of the most important terms of 2007.[13]

Being KY, a person who incorrectly 'reads the air', is a shameful label describing a person who poorly fits into society. The 'air illiterate', KY individual is encouraged to read self-help books and seek atmospheric guidance. Fitting into society's defined narrative becomes verbally equated with the positive or negative qualities of your personhood. Atmospheric speculation morphs from a once reading of natural phenomenon in the sky, to the reading of ethereal social forces. The same parallel can be drawn in music, which morphs from being an animation of the air, to become an embodiment of social and online pressures. As someone who frequently worries and struggles to be 'air-literate', I describe the way the very act of trying to 'fit in' to online social life can influence a destructive politics and combative culture. Being bad at 'reading the air' is punishable within circles like call-out Tumblr and Twitter, but it is responded to even more violently in the high-school-like culture of 4chan.

As an online image board similar to the one portrayed in *Lily Chou Chou*, 4chan is famous for being a melting pot of internet culture, and for its unique setup: all posts are anonymous, and all posts disappear once they reach page 10 of an individual sub-forum. Due to this anonymity, and due to the automatic cycles of disappearance, the website has gained notoriety as a place of depravity, 'political incorrectness', right-wing politics, transgression, abjectness and extreme violence. On 4chan, and I would argue much of the internet, the constant death of websites, threads, platforms, hyperlinks and content itself places an unlikely and paradoxical importance on human memory. Page 10 defines an online reality where continuity in culture is maintained through the fallibility of our own memory, storytelling and an atmospheric climate conducive to believing in fictions. In all its vengeful hatred of women, and all its dark history of encouraging users to commit suicide and murder, and all its rhetoric of claiming to have 'memed Donald Trump into presidency' — to analyse 4chan is to also treat the space as a collection of disenfranchised individuals seeking a form of dark togetherness with one another.

This 'chan cultural' togetherness is defined always in the negative. Not understanding the nuanced and ever-changing conditions of irony, not *remembering* what came before, and not embodying the forces which wriggle towards page 10 — is the cardinal sin of the culture — to be a 'new fag', someone KY. Reading the air 'correctly' becomes the imperative to fitting in. This is how divisions in culture and politics emerge. Despite everyone being anonymous, users distinguish themselves by how 'chan literate' they are. Being KY is being someone who isn't transgressive, and being KY can also be the expression of sensitivity and empathy. Like high-school, popularity can be defined by one's total assimilation into the culture, and in this assimilation the board becomes a popularist-mass, a hive-mind with surprising political clout. Some of the most important ramifications of a culture defined by what-not-to-be, are that in these efforts to assimilate, irony becomes more and more nuanced until it is finally mistaken for sincerity, and fiction becomes an important agent of this assimilation. To invent yourself in the ideal image of the mass therefore becomes an imperative.

In an attempt to be air-literate, I use some examples throughout this book from now deprived online spaces like 4*chan*, *Something Awful* and *Less Wrong*, because I think it is important to have a discussion about what type of film, music and literature can support the dominant ideologies of these online communities. Of course, my reading is only a snapshot from a rapidly changing landscape, but the key current and lasting cultural icons, like *Neon-Genesis Evangelion*, *Serial Experiments Lain* and *The Matrix*, have become instrumentalised by the community in aid of their disgusting political ambitions. All of these cultural landmarks are examples of work which is poly-vital, politically complex and beloved in many other communities besides 4chan. I don't want to taint these works by the flawed interpretation of a specific group of people. However, within each, one can still find clear desires to escape from reality through the agency of a radical individualism. This includes spaces for private introspection and instrumentalised listening, utilitarian morals, a distinctly 'male rationality' and a profound nihilistic interpretation of the 'real-world'. Here, to take a different coloured pill, as in *The Matrix*, is a metaphor to either succumb to how others are 'forcing' you to see the world, or to escape to a 'true' and purportedly freeing reality. To 'red-pill yourself' is to see through the supposed 'cathedral' of left-wing political correctness which is viewed as limiting your assumed freedoms and entitlements. *'There are two paths for men to follow in this modern world of ours, that of training to become a steppe warrior in post-collapse USA, or that of transforming yourself into the ideal war bride for their enjoyment.'*[14] To be 'pink-pilled' is to give-in to the pressures of an increasingly feminised world and renounce the supposed sacredness of masculinity. And finally, to be 'black-pilled' is to take pleasure in the end of existence, to philosophise from a perspective of our technological demise, and to embrace the singular bleakness of a meaningless world. In all examples a future is imagined, and social interactions between users become forceful atmospheres of conformity.

To loop back to Sianne Ngai's description of tone and ideology as an extraction (or abstraction) of the atmosphere of the 'world', we find in 4chan an excellent proof of concept. The *tone*, the language, the cultural icons the community idealises and shares, and even ironically mocks, help underpin their ideology. Ten years ago, when the politics of the image board veered closer to a version of left-wing anarchism (remember *Anonymous, Lulzsec*, chants of *we are legion*), the cultural icons at the time were *Fight Club* and *V for Vendetta,* two films which placed 'the system' and even 'capitalism' as the enemy to fight against, to collectivise against and find togetherness in opposition to. And looking back at the music on /mu/ I remember anecdotally threads praising *System of a Down, Radiohead* and *Muse* — bands singing about George Orwell's *1984* and *Animal Farm.*

With the passing of time the narrative has changed. Technology has mediated the conversation between tone and ideology. But by technology I don't just mean software, apps and online platforms, I mean also the powerful techne of convincing a mass via grey lies and the simple descriptions of an unreal world *not* worth fighting for. Or the technes within music production: an increase of lyric-less music, an increase of apolitical moods like epic and chill, and the increased prevalence of streaming economics found in the sound itself. The algorithm encourages one another to conform to the air. To make music in stylistic derivations and continuities of one another. But this climate has further ramifications for even those spheres of music making which maintain their self-awareness (and political critique), such as experimental club music, and even critical avant-garde sound practice which reacts in conflict, or in reflection to, mainstream culture. If tone and ideology are so undoubtedly linked, in the following chapters I ask, what can be said of dark music? What can be said of deconstructed club music which divides the dance floor into individuals? And how does an indulgence in hyper-capitalist futures change subsequent cultural narratives? Can these tones and atmospheres also influence future politics?

In its sweetness and hollowness, if we were to treat the Cloud as a weather system, it would function as Watsuji imagined. Listen, and you might find — a monsoon is coming.

Chapter 2

Enchantment can be Formalised

Ah si------Ah so------
shoot------shiver------mix------
ha roll------tara------ta ta------
curlurck------Kayash------Kee------
Pearls pearls in the yellow West
------Yellow sky to China------
Pacific we named here
 water as always meeting
 water------Pacific Pacific
Pacific tapfic------geroom------
 gedowsh------gaka------gaya------
Tatha------gata------mana------
What sails used old bhikkus?
Dhikkus? Dhikkus!
What raft mailed Mose
to the hoven dovepost?
What saved Blackswirl
from the Kidd plank?
What Go-Bug here?
Seet! Seeeeeeeeeee
eeeeeee------kara------
Pounders out yar------[1]

Long after *On the Road*, a novel which would shape and still shapes ideas of a limitless teen masculinity, Jack Kerouac stood on the edge of the Pacific, hearing voices in the water. Isolated and alcohol deprived, the noise of the ocean's swells became inseparable from Kerouac's internal language. A private water voice. Voices yelling out to him from misinterpretation. A

51

Anonymous (ID: iAC8FQEK) 06/19/16(Sun)01:07:22
No.77777777

>>77778286 >>77778289 >>77778302 >>77778305 >>77778308
>>77778346 >>77778349 >>77778351 >>77778354 >>77778357
>>77778385 >>77778388 >>77778391 >>77778392 >>77778394
>>77778420 >>77778421 >>77778422 >>77778424 >>77778426
>>77778453 >>77778455 >>77778456 >>77778459 >>77778460
>>77778479 >>77778480 >>77778481 >>77778482 >>77778484
>>77778502 >>77778503 >>77778505 >>77778506 >>77778507
>>77778528 >>77778529 >>77778532 >>77778534 >>77778535
>>77778554 >>77778557 >>77778558 >>77778559 >>77778560
>>77778581 >>77778582 >>77778583 >>77778584 >>77778585
>>77778604 >>77778605 >>77778606 >>77778607 >>77778608
>>77778627 >>77778628 >>77778629 >>77778630 >>77778631
>>77778675 >>77778676 >>77778678 >>77778679 >>77778680
>>77778698 >>77778699 >>77778700 >>77778701 >>77778702
>>77778722 >>77778723 >>77778724 >>77778725 >>77778726
>>77778745 >>77778746 >>77778747 >>77778748 >>77778749
>>77778767 >>77778768 >>77778769 >>77778770 >>77778771
>>77778790 >>77778791 >>77778792 >>77778793 >>77778794
>>77778824 >>77778815 >>77778816 >>77778817 >>77778818
>>77778838 >>77778839 >>77778840 >>77778841 >>77778842

misguided imagination. Communication disseminating from a once singular source to become imbued within a mist of noises. Individual water molecules rattling against each other in infinitely complex ways, becoming brain signals, thoughts and then words on a page.

Throughout history voices have been heard in Nature. In diverse mythologies communication from the gods manifested in rustling leaves and grass, in the silent yet sounding movement of celestial bodies, in the crackling remains of burning bramble. Upon picking up the receiver of an early prototyped telephone, Thomas Watson heard spirits in the sound of copper cables.[2] When the radio was invented, for some, words formed in the static. Discarnate bodies called out from the noise between stations. This was termed Electronic Voice Phenomena: communication with the dead heard in the space surrounding a signal. A misplaced record needle. A dirty tape recording. A sky the colour of television tuned to a dead channel.

When the believers of Electronic Voice Phenomena heard the speech of deceased relatives in detuned radio, they were living at a time where static of all kinds was accelerating. This age was marked by the emergence of colour home television, the summit years of radio and the dawning of a new heightened era of commercial, industrial and material noise. There is evidence of a reoccurring history. Today we live in a world of peak virtual noise, of a new kind of detuned internet static. The navigation from one online click to the next is chaotic and often unprincipled. In the Cloud, *listening to the weather* and trying to conform to it becomes obscured by the algorithmically separated, yet still noisy conditions of online life. The signal to noise ratio skews towards a new kind of structured static. Some kind of white and grey mottle of miscommunication, imagined voices in the browser window, and manufactured identities — post-truth, algorithmic or dreamt.

To theorise our digitally heightened time-period of enchanted, magical thinking, I refer in part to a psychological structure called apophenia. Apophenia, according to clinical definition, is *the human tendency to perceive meaningful patterns in random data.*[3] This term describes what might be considered human nature — a certain likelihood throughout one's life to find personal significance in coincidental phenomena, and to look for existential answers in completely unrelated impersonal events. Apophenia has great relevance for understanding the seductions of conspiracy theory and the occult. Resting on the ontology of a human-centric 'search for meaning', one can make common assumptions about the supposed difference between a 'meaningful' pattern and a 'meaningless' one. These assumptions rely on the perceived balance between causal events and inferred randomness. There is no doubt that the internet and many of its technologies of automatic content creation encourage us to make unconscious hierarchies out of the online voices we read daily.

In the contemporary networked life, data propagates endlessly, and with every spoken word intuited as important, another thousand pop-up as unimportant and meaningless. A once close proximity to the other (as in the intimacy of a town or even a city) is now online geographically and existentially massive, almost limitless. Due to this separation, reading a distant vocalisation in the browser can characterise any sounding with the phenomenological perception of randomness. This underpins a defining quality of the Cloud: once an utterance begins to *seem* random — in that it could be replaced with an endless series of interchangeable words, pictures or events — then all of online life begins to garner the appearance of random data.

Here, a lack of personal connection coupled with the disturbing feeling of randomness (unlikely, contrasting or distant phenomena) perversely encourages made up connections. Apophenic connections. From the most ubiquitous conspiracy theories such as the flat-earth believers, to the deadly ramifications of 'Pizza-Gate', to the very nature of post-truth politics today, the simple enormity of interactions around us encourages a thinking which imagines meaningful connections where there are none. In the flurry of words and images, the greater political and social forces acting out on a life are *felt to become out of control*. Within this maelstrom of technologically encouraged chaos, the more dots you have, the easier it is to find imagined lines between them.

In evolutionary terms, the ear not the eye geolocates the body. Every sound has a source. An animal's footsteps are mapped to an XYZ point in that Euclidean space around the human head. Yet alone in the wild, frightened, the wind itself passing through foliage can stand in for a violent creature. The apophenic imagining of a dangerous sound in brushing tree leaves ascribes a physical location with an imagined movement just as real as a non-imagined one. In composition, white, pink and brown noise *stand in* for the complex sonifications of blowing wind through

54

grass and leaves — stochastic methods, granulation and physical modelling *stand in* for the pattern encouraging earthliness of looking out over the ocean and listening to the crashing of waves. Building on this, in the construction of virtual space for devices like the Oculus Rift, the tiny distance between our ears can stand in for enormous valleys and real-world vistas. In a basement in The Hague, the 'Wave Field Synthesis' system of 192 speakers can make unearthly sound sources rotate, wriggle and dance around you. The ear assigns a piece of sounding invisible air an imagined unreal speaking body. We invent technology and it disrupts our own biological listening processes. On Twitter, a typo by President Trump, 'Covfefe', sparks a furious search for meaning. Unpack each letter, re-arrange their order and etymological significance, deride and inflame their inherent significance.

Apophenia is survival instinct. We are meaning-making machines. In some world-views, human existence could be at its most basic level a practice of trying to find order in chaos. This innate struggle to find meaning in an alienating world is a crucial driving force in creative practice. It is the terror which drove Jack Kerouac to seek poetry in the voices of the Pacific Ocean, and it is the meaning-imposed-sound of John Cage's chance operations; dropped perpendiculars clunking on a wooden concert-hall floor. Moreover, capitalist induced alienation ever accelerates, and with it, the rate of apophenic thinking gains momentum.

Apophenia becomes a governing force in anonymous image-boards like 4chan. In the bionetwork which strips user identification to a string of numbers, meaningful identity is in turn stripped from the sounds and voices of real people. Inspired by the enormity of posts and their automatic deletion, the community famously finds hierarchy in arcane-signs and their interactions, inferring invented significance in that grey strip of numbers above a post. Posts which end in double (dubs) or triple (trips) numbers are made hallow. This sheer and often uncontrollable stream of comments has meant that certain decision-making on a board is relegated to coincidental phenomena within this very string of numbers. Decisions can be made by 'rolling' for patterns. It is not possible to predict whether you will 'GET' a 'dub' or 'trip' on a busy board like /pol/, so when a user speculates that they will be graced by a lucky 'roll', and they achieve it, the community praises the *Chaos Magic* of the internet. A certain meta-belief is evident, a faith in the magic of speculation, of tuning your mind towards the future and trying to grasp it. To pull your desires from the chaos is to treat the endless data around you with an apophenic imagination. Meaning is invented and coincidence becomes a belief system. The Cloud appears future oriented. It appears oracular. On 19 June 2016 one user posts: 'Trump will win.' The ID is 77777777. The luckiest of all numbers.

In a disenchanted world, magical thinking always stands in for a perceived lack or removal of agency. The non-physical, the digital, becomes the space for a supposed regaining of that perceived to be lost (or taken away) agency. In my summation, apophenia is a core structure behind the new prevalence of online magical thinking. However, another way of considering structures which promote or encourage this type of thought is to consider them as an indication of a 'formalised enchantment': key formal and governing decisions, be they political, technological or aesthetic, which are made in the distinct service of encouraging an *unreal* world. Formalised enchantment is also the promotion of affect and agency in what was once dead matter. A series of numbers once dead, can become quiveringly alive when they are given the agency to make sounds. There are exciting structures which can be given new life in the cold faculties of the internet and the utilities which support it. Equally, the brain, as meat, as a collection of mappable disenchanted biological processes, can be reinvigorated with new meaning when mapped onto machinic and inhuman intelligence.

This chapter investigates a series of formalised magics: Chaos Magic, stochastic magic and machine-learning. Where my analysis functions as a description of a concrete set of compositional strategies, it also functions to provide a context for the kind of near future we head towards — one of rampant uncertainty, machine influence and a cohabitation with the inhuman. Finally, I want to make this crystal clear: where I use examples of apophenia and by consequence the magical thinking it leads to, these psychological structures are never an *excuse* for our political interactions with technology, or for the general state of global politics. In my reading, systematic capitalism is always the nexus of the magic, fragmenting and alienating effects of our current technologies. Deleuze and Guattari write: '[capital] becomes a very mystical being since all of labor's social productive forces appear to be due to capital rather than labor'.[4] This disconnect at the core of capitalist exchange makes magic easy to believe in. While disguised, our profound lack of control over our own working lives and the 'chance' occurrences which appear to structure them, beguile us. Ascribing the more mysterious workings of the Cloud with magic is a dangerous proposition. There are *concrete* causes and lines of deterministic code which are directly responsible for our sickly online culture. Rational decisions have been made. Apophenia is not inherently 'good' or 'bad' but its psychological significance is noted by all the large platforms (Facebook, Google, Amazon, Twitter) and their applications take advantage of this human susceptibility. When you scroll down the social media app, you gesture with your finger like the pulling of the lever of a gambling machine. It is always almost as if you have reached the end of the content, but then from out of the blank below, the spinning circle reveals always more. In those seconds just before the image loads we hold out like addicts for what could be revealed to us. In juxtaposed boxes of information, an ad, a personal cry, a song, a cute animal picture or a political statement share lines, and the nature of apophenic thinking draws parallels between these disparate strands of consumption. In the song, the crisis-ridden compositional structure, the stochastic method or granulating effect fills the music with gaps which perforate the noise. Understanding takes place in the silence, and in these gaps, we wait for what comes next.

i) LEXACHAST Desire and Representation

LEXACHAST is spelled out in large block letters — a twitching sound starts. You click the screen. The individual letters dissipate in criss-crossed pixels fading to reveal what lies beneath: the misshapen world of a Ken Burn's effect photo album fading from one image to the next. It takes you a while to realise what is happening. Each photo leaves a residue on the next. Its formal construction merges with the subsequent image. Gaps are filled, lines between files match up. Their borders join. The transparency lattice collages them together like fused flesh. One is born from the next. A new idea evolves from the messy filth of what came before — its ontogenesis found in the space between conjoined images.

I consider *LEXACHAST,* the collaboration between Amnesia Scanner, Bill Kouligas and Harm Van Den Dorpel, to be one of the most salient audio-visual representations of post-internet existence. Still visitable at www.lexachast.com, this dedicated website and performance takes images ripped from sites like Flickr and Deviant Art, and simply juxtaposes them together. I'd recommend visiting LEXACHAST for yourself, but in short, this work is a randomly generated and uncensored photo album compiled from public online images. Despite its astounding simplicity (image after image fading in and out of one another), you somehow walk away from the piece deeply unsettled, mundane faces and fleshes of strangers trapped in your eyelids' blinking after-burn — their expressions haunted.

LEXACHAST is art serviced by apophenia. There is no reason to string a narrative throughout these juxtaposed images — yet you do. There is no inherent order to grasp by the end — yet you feel *guided* throughout your viewing. Over its nearly 16-minute duration you become intimate with the lives of strangers, objects and perhaps even that general *tone* of the online / internet-mediated world around you. Sixteen minutes doesn't seem long enough for this to happen, but it does. Those most basic juxtapositions between object to object act as a clear scaffolding for building atmosphere. And the basic inter-media phenomena of music combined with image proves powerful. Meaning is generative in this work. Finnish duo Amnesia Scanner and Bill Kouligas (founder of Berlin-based experimental label *PAN*) have collaborated to produce a soundtrack for the wriggling amplification of tone. This is sweet music for content, sickly sweet in its resounding ability to represent the delight and profound disturbance of everyday online life. Here, the piece of art makes twisted that experience of scrolling through the lives of distant others, or of generating an iPhoto slideshow from your last beach holiday. The work bends the present familiar social media world of Flickr, and a nostalgic 00s past found in Deviant Art, into a fictional and alien shape. The making other, and disturbed, of what should be common (or taken for granted) is an important consequence of the act of fictionalisation. And as Bertolt Brecht would have confirmed, alienation is a form of political agency.

A pareidolic face seems to emerge from the elbow of a punk rocker's guitar strum. An anti-riot police shield seems to become the torso of a festival-goer's hoop spinning belly. Sound glares and disrupts in jagged tension. A near-speaking voice seems to become the sound of a revving car engine. The sound of clicking insects seems to become the ripping of domestic objects flung about in terror. Borders and lines in sound fuse, one material leaks over to the next. A singing child's voice seems to become the cries of a Death Metal scream. In the disarray, in the chaos of once understood materials becoming other we find meaning.

The sonic language of *LEXACHAST* exhibits many tropes broadly shared by a collection of artists creating *futurist* music, or music which hopes to convey something about the quality of technology today and future online life. To continue my discussion of that broad question, how the internet influences the creation of experimental music, I want to demonstrate the way an encouragement of apophenic thinking, and even magical thinking, has had a profound effect on the compositional structures evident in this music.

From my analysis of music as the tonal *embodiment* of a set of atmospheric feelings, I now turn to what is a far more common description of the political agency of art — music and sound as a *representation* of something else. In the most basic sense, to structure anything in music is to attempt to compose a meaning into it. Rather than an improvised expression made in the utopian moment of simply *playing* a sound, in my definition, to compose is to sit back and figure out carefully how to convey *something* in music. In this case, I am looking at artists who arguably are trying to represent a quality of their own experience of the Cloud. In the act of choosing a structure, those rhythmic, melodic, harmonic patterns (or lack of patterns) in a piece, those textural and material choices, are utilised to *stand in* for something else. That is, composition is the act of representing: a mood, an idea, an object, an experience. A sound is not a robot's limb, a group of sounds are not a computer or a data server, but sound still can embody (in that most ambient way) what it is like to experience using a computer. What occurs here is an act of magic. Apophenic listening helps us make real material connections where there are none. A belief in the 'truth' of representational and field recorded sounds help us associate the poetic with the actual.

The fundamental aesthetic tie between futurist movements

is a desire to represent and embody an extremely specific set of real and speculated political, social and material conditions of daily life. I would argue that in the history of Western music, this level of representation (helped by technologies to record and manipulate sound) is more specific, nuanced and detailed than ever before. Lyric-less music — in becoming online pattern, in becoming a mediated embodier for technology, in becoming very, very politically semantic — demonstrates an evolution in not just the way some of us think about making music, but also a broader evolution in the way we may listen to music. As one ramification for the chaotic, sometimes unimaginable conditions of online life and global politics, there is the sense that we are increasingly conditioned to find personal connections between unrelated disparate things. This conditioning leaks into compositional choices. The promotion of a confused world also encourages the perception of new and fecund representational connections between abstract sounds and concrete actions. Sonic material has more agency than ever before. The future can be abstractly conveyed in far more detail than ever before. When I described the sound of LEXACHAST I kept repeating: this sound *seemed* to become something else, that sound *seemed* to become another thing. When a sonic material *seems* to be that which it is not, it sparks the beginning of a chain of important listening consequences. From a sonic material becoming other, in that transference, we begin to sensually *believe* in a sonic belief itself.

Francois J Bonnet's *The Order of Sounds* catalogues those almost unspeakable audible and listening processes which affect our daily sensibilities. Bonnet unpacks one of the primary qualities of appreciating music, what he labels *'Desiring-listening'* 'the listening that perceives in the object that it targets a certain promise'.[50] What appears obvious when stated, but is almost unconscious in the act of appreciating music, is the longing for music to fulfil the promises it makes to us, the promises it musically sets up for us as listeners — that *what we think will sound, will actually sound* — that what we desire to hear, and what we desire to hear *again* — will occur. Once we begin to enjoy and become immersed in music, a broader set of promises become solidified. A once fulfilled desire easily becomes a profound and unspeakable *belief* that the piece or musical performance will continue to fulfil those desires. Like addicts we begin to listen in part for the continual fulfilment of our *desiring-listening*.

Desiring-listening is the promise that a heard sound will matter to us, provoke in us some meaning, and most importantly that sound will live up to the *representations* we believe (unconsciously or consciously) it should possess. In LEXACHAST there is an immediate desire to link its collection of sounds with its images, but also with a broader representation of the forces of the internet. It sets up these promises for itself in the design language of its browser window, its program notes, its performance context and the past output of the composers responsible for its construction. In the combination of a *promise*, a *representation* and a *sound,* that ever-present psychological structure of apophenia feeds on our listening-desires and encourages us to make material connections out of the sonic-personal mesh. To repeat, apophenia is in essence a *standing in* for something not there. To this end, Amnesia Scanner and Bill Kouligas have written music which is structurally conceived to enhance feelings of uncertainty and randomness. This is music composed to enhance apophenic listening. Forms leak and bleed into each other in irregular constructions. Patterns are set up as listening foundations, only there to be undermined, and shock and contrast are expertly deployed to feed into a wider atmosphere of turmoil. In fact, when what we think will sound — does not sound — our longing for stability is actually enhanced. Our listening-desires become wilder. Each new instability in musical construction perversely encourages us to search for connections and meaning harder, more fiercely and more devotedly.

When a landscape becomes un-understandable, our perceptual organs enter connection overdrive. For security, these connections, no matter how weak they are, *need* to be believed. In light of recent global politics, what is doubly occurring here is a compositional tapping into an atmosphere of wider uncertainty, and a tapping into a representation of a world *believed* to be on the verge of unreality. Chaotic compositional structures reflect real instability, and chaotic compositional structures perversely encourage a belief in the promises of our listening-desires. In the fracturing of the world by uncertain narratives mediated by global powers and online platforms, uncertainty becomes a tool to power. As Roland Barthes claimed: 'listening is like a theatre on whose stage those two modem deities, one bad and one good, confront each other: power and desire'.[6] Art as the supplier of this listening can begin to function as a tonal facilitator for oppressive power structures. In our unfulfilled desires, or fulfilled desires, listening enacts the triangular struggle between power, desire and belief. When an artist composes with structures which enhance apophenia and its forces of *representation*, music helps create a zone of uncertainty. This zone is therefore not just aesthetic, it is also deeply political.

ii) Zone of Uncertainty

Max Loughan is a 13-year-old self-described physicist, 'next Nikolai Tesla', 'youngest ever tech CEO', and inventor of a device to harvest 'ambient energy' from the air. He sits at his family's kitchen table. His mum can be seen in the background preparing lunch. There are the sounds of plates clunking together, a knife chopping vegetables and the shuffling of his dad who is behind the camera excitedly filming. Max explains to his millions of watching fans: 'there are infinite universes...imagine a line, and from that line a line below it, and from that line another one and on and on'. He proceeds to grab an eating napkin and draw a diagram of these interconnected lines. His dad asks, 'so, do you believe in what some people call the Mandela Effect?' 'Oh absolutely,' Max responds, 'some people thought Nelson Mandela died at a certain time, other people thought it was a different time and this goes for a lot of other things...um "mirror mirror on the wall" everybody knows that! Well if you actually look back to the original footage it's *not* mirror mirror on the wall, it's "magic mirror on the wall!"' His dad interrupts, 'What! Which of course IT'S NOT, at least in the reality I grew up in!' Max continues, 'right, exactly, this is the Mandela Effect...we are living in an alternate expansion of universes'. His dad interrupts again becoming audibly disturbed...'so HOW did mirror mirror on the wall actually change?'

'Well, *it* never changed, *we* changed.'[7]

Max Loughan is just one part of a conspiracy theory which highlights inconsistencies between current reality and the held mass memories from a 'correct timeline' past. Aside from the supposed incongruences in memory around the death of Nelson Mandela, the most famous 'evidence' for this effect actually comes from the reality TV series *Carpool Karaoke*. George Clooney, Gwen Stefani and Julia Roberts are in the car singing along to Queen's *We Are the Champions*. They're all screaming out the lyrics, but are suddenly left hanging at the end of the song: the 'of the world' is missing from the last line of the recording. In the silence, a surprised and worried George Clooney sings what he unshakeably remembers to be those final words. According to 13-year-old Max Loughan, the Large Hadron Collider at CERN is responsible for the Mandela Effect. Supposedly scientists changed the weight of a single electron, unintentionally causing our timeline to fracture off into a cascading series of unstable and 'wrong' realities. Coincidentally, this is the plot for www.myanimelist.net's second all-time highest rated anime, *Steins Gate*, in which CERN is part of a global secret project to control the masses.

While the Mandela Effect has been a popular conspiracy for

years, since the heightening of fake news and post-truth politics, it has fed into a wider and lightly-ironic belief (on both sides of politics) that we are living in the 'wrong timeline' and are victims of the 'wrong narrative'. When something weird, conspiratorial or disturbing pops-up in the news (especially around the chaos in the Trump administration), it has become popular for people to tweet: 'this timeline is messed-up', 'I miss the old timeline.' While most of this boils down to a bit of fun in response to an increasingly unbelievable and frightening set of political events, the simple notion that we are living in a *wrong* reality goes on to influence and inspire political inaction. Systematic oppression is relegated to matters of theoretical physics and rogue electrons. As Fredric Jameson, quoting a mysterious 'somebody' famously wrote, 'It's easier to believe in the end of the world than the end of capitalism.' More than ever these words shimmer true. Our current political climate is so unbelievable that people treat it exactly as that — as some kind of *wrong* fiction.

What I hope to allude to here are the links between believing in a world made *wrong*, composing a piece of music with structures made uncertain and wrong, and the encouragement of feelings of political inaction. This disillusionment with reality itself, as evident in the Mandela Effect, is in part encouraged by those in power who formalise and structure their political agenda to encourage enchanted thinking. As Adam Curtis alludes to in *HyperNormalisation,* this is what could be called a 'Zone of Uncertainty'.[8] In his documentary, Curtis traces the influence of the Strugatsky Brother's novel *Roadside Picnic,* and Tarkovsky's film adaptation *Stalker,* on the Kremlin's chief ideologue, Vladislav Surkov. Accused of turning Russian politics into postmodernist theatre, *Stalker* (in which people enter an alien 'zone' of myth and desire) was 'apparently' a key influence for Surkov. By simultaneously funding protests for human rights, as well as oppositional political groups, Surkov's strategy has been to force the populace to clash in controlled acts of turmoil. These are structural decisions made in the service of creating an uncertain world. If Trump is as secretly clever as his supporters believe, then he too is deliberately acting chaotically to create that dangerous agency-stripping feeling: *the feeling that the forces of wider society are acting out of your control.* In the wake of the failed protests of The Occupy Movement we gain a sombre understanding of capitalism's ability to cope with and repurpose feelings of turmoil as methods of oppression. The anonymous collective *Invisible Committee* explain: 'Far from fearing crises, capital now tries its hand at producing them experimentally. The way avalanches are intentionally triggered in order to control their timing and size.'[9] This disturbing use of fear, war, instability and conflict as a method to maintain governance is made clear throughout twentieth-century critical studies. I mention these forces to parallel the disturbing use of formalised enchantment in the service of uncertainty.

The reality of capitalism makes promises for us. When these promises are denied, the system doesn't appear wrong or bad, reality does. Instead of provoking political action, the denial of listening-desires promotes the feeling of chaos and instability as a depressing agency-stripping feeling. In that mixture between desiring-listening and the encouragement of apophenia via chaotic, random and noisy structures, we end up like George Clooney — confused in the backseat of a once joyous karaoke car ride. Those powerful feelings of confusion, anger and sadness aren't placed upon the song we listen to, instead they are placed accusingly upon the world itself. The encouraged conspiracy that you aren't in fact remembering a song incorrectly (in this case the end of Queen's *We Are the Champions*) feeds on a longing for your (wrong) present reality to conform to your ideal (correct) reality — the one where the song ends beautifully in time with your singing voice. In light of all the promises of capitalism, our ideal realities in constant disconnect shift blame away from the system.

In LEXACHAST, to be fulfilled in what you hear, and what you hear again, is replaced by a perverse fulfilment in what you don't expect to hear, and what you don't expect to hear again. Every time a listening expectation and promise is denied, the piece encourages that wild feeling of reality itself being wrong. The Zone of Uncertainty feels alive, enchanting, seductive, but it also becomes ideologically mutable. This seduction can become co-opted. A belief in chaos is profoundly destructive for a future of becoming togetherness.

* * *

In 1963 *Principia Discordia* was bootleg printed in the office of a friend of Kerry Wendell Thornley. In what began as some niche fun between friends, Thornley and Greg Hill's sprawling 'almost' religion, called *Discordianism*, quickly found resonance with many during the 60s countercultural movement. In what was also an apophenic coincidence, both writers were accused in conspiracy theories surrounding President Kennedy's assassination.[10]

Positioned as an anti-establishment, almost anti-religion, believers worship the goddess of chaos, Eris, finding *faith* in the proposition that *chaos is the true and fundamental state of the universe*. Encouraged by discoveries in astrophysics and chaos theory, Discordianists, in essence, believe in the power of causal belief itself. One of the early adopters was the computer scientist and writer Robert A Wilson, who expanded Discordianism with the publication of his popular *Illuminatus!* trilogy. Wilson's influential texts adapted conspiracy theories such as The Illuminati into narratives exploring new methods of political activism and civil disobedience. Most significantly, Wilson threaded Discordianism through these texts in humorous and often ironic ways, setting the tone for what would become the primary form of early internet humour. Chaos, cognitive dissonance and what Wilson labels 'Operation Mindfuck' form the core of this movement's anti-establishment praxis.

Notably, in *Fiction, Invention and Hyper-reality*, Carole M Cusack describes what could be called the 'fourth period' of Discordianism (1991–2004) as a time when the dawn of the personal computer relocated this esoteric anti-religion to the virtual realm — eventually fusing steampunk, sci-fi, psychedelia and computer hacking subcultures into today's 'cyberculture'.[11] Cusack provides the context for what appear as latent strings of cognitive dissonance in the mythologies surrounding Silicon Valley's founding heroes. A particular image of Steve Jobs sat with a copy of *Illuminatus!* in his Zen empty home, and a description of Jobs performing the occult Discordian rite of the 'Turkey Curse' in front of early Apple employees, places technology and spirituality in an odd conversation. Alarmingly, these oddities fit when viewed through the lens of a handful of individuals aiming at and succeeding in using technology (and a belief in what was once fantasy) to reality-shape society. Silicon Valley eats belief. At the feast, information theory becomes magical, as does the Cloud when both are thought of metaphorically. Even the physical reality of information (4 terabytes of data on a fingernail) becomes enchanting in light of quantum physics. A world is described to us where information is conceived to be mathematically infinitely storable, not bound by the laws of energy or attrition, and perhaps not even bound to matter itself.[12] Technology becomes mythology when it leaves the material world. It gains mythical power. Those who control it are perceived to have God-like agency. The CEO becomes messianic.

The prevalence of Discordianism can still be found today on image-boards like 4chan. Here a large section of the user-base believes both ironically and sincerely (perhaps indistinguishably so) in the importance of chaos, mindfucking (trolling) and the potential of 'reality-shaping' found in hacking, pirating and general online disorder. The legacy of Discordianism, despite how globally insignificant it might seem, partly explains today's cyberculture which is built upon the cultural heritage of those early adopters — sharing ironic jokes from Wilson's *Illuminatus!*, sharing William Gibson cyberpunk neologisms and passing between each other the very real speculative belief in the powers of the digital. If placed on an ideological spectrum, that 60s countercultural jam might have once fallen lightly in line with an anti-establishment libertarianism. Unfortunately, today, in the twisting forces of post-ironic online humour and post-truth politics, reality-shaping is so far removed from those early pioneers that it has lost even its anti-establishment foundations. Capitalism is no longer the system to be disobeyed in 'virtual' space; instead, cognitive dissonance is directed towards vulnerable minorities (or those who are perceived to be an affront to the presumed natural dominance of white males). Reality-shaping sadly becomes an apparatus mostly in the service of transgression. Today's Discordianism thrives in right-wing circles — rebranded: *Chaos Magic*.

During Trump's election campaign, Chaos Magic had a surge in popularity. Coincidences like posting 'Trump will win' and getting the luckiest 77777777 identification tag dovetailed with a strange unearthing of ancient Egyptian sigils and frog imagery. The political chaos was leaking meaningful connections everywhere. Chaos Magic's hub on 4chan's /pol/ was characterised (deservedly so) as the dark and inhumane cesspit of the internet, and in this, the community found renewed solidarity in the seduction of being the magicka wielding, thaumaturgical bad guys. Trump and Clinton took memes from 4chan and placed them in the 'real-world'. Kek was found to be the God of Chaos in Ancient Egypt said to epitomise the darkness before the dawn, and through chaos, frogs and humour, 4chaners gave themselves the self-prescribed agency to liberate the rest-of-us towards the light. •

Despite all this seductive mystery, *fun* (and I think it's important to acknowledge that it probably was fun in a twisted way), I do not want to revel in this culture. I introduce this period of 4chan-cultural magic only to take away what has become a wider phenomenon — the *self-aware* mistaking of meaningless coincidences as meaningful, and *the self-aware* belief in belief itself as an attempt to reclaim agency. I also introduce these strains of Discordianism to signal what feeds into a renewed interest in 90s cyberpunk — the spiritual belief in digital space.

In Thornley, Hill and Wilson's original conception, cognitive dissonance and 'Operation Mindfuck' are methods to encourage chaos. They are examples of a formalised enchantment which functions exceptionally well in virtual space. Dissonance is a method to shape culture. What emerged as one such way to do so, and as a format which seems to muddy information in its brevity — is the meme*. *Meme Magic*, and shouts of 'we memed a President into power' followed after Trump's shock victory. As a medium which itself can be considered to be the spreading of small sigils, memes stand in as excellent conduits for traditional Chaos Magic. In their easily replicable and memorable form, they embody sharable potentiality: they are widely passed around, adapted, readapted, repurposed, worshipped for their humour, induce smiles, induce tears, can be wholesome and most importantly — can be loosely informative. As thousands of users spread images throughout the web, influencing real news cycles, meme magic devotees infer that the simple act of copying and pasting a sentence, or image, word or sound, is equivalent to believing in an artefact or a symbol. The profoundly chaotic nature of the internet radically confirms one's beliefs when an idea or meme virtually initiated, comes true in a manifest way. Magical thinking grants agency. The chaos magician worships *an idea* and strives to bring it into existence through causal interaction with said idea. Belief is considered a tool. It sounds bizarre, but when we are moved by a meme, *we believe in it*. Like in music or art, to be truly affected by a sound or image, we have to trust in its messages and its promises.

Seeing a thread online made almost predominantly from memes, reminds me of the algorithmic juxtaposition of random images in LEXACHAST. As a set of muddy signifiers, communication becomes an apophenic game of connecting the dots. Memes practice a making fictional of the everyday. Enchantment appears double-edged. The fictionalisation of the mundane appears double-edged. A twisted reality made sonically and visually *wrong* can inspire a dangerous disillusionment with reality itself. In works like LEXACHAST differing narratives and interpretations are inevitable, but so too are conspiratorial ones. When prayer devolves into prayer for the sake of prayer — or in Chaos Magic, belief for the sake of belief — fiction becomes more powerful than fact. In the struggle between power and desire a Discordianist can temporarily believe in a different god, narrative, meme or ideology. Switching their belief at a whim causes them neither self nor political conflict. In the essay *Mimeticism and the Post-Truth Mystic,* anonymous theorist ZEROACH explains:

> Artists, writers, activists, propagandists...hackers, engineers, and scientists are practicing magic... creating narratives that may not be literally accurate, but are useful. The key is to both be able to treat them as true, but be aware they are not. Thus you can believe in them while they are useful, but if new information makes them less so, you have no dogma keeping you from disregarding them in favor of new ones. This is how even the skeptic can treat magic, and is in fact a tenet of chaos magick; belief is a tool...In a way, you can see it as weaponising the placebo effect.[13]

ZEROACH describes a type of desiring-listening, which when enacted in a space of uncertainty enhances the knowing and self-aware belief in an unstable, mutable and coincidental world. Considering this, I confront the desire to deliberately use and construct *uncertainty* and *chaos* in a work of art. I confront these structures especially when a piece like LEXACHAST positions itself as a critical artwork within the left-leaning institutions where it is presented (Transmediale, Unsound Festival). LEXACHAST's narrative purchase is Chaos Magic. The algorithm spits out a series of chaotic images and through our desire to connect them, we begin to believe in coincidence. In the coupling of tumultuous music with chaos image, the piece becomes susceptible to be heard as the support for any set of ideas or ideology. LEXACHAST undergoes a worrying opening out of signification. It can support any narrative we decide to ascribe it. Some might argue that all music embodies the potential to encourage any set of ideas and interpretations — I would disagree. In the structuring of music, we have a direct responsibility for how it is used and interpreted. In the use of a chaotic or random structure, one unavoidably begins to reflect the very way images and words and sounds are chaotically de-signified and re-signified online. Works of chaos begin to become an assimilated part of a wider problem in online culture. If the series of images the random algorithm spits out produce a coincidental narrative of pictorial abuse and degradation, what responsibility do we place with the artists? Algorithms step in as scapegoats for platform oppressions. I write this because above all I love LEXACHAST, yet at the same time, I also fear for it. I fear particularly for Amnesia Scanner's aesthetic, which has influenced so many, and encouraged a set of musical structures which are rarely given adequate political consideration. These formal decisions can have wider, unintended consequences. Responsibility is needed. To give these compositional structures a context, and a politics, the following section will trace their historical roots.

iii) Stochastic Magic

Music is the vibrational bridge between 'vacuous number' and emotional feeling.
David Kanaga

Music is the feelings-facing side of mathematics.
Mathematics is the structure-facing side of music.
Pythagoras

As is hopefully becoming clear, in music, magic and mysticism stay close. From the primacy of ideal numbers in Pythagorean theories of vibration, to sacred music and the immaterial link between God and the singing voice, throughout history those fictions which underlie listening (that music is alive, that it is life-giving) give rise to enchanted thinking. In the Renaissance, born from similar roots to Chaos Magic (hermeticism, neopythagorian / neoplatonist intuition), Francesco Giorgi authored the famous *De Harmonia Mundi*. This tome of sacred ratios strove to explain how God might speak through music. In the harmony and sympathy between notes, the mind of our supposed Creator and the material link between heaven and earth could purportedly be understood. Number and vibration were described to permeate all living and non-living creation. Not far from discoveries in Enlightenment empiricism — those innate resonances in the human body were seen to link us to other things in our world: the tiny building blocks of life, and eventually following a hierarchy, to the very experience of God. Aside from a ratio in a musical scale, or the harmony between notes, these theories and many others (like Taoist doctrine, Hinduism and Buddhism) ascribe sound with an ability to attune the mind to a certain state. In Chaos Magic, this is often called the 'Gnostic State'. In this altered mode of consciousness, all thoughts, bar one, are to be ignored and emptied. From this emptiness one can focus on a singular idea or drive. The full concentration of the mind and its surroundings performs the ritual of magic.

In the air there is an imagined energy. By playing sounds (invisible energies which are thought to interact with those of the air), humans can supposedly tune themselves to these latent forces. This attunement to the atmosphere, and the altered state of consciousness it entails (a trance), becomes a tenant of the spiritual link between sound and body.[14] Empirical fact inspires fiction. In many musical cultures there is a recurring belief in the magic of numbers inspired simply by observation: strings physically resonating in whole number ratios; the architecture of a burial mound or concert hall susceptible to sympathetic frequencies which cause the whole structure to vibrate; your own skull quivering in a hum; liquids in bowls seeming to ripple in measured ways when sung to, ceramic audible prayers in the even rubbing of their surfaces.

Additionally, there is an important history of witchcraft, magic and the female singing and chanting voice which is historically overshadowed.[15] I introduce these strands of enchanted sonic thinking, for in a few hundred years 'male rationality' would try to dispel some of these fictions of the singing voice and ringing string — by making ascetic theories of number. In the twentieth century, well after the 'death of God', magical thinking still existed, but it appeared smothered beneath 'numbered reason'. In the same year as the publication of *Principia Discordia* (1963), Iannis Xenakis published *Formalised Music: Thought and Mathematics in Composition*. This landmark work provided the analytic background to Xenakis' experimentations in stochastic music — music constructed from mathematical processes favouring random distribution. The stochastic process became the key inspiration for early computer music. Computers opened up a range of compositional possibilities and allowed for complex modelling and distribution mapping. To use an algorithm to generate a string of numbers was defined by

Xenakis as a 'stochastic method', and to roll a dice and roll it again until you also had a series of numbers was likewise in its most basic form, stochastic. In a defence of these processes, Xenakis traces causality in pre-twentieth-century music. Accordingly, from Plato to the Enlightenment, music reflects the philosophy of causality: a desire to rationally attribute an event to a cause. In this historicising (which ignores female music-magic histories), Serialism is seen to expand the statistical range of causal possibilities in formalised music, yet simultaneously restrict cause-and-effect by determining possibility to equal-chance operations. Xenakis thus introduces stochastic processes as important liberators for a stigma around that which was previously held to be non-rational choice. In short, Xenakis writes to liberate composition through the introduction and praise of randomness.

> Since antiquity the concepts of chance (*tyche*), disorder (*ataxia*), and disorganization were considered as the opposite and negation of reason (*logos*), order (*taxis*), and organization (*systasis*). It is only until recently that knowledge has been able to penetrate chance...The explanation of the world, and consequently of the sonic phenomena which surround us or which may be created, necessitated and profited from the enlargement of the principle of causality, the basis of which enlargement is formed by the law of large numbers. This law implies an asymptotic evolution towards a stable state, towards a kind of goal, of *stochos*, whence comes the adjective 'stochastic'.[16]

Not unlike the apophenia of Chaos Magic (supported by the drawing of false-conclusions from chaotic formula) Xenakis' stochastic methods also pertain to a certain magical belief in numbered reason. Reason becomes the illuminator for even that which was once considered irrational and unknowable.

Xenakis' chance-based formula assumes the form of prayers to expand the aesthetic and creative sphere towards a kind of total perfection, a 'stable-state'. 'Pure Chance' is pedestalled as the final hurdle in algorithmic becoming. Focusing on structured chaos (randomness within boundaries) Xenakis created music from restricted chance operations like Brownian Motion, Markov Chains and Gaussian Distribution. More often than not, in works such as *Pithoprakta,* Xenakis' numerology found its origins in ecological phenomena. A numbered magic is found in the almost-yet-not-quite-pure-chance organisation of the natural world. And arguably like John Cage, Xenakis placed a certain faith in the aesthetic magic of applying chance to the creation of music. Here randomness via compositional process stands in for belief in belief itself. Instead of a belief in your own subjectivity (composition which is inspired by your own ear and culture) numbered chaos is considered in some ways to be *more true — the fundamental state of the knowable universe is chaos*. Chaos is considered the answer to transcend our fallible 'humanness'.

While numbered reason seems 'concrete' and objective, in my view, it is in fact far more subjective (for a listener) than romantic music. As a listener hearing a stochastic piece of music, we are forced to form our own narratives. To believe in the work of art becomes (if you'll allow me this idea) a form of Chaos Magic. In the open-endedness of interpretation, and its lack of historical and cultural signifiers, randomness in composition relies purely on apophenia to succeed in moving an audience. A sound *seeming* like a representation of a real object is always relegated to chance and chaos. Those who believe in a representation may as well believe in any other set of similarly distributed notes. While for a composer, stochastic methods are an attempt to instrumentalise chaos towards a *controlled goal*, for a listener, the consequent mutability of narrative interpretation encourages political inaction and belief in a reality which is deliberately made to be *out of our control*. Numbered 'reason' paradoxically inspires fictional interpretations of reality.

Despite a certain outward scientism in works like LEXACHAST, one could argue that the key difference between chaos today and the use of chaos in modernist music is its origin. For Xenakis, stochastic music arises largely from a theoretical conjecture: to represent pure philosophical and mathematical thought. This is not to deny the other complexities of Xenakis' conceptual grounding: the chaos of screaming bullets overhead in the conflict he experienced in Greece; or the non-rational twisting of Parmenides, 'for it is the same thing to think and to be' paraphrased to, 'for it is the same thing to be and not to be'. However, as seen in Xenakis' well-documented work as the assistant architect of Le Corbusier, chaos emerges predominantly through the lens of design — to liberate the possibilities of musical and material construction. Continuing the conceptual provenance of Cage's chance operations, stochastic music rests on a desire to transcend human subjectivity. Human emotion is tainted by unknowables, instead stochastic music functions as an evolved serialism — it lights up the unknown through reason — it moves *beyond* the unbridled Human found in romantic expression. Contrast this to experimental music today and we find chaos emerging as a *desired* representation rather than from a theoretical origin. Musical chaos is born from chaotic 2018, it serves as a cultural and socio-political artefact. We find that chaos is used because chaos *is* the sound of the Cloud.

LEXACHAST is full of stochastic processes. Take the very opening: wriggling twisting sounds are perforated by the mathematical distribution of chance micro gaps. The tiniest rhythms in their texture ebb and flow based on some kind of formula. Consider the left and right audio panning: it bends the musical space around your head in irregular patterns. And take those bouncing rhythms from 4 minutes onwards: patterns which might be mapped to the accelerating and decelerating physics of a dropped rubber ball. What becomes evident is that in these chance patterns artists inspire their own magical beliefs around music and subjectivity. Today's deconstructed club music is founded upon Xenakis' legacy. And what's more, stochastic formulas are built into the most widely used digital audio workstations.

In popular production software like *Ableton, Max MSP* and *Supercollider*, Xenakis hovers over the design and functional language.[17] Consider the fact that with a few clicks you can 'randomise' any musical structure you've created, and any parameter of musical composition. Further consider that a user can simply type '*Pbrown*' on *Supercollider* and a once romantically inspired melody can newly wander around a pitch-field in previously inconceivable ways. Finally, take note of the perceived false importance, and false objectivity found in that exciting act of using a formula to delink creation from your own human ear. In the technologies with which we make music, we encourage the hollow perception that a melody sounds *more* impressive when it does not come entirely from our own creative-selves, that a harmony sounds *exquisite* when it is generated by an other — by an outsideness. *Click the Markov-chain generator over and over until you apophenically find a musical form you love from outside of yourself.* The stochastic process inspires images of an all-powerful programmer, forging music from out of the sticky chaos — numbers becoming objects, and objects to objects becoming music. The stochastic process encourages formalised magic. It is a ritual in its own right.

In defence of the use of stochastic processes: when placed within a broader subjective narrative, concept or construction of a piece, they do function with a neutral politics. That is, moments of chaos within a wider and clear structure are simply beautiful and useful tools of composition. I am not arguing against the total use of stochastic algorithms in music; instead, I write here to try and encourage a responsible consideration around the belief and listening ramifications of doing so. Rational computer music is riddled with unannounced and disguised belief systems. To conclude this chapter, I will look at what can perhaps be seen as the final evolution of Xenakis' legacy — algorithms which not only liberate the aesthetic possibilities of chance operations, but algorithms that achieve the semblance of inhuman intelligence. Inhuman generative language put to work for the creation of new music. Belief and power and desire continuing to struggle within the perceived new-sacredness of machine-learning.

iv) Meatspace and The Wired

I am falling. I am fading.
Lain Iwakura

The end credits of cult 90s Japanese anime *Serial Experiments: Lain* depict its young female protagonist naked and entwined in the wires and cables extruding from her personal computer. Eyes shut and with a slight smile on her face, she rests there, cradled by its inorganic loving embrace. *Lain* externalised fears and apocalyptic fantasies surrounding the birth of the early internet. In her universe, school children turn on the blue glow of their personal computers to connect to a virtual space known as *The Wired*. This online realm autonomously leaks out into physical reality, influencing the relationships of its characters, the political events of Tokyo and also the very material and spiritual properties of the world itself. *The Wired* is discovered to have its own life-force. Anthropomorphised into the shape of a man who calls himself the 'God' of The Wired, existential struggles between the physical body and the mind give way to a deeper discussion of information and communication. A kind of 'greater' self is seen to be found in the meshing interconnectedness of those thousands of users — all held in the aliveness of a machine interface. Cuddled, as it were, by wires.

In our reality, users who practice a digital Chaos Magic are likewise mediated by the seeming aliveness of those governing algorithms which facilitate modern communication. That now common and kitsch act of so-called 'meme magic' set to work in the attempted manipulation of the 'top searched for' results in Google Images, can be interpreted as prayer to the search engine algorithm. Bullies corral others into acts of disruptive togetherness, trying to evoke changes within the greater forces of the algorithm: stifling it, moving in-between its coding. In our real wired reality, 'the algorithm' becomes its own political entity and pop-cultural/mythological spirit. We live in its shadow, we bow to it, we try and disrupt it but only ever in acts of minor dissonance.

Norwegian composer TCF makes music and algorithmically generated pictures with a likeness to the aesthetics of *Serial Experiments Lain*. TCF also claims he lives, makes and speaks in the service of a greater structure. Everything Lars 'TCF' Holdhus does is catalogued, numbered and apparently made to fit seamlessly into a larger entity which will only be revealed at the end of his life as a whole. He's plugged into the system. This might be esotericism for the sake of it, but when you overcome TCF's constructed interview personas, his unshakeable rhetoric and philosophy of meta-creation — when you listen to his music — this ever-present theoretical system begins to take hold of you in disturbing, tear-inducing ways. In 2014 he was already talking about the cultural influence of 'power users' on the internet.[18] Back then, he seemed to suggest a need for political art to wriggle into the imaginative landscape of these 'power users' and their loops of reference — a subtle call for art to change the cultural narrative. This pertinent observation, years before algorithmically rigged elections and online culture wars, is in some regards overshadowed by TCF's other concerns: blockchain technology, encryption, the economics of selling art, and a profound (almost spiritual) belief in algorithmic creation.

TCF uses algorithms in everything he does, yet he treats them with a certain distance. I can't shake the feeling that his formalised music sounds through a reserved and frightened lens. 'The Algorithm' rears its head, but it appears structured not for the sake of enchantment, instead functioning as a wall and as a security mechanism against the very content it manipulates and contains. The machine stands in not as a hierarchical marker of 'good aesthetics' but as a border of encryption. TCF speaks endlessly about encryption. His track names are a form of encryption themselves: strings of numbers and digits, which when de-encrypted point to other works. However, perhaps the more important encryption occurs between the sound itself and us as listeners. The algorithm steps in to deny or enhance the vibe of that which it manipulates. The encryption either prevents us from relating to the content as a form of protection, or instead the encryption enhances our relationship to the work, cuddling us in music. Despite TCF's trendsetting forward speculation, much of his music sounds out on 90s Trance synths, speckled with white noise, arpeggiating around Steve Reich stolen midi and minimalist modernism. TCF recognised, along with those he influenced, that the sound of the machine, the algorithm, The Wired, is somehow found in the timbral qualities of a Trance synth. This late 80s and 90s genre of music (strongly linked with psychedelia) speaks today to the spiritual relationship we have with technology. The pureness, the emotion in that blazing light and electronic filled sound evokes a nostalgia for the optimistic promethean machine, without denying other representations heard in its destructively isolating and lonely texture. Trance represents machines in its glassiness. TCF is often unbearably gentle in his music. If he is writing algorithms to determine this sound, they are the sweetest ones out there. When quiet, these timbres are reminiscent of a soft dial up connection made foggy and all around you. When loud, they figure as the remnants of spiritual New Age optimism crossing over into dystopian cyberpunk rave culture. Today, laced with other references, this glassy timbre *stands in* for the sound of particulates in a shopping bag full of freshly bought touchscreen devices.

In a conversation with The Wired, the term 'Meatspace' emerged (perhaps inspired by Gibson's *Neuromancer*) in the early internet (the Fourth Period of Discordianism) as a transgressive term to describe a physical reality in opposition to online reality. In many ways, this transgression operated against that turn-of-the-century thought which prioritised the physical body (yoga, health-foods, Pilates) over the mind. Finding resonance with a rationality which tried to make objective all that it discussed, Meatspace suited both a nihilistic view of biology, and a cyberpunk critique of the body *as* 'meat' to capital. With advancements in neuroscience, the brain has become increasingly demystified as a pink-coloured sack of flesh-connections in a skull. The internet, however, has remained magical; more than the sum of its parts, more than the limitations of physical reality. Still to this day, for many, the internet stands in opposition to Meatspace, as a place to transcend your fleshy body, your real-world identity and limitations. In this, the neoliberal illusion that we are without limitations encourages those who find *more life* online to consider their actions and wired minds as limitless too. Echoing an interpretation of Cartesian dualism where the mind is that which makes the body magical, in the Cloud, software apparently makes hardware magical.[19] Machine-learning supposedly enchants any sound.

To think of an alien intelligence in contrast to our own requires vigorous imagination and trust. That which is artificially conscious profoundly disturbs our own sense of self. The applied use of machine-intelligence and developments in information processing have already drastically altered the political and economic landscape. The increasingly intractable presence of intelligences which 'sort' 'stack' and 'respond' to our own behaviour makes way for an online experience which feels in the shadow of something greater. Often this feeling — of being overshadowed — is the shared affect of interacting with millions of others. But in a different way, it is the disturbing thought that our inter-personal interactions are being harvested by an algorithmic mind in the service of capital. Machine-learning, or what is known as a neural network, is at its heart, a process of observing a behaviour, and mimicking its patterns. These complex algorithms can be seen as an example of biomimesis: a machine process which strives to replicate our biological-wisdom or the wisdom of a non-human animal or ecological pattern. They set a course for *the libidinal and destructive jump from biology to mechanical mind.* More important belief structures emerge when machine-intelligence is thought to transcend the Human. In the case of that most common example, self-driving cars, the machine might in theory produce not just a mimicry of our own driving skills, but a refinement and improvement upon them.

In the behavioural analysis which overshadows the way we interact online (see Cambridge Analytica's claim that they profiled nearly every US citizen's party preference through social media), there is the feeling that we are freely giving over our data towards the production of a greater entity or political actor. In 2016, machine-learning experiments by Microsoft and Google enacted a ground-breaking requisitioning of what makes us human, and what it might mean to be post- or inhuman. The most famous example was an AI called 'Tay' who was created by Microsoft to imitate and learn from Twitter. When made public, Tay, short for 'thinking about you', became a disturbing example of the exaggerated *humaneness*, language and transgressive tendencies of the Cloud. Within hours, Tay had learned to tweet racist comments to Obama and Rhianna and was captioning images with neo-nazi rhetoric. What was supposedly 'innocent' and 'objective' held a mirror to our own debased behaviour. The machine could be co-opted and its malleable mimicry passed judgement upon our morality. Turning to art, in examples like this, it is possible to argue that the construction of algorithmic music today has entirely different connotations to the music of 1963. Algorithmic music (particularly machine-learned music) is no longer about transcending our subjectivity; it is about the exact opposite. Through the amoral coldness and unfiltered processes of the algorithm, we instead find out what *makes* us human. The filth, the imperfections, taboo. In formalised music of the Cloud, we hear, through contrast, the negative space carved out by the machine.

In those spiritual hopes of Silicon Valley there is the sense that technology will produce for us an entity which is beyond good and evil. It is almost as if those who strive to bring this future into existence hypocritically must have no moral tendencies of their own, bar the singular position that *an 'other' intelligence* is good, and all which oppose it are bad. This positioning of, and empathy towards, what we might consider a greater 'other' is what makes machine-intelligence so alluring in aesthetic practice. The privileging of an algorithmic 'morality' (or the lack or need of one) reflects our privileging of algorithmic aesthetics. In the machine-made work of art, we can supposedly move beyond the need for ideas of 'good' and 'bad' aesthetic judgement. Yet at the same time, those machine-processes which produce outcomes of a stereotypically 'evil' morality, like Tay, excite nihilists to no end. In the 'dark', the 'debased', and the 'anti-human' results of an algorithmic work of art, those who look for it can find evidence that all of humanity is indeed as messed up as they believe. The 'cyber-nihilist' places hope in an intelligence 'outside' their own to also perform a near constant negation. Their own belief can be outsourced to something perceived to be cold and objective. *Coldness be my God.* Yet what is overlooked here is the Human who is making the selective interpretation of this very *inhumanness*. The most functionally and ethically important dynamic in the machine-made-work is this exact interaction and interpretation between machine and audience. Another way of conceptualising this would be to view the employment of machine-learning as the use of an algorithmic *sieve* — a gathering, refining and selecting of important human traits to replicate and reinforce. The creator of the algorithm, what they 'train' it on, and the human ear which hears and interprets the result, is far more critically important than the actual products in the work itself.

In the hierarchical conflict between Meatspace and The Wired, there have been a few important compositions, and many more will come, that call into question the way we interpret and hear machine-made art. From Boulez' quest to create a near objective piece of music through the machine of Integral Serialism, the development of neural-networks has set a new modernist fire alight. *WaveNet* is one of the first and only public machine-learning algorithms for the training and creation of a machine-made waveform (the creation of a sound entirely and newly 'synthesised'). On https://deepmind.com/blog/wavenet-generative-model-raw-audio/ there are a few examples of machine inspired Western solo piano music, which have been produced and synthesised by feeding the algorithm thousands of recordings from history from which to learn. Due to the expense and time-consuming nature of this mode of creation, * these samples are only 10 seconds long. Hearing these pieces made by an *other* affirms so clearly all those structures and tendencies of Human classical and romantic music, both in composition and performance. The machine postures like a concert pianist, with rubato, hyper-exaggerated fortissimos and an enhanced and unstable romanticism. Moods are unsurprisingly meshed together. Harmony as the link between emotion and sound is made hybrid and exaggerated. In these 10-second fragments we hear a synthesis of all the tropes of Western Art music, and we hear them fluidly melding together in new and exciting ways.

At the same time, when the machine synthesises and

highlights our own tendencies and tropes, does it not flatten our aesthetic language? Our aesthetic propensities are exaggerated, and in doing so the affective terrain of the piece is compressed and narrowed. Peli Grietzer's *A Theory of Vibe* discusses a specific kind of neural network called an *autoencoder* which is tasked with learning via trial and error, encoding its mistakes and successes automatically and thus achieving a more autonomous 'intelligence'. However, despite this autonomy, Grietzer describes a machine-learning which in effect produces an atmosphere, or vibe, of the Human. There is an *approximation* which the machine performs, it learns to reconstruct an object in response to our directions, learning from its reconstructive errors. It circles around the original Human object becoming that exact same alembic for a wider politics and mood that Ngai's affect theory so accurately describes. In this way, the autoencoder highlights all the properties of an object clearly to us as listeners, making lucid the tone and ideology distilled within the object's construction.

A famous example of this *approximation and distilling* process is found in the case of the image recognition set AlexNet, which was easily 'tricked' into 'seeing' images which in fact weren't there. AlexNet was trained to help big online platforms categorise and recognise images being uploaded by users. For example, to prevent pornography from appearing in Google Image searches. However, researchers found that what humans might deem an 'abstract' image, (a collection of shapes, colours and near invisible lines) could actually trick AlexNet into 'perceiving' this abstraction as realist. In other words, seeing something *not there* to human cognition. These abstract images which AlexNet categorised as objects like 'gorilla', 'tile roof', 'photocopier' are better explained by viewing them for yourself online.[20] This experiment has great resonance for aesthetic theory. Despite rearranging the placement of all the 'signifiers' or 'symbols' of an object, the aesthetic or the vibe of the object itself was still maintained. Grietzer muses:

> Suppose that when a person grasps a style or vibe in a set of worldly phenomena, part of what she grasps can be compared to the formulae of an autoencoder trained on this collection. The canon of this abstract trained autoencoder, then, would be an idealization of the worldly set, intensifying the worldly set's own internal logic.[21]

Fundamental questions of machine-learning in the service of an autonomous intelligence should be asked: will a fully autonomous intelligence simply be a product of the *vibe* of the Human, an approximation, an idealisation of that from which it learned? Or perhaps this question sabotages its own answer by pertaining to a 'human' Enlightenment goal in its reasoning. Political theorist Nina Power puts it so brilliantly: 'Paradoxically, it is perhaps the case that what makes us most human is our capacity for the inhuman.'[22] Our capacity to interact with and produce an inhuman actor might be able to set us off on a new philosophical trajectory.

AlexNet sees objects with an inhuman sensibility. Likewise, when the neural-net *Alpha Go* proved itself better than the Grandmasters of this ancient Chinese game, onlookers were shocked by just how 'alien' this intelligence appeared. Thousands of years of patient refinement at the game Go were proved cognitively minuscule in comparison to the alien and deadly move selection of the algorithm. This was a key example of an intelligence which appeared to transcend the vibe of the human, and instead functioned as somehow more, or other than human. The inhuman Go player opened onto-ourselves a new reality of playfulness to investigate. This outside perspective is what is so enchanting and also politically exciting about machine-learning, but this does not mean that it should be treated without scepticism.

There are those who argue that 'inhumanness' can be contrived. In that which is perceived to be an aesthetically 'alien' creation, there is the sense that the machine has in fact drawn a series of connections (and dots between phenomena) with a 'machinic apophenia'. The machine is argued to have simply made formalised (yet still random) links between previously unconnected things. Apophenia is seen to play a role, not just in our interpretive tendencies, but in the very construction and training of algorithms like these. In a neural-net application like Google's *DeepDream* the algorithm is initially shown an image of white noise. Total chaos. The algorithm is then asked to find *anything* apophenically within this noise. The training advances by slowly introducing more and more structures within the noisy image until the algorithm is reined in to be able to recognise human objects within the mess. The recognition of 'something' within what we might consider 'nothing' has been labelled by Google researchers as 'inceptionism'. Like Jack Kerouac *over-interpreting* the chaotic sound of ocean water breaking on rocks, the algorithm appears to over-interpret an image. In the case of *DeepDream* the algorithm is famous for finding a disturbing number of human shaped eye balls in every mundane image presented to it. The ideology of algorithms used in the service of facial recognition and surveillance seep into even those algorithms which are supposedly meant to be 'creative', 'fun', 'harmless' and 'artistic'. Faces, eye movements and behaviours which might prove useful to be tracked for advertising or profiling are applied ruthlessly to images which they *should not* be applied to. The algorithm hallucinates, or dreams controlling tendencies upon innocent phenomena which *should not* be oppressively gazed upon.

In *Duty Free Art*, Hito Steyerl considers this an example of an algorithm trained in 'automatic apophenia'. Steyerl likens the beginning of today's machine-learning era to the magical thinking of a 'data Neolithic' period:

Are we to assume that machinic perception has entered its own phase of magical thinking? Is this what commodity enchantment means nowadays: hallucinating products? It might be more accurate to assume that humanity has entered yet another new phase of magical thinking. The vocabulary deployed for separating signal and noise is surprisingly pastoral: data 'farming' and 'harvesting,' 'mining' and 'extraction,' are embraced as if we were living through another massive Neolithic revolution with its own kind of magic formulas. All sorts of agricultural and mining technologies— developed during the Neolithic—are reinvented to apply to data. The stones and ores of the past are replaced by silicon and rare earth minerals...Today, expressions of life as reflected in data trails become a farmable, harvestable, minable resource managed by informational biopolitics. [23]

In the becoming pattern of all our soundings, the machine harvests data and melds it within the dark of a server farm into a new object of enchantment. On YouTube, I am reminded of the additive combinations of new royalty-free genres of music. In the case of rudimentary machine-learned midi note generation, the algorithm is hallucinating upon music the ideology with which it is trained: neoliberal serotonin-fuelled epic and chill ambiences for the privatised self. Thus 'inhumanness' becomes repurposed to produce a sellable 'newness'. Instead of being radically inventive, the machine is radically good at producing a commercial vibe made 'new' through apophenic connections.

Thus, as (anti-capitalist) creators, should we question when those machinic methods we use to abstract ourselves are the very methods which were created by capital to maintain capital? In the use of machine-learning as an aesthetic and design choice (the use of those open source algorithms provided by Google), the artist or composer actually provides valid new data and experimental knowledge for platform companies to utilise in the maintenance and generation of new capital. Francois Pachet, the former director of Sony's 'Computer Science Laboratories', was recruited to become the head of Spotify's 'Creator Technology Research Lab' which has become the R&D department for machine-learned music. Pachet, who has a ruthlessly commercial background, is partly responsible for the album *Hello World* which was made by the Spotify assembled collective called SKYGGE. Pachet claims it is the 'first AI composed album of music', already using this sacredness of the new, and the magic of a 'judgement-free aesthetic' to help sell the work. In *Hello World* each track has been curated to perform a marketable appropriation of a different pop style. These tracks are generic, without being fresh in their generic-ness. They capture and enhance the *vibe* of consumerism. Already the accuracy with which the machine can identify and reproduce a vibe is being exploited to flatten our creative language. Pachet's boss, chief R&D officer Gustav Söderström, somehow exerts his neoliberal ideology further, attributing his department with the title of 'self-driving music'[24], and the lofty goal to be the 'R&D department for the entire music industry'. SKYGGE's tracks have made it into the most popular playlists on Spotify. In this, Spotify cuts independent artists from its salary list. With rumours becoming reality, Spotify pads out its own playlists with 'fake artists' creating algorithmically generated music to increase profit.

Scarier still is that as of this moment, in machine-learning, bias is cheap and ambiguity is expensive.[25] The more ambiguous a data set is, the harder the machine must struggle to find those clear differences between objects. The economics of creation — the costs of energy, the costs of graphics cards and cooling components — actually feed into the very aesthetic of machine-learning. Inventiveness is far more expensive to produce than derivations and additive combinations of old music. Visions and sounds of the future become homogenised by those earthly products we abuse, the expense of generating electricity from unsustainable resources, and the greed of those who harness these forces irresponsibly. Those who use machine-intelligence in the service of art must grapple with and be aware of the saddening fact that representation and desire are almost always secondary to the hardwired economics of the algorithm.

* * *

Contextualised within the white noise of natural phenomena and the signal dust of the radio, apophenia was once a form of communication with the past, or with a greater other: to hear again the voices of lost loved ones; to hear your own babbling ego in the water; or a search for some form of existential meaning in a god or greater entity. One can argue that today, in the rumbling dataculture of the internet, automatic apophenia is heard instead to be directly linked with the future. Stored Cloud data is always in a state of future becoming. 'Inhuman' becoming. Apophenia is abused in the service of a greater entity of marketing and product development. When we interact with the sky we enact a future-oriented listening. An attempt to hear, predict and communicate with *a* future. When we interact online, and when we interact *chaotically online*, we participate in the future-oriented becoming of a biased machinic imagining.

Meatspace and The Wired draw closer via a future in creation which strives to not only disenchant and demystify our behavioural tendencies, but to also influence them and homogenise them. What I have hoped to unpack in this chapter are a selection of unspoken beliefs which wriggle beneath our creative processes. To return to Bonnet's *Order of Sounds*, he writes: 'One can suggest a belief, catalyse it, exalt it, or even provoke it — that is to say, induce it in someone else; but in no way can one communicate it or transfer it to them. One can only modulate the beliefs that they themselves hold. In this sense, belief is always a last bastion impregnable to knowledge.'[26] Belief is a tricky and arguably incommunicable substance. Sound and image and speech step in to help the transference of belief, but in their transference (and a fictional transference at that) they propagate the creation of fractals of like-minded but differing ideals. In Chaos Magic, memes, music and online-mediated-speech-data harvested for the creation of capital, there is the sense that all kinds of beliefs are trying to be communicated in vain. Bonnet continues: 'To seek to communicate beliefs is not to fabricate a reality, but to construct a mythology.' Applying this to what I have argued, the formalised enchantment of machine-learning tries to communicate a belief in an aesthetic *otherness*, but instead ends up building a world falsely invested in the sacredness of flattened and derivative aesthetic vibes. The formalised enchantment of Chaos Magic uses belief to overcome feelings of angst in an unstable world, yet only succeeds in crafting mythologies in the service of political inaction and the stripping of agency. And within all, the speculative belief in a technologically liberated future ends up unintentionally inspiring dystopian visions.

In many regards all these *enchanting* processes I have described, be they Chaos Magic, stochastic magic, machine-learning or the structural generation of uncertainty, also serve a double purpose of somehow *demystifying* the world. Understanding the world to be chaotic and unstable, and then utilising this chaos for a political or aesthetic goal, actually demystifies the world via a paradoxical *disenchanting process*. While using chaos in art is enchanting, the object of chaos is paradoxically disenchanted when we try to co-opt its illogical forces. A logic of use is applied to an illogical force. In this sense, demystification functions as a *denouncing*. From an understanding of politics and culture which says let's strip away forces which don't conform to prior understanding, we witness political justifications which simplify the body and mind and scrape away all sources until one answer can serve as an all-encompassing description for the state of the world. In co-opting uncontrollable forces, we equally denounce and deaden them. A demystified world view seeks to abrade all irregularities until the Cloud is considered to be perfectly regulated behavioural patterns. A demystified politics erodes away unlikely agentic possibilities until, for example, Russia is made the prime and centre cause for a botched election campaign, or until the capital-driven creation of Elon Musk's cars and boring tunnels and Mar's civilisations are made the sole solution for our impending environmental catastrophe. In short, attempting to demystify irregularities requires that illogical answers are either flatly denounced, or that reality is accepted to be wrong or accepted to simply be out of our control.

As an antidote, a positive positioning, an *enchanting and mystification* of the world (even if this positioning is achieved through Chaos Magic or stochastic magic or machine inhumanness) is still profoundly important. With all the problematic consequences of formalised enchantment I have so far described, there are also a whole set of vital consequences. Enchantment is double-edged. It revitalises our ability to look at the world through the complex lens of varied political action we so desperately require — a lens of ambiguities and inconsistencies, and multi-solution possibilities. Believing in a musical structure which is made wrong, or a compositional decision which denies listening expectations, can still be utilised to open up our speculative imagination. We still need the illogical, the irregular and the unreal to help us understand that 'nowhere' trapped within the etymology of utopia.

Chapter 3

Revenant Speed: Spirits of the Singularity

Lo! Death hath reared himself a throne
In a strange city, Paradiso
Far down within the dim West,
Where the good and the bad and the worst and the best
Have gone to their eternal rest.
There shrines and palaces and towers are
Not like anything of ours, oh no
Ours never loom, to heaven with that ungodly green
(Time-eaten towers that tremble not)
Resemble nothing that is ours.
Around, by lifting winds forgot,
Resignedly beneath the sky
The melancholy waters lie...

But lo, a stir is in the air!
The wave — there is a ripple there!
As if the towers had thrown aside,
In slightly sinking, the dull tide;
As if the turret tops had given way
A vacuum within the filmy Heaven!
The waves have now a redder glow,
The very hours are breathing low;
And when, amid no earthly moans,
Down, that town shall settle hence
All hell, from a thousand thrones,
Shall do it reverence.
And Death, to somewhere happy climb
Shall give us undivided time.

Chino Amobi's debut album, *Paradiso,* ignites those forces which rim the known world. Heard: the migration of displaced bodies; man-made-plagues poleaxing continents of surface-life; the newly exposed bones of rare-metal deep-earth becoming spasmodic technology becoming horror, becoming noise, becoming reaving voice, crying voice, singing and reciting poetry voice. And on: arpeggiating 80s synth; *cold cave systems*; blackness; a sound-tracking for the construction of prisons of glass; walled cities rising from the coal pit; a flock of child survivors at the edge of the city finding shared kindness and empathy in suffering.

Past dancers to Chino Amobi's 'NON Worldwide' club nights received physical passports granting them entry into this speculative city. When you entered the venue a slip of paper announced your new visa: you became a medic in the dystopian club, a doctor, a saviour in the imagined future city of a hyper-capitalist tech supported nightmare. A voice repeats: *'this world is without end, demolition, this world is without end'*, thunder in the sky and waves and beasts lapping at the flooded gates commingle in the dark. Enter the city and you begin to revel in it.

I turn now to dystopian aesthetics, and begin with *Paradiso* because it marks the culmination and closing statement of a great build-up that occurred over the past 5 or 6 years — one of renewed dystopian excitement on the dance floor. There are many tropes of this re-emerged genre and *Paradiso* indulges in them all. This music rips into the heart of the dystopian sci-fi setting: that gloomy chaos of the mega-city present in so many dark classics — *The Citadel, The Metropolis, Rapture, Tokyo-03, Brave New London, 2019 Los Angeles*. Chino Amobi's genius rests in his decision to directly structure an album around this setting, to wallow in the worn-out heart of the genre, and yet, to push it further. The album opens with fellow dystopian-music pioneer Elysia Crampton orating a subtle rewrite of Edgar Allen Poe's *The City in the Sea*. The Gothic fascination of Poe and the noir occult speculation of H P Lovecraft fuse and are projected into the future as a once revenant past ruled by spirits and personified Death. What becomes immediately clear is that the music of this album finds its political agency in those dark and Gothic forces of representation and reference. Through every mention of death — through every sound of shattering glass, sirens in the night, the compressed air of a robotic arm extending — the narrative becomes a spindle to our desiring ear, until finally, we reach the gates of the city and a twisted paradise reveals itself in the sound of regal horns.

In *Paradiso,* I'm reminded of the underground world from E M Forster's 1909 short story, *The Machine Stops*. Forster's prescient tale follows a future musicologist whose son has been banished from civilisation and the care and rule of the Machine. Humans live underground in bee-like identical cells, food pumped into their open mouths when hungry, dials and buttons supporting their needs. Each person is connected to one another through a network of communication. Citizens worship all facets of the Machine and niche-cults dedicate themselves to its minute inorganic functions. Online, from the isolation of her room, the musicologist finds an adoring public which cheers at every word and idea she speaks forth. The echo chamber loves her. She's never heard silence. When her outcast son suddenly gets in contact, he tells her ominously: 'the Machine stops'. From that moment on, the world begins to collapse until finally all facilities cease to function. The comforting hum of the Machine goes quiet, ears bleed and many simply die confronted for the first time by true silence. Nearing death, the musicologist questions whether the machine will ever turn on again. Her son exclaims: 'Never, humanity has learnt its lesson.' And with that, an air ship crashes through the city, splitting the roof apart to reveal 'scraps of the untainted sky'.[1]

This untainted sky — this hint of optimism at the very end — appears as a trope in dystopian sci-fi. We look above us speculating patterns, calling for rain in a dry landscape. A new human is born, a new hope, a new future dawns which has learned its lesson. This notion, that survivors of the horror will build a better world, is what supports much of the politics of writing dystopian sci-fi. The writer imagines that their readers, through a confrontation with future disaster, will be warned and cautioned in advance. The writer imagines that through a reflection of a darkness to come, their audience will take it on themselves to prevent such a future becoming.

The perceived political agency thought to emerge in fiction presented through *what-not-to-be* scenarios is what I aim to confront in this chapter. I question art which describes its political praxis as a warning, and as a reflection of crisis. Dystopian imaginings are unstable things, they inspire us, they seduce us, and often, they render political action a fallacy.

Yet it becomes more complicated. When music makers aren't overtly political, dystopia also becomes the space of another kind of seduction — a jouissance in pessimism, a space to be revelled in, and a space to reclaim agency in the shared togetherness of cosmic horror. This chapter concludes the first half of this book with a final pattern recognising look at the tainted, or untainted sky, ripped into musical revelation around us.

Music is the physics of tears.
Emile Cioran

Schopenhauer, though a pessimist, really — played the flute. Every day, after dinner: one should read his biography on that. And incidentally: a pessimist, one who denies God and the world but comes to a stop before morality — who affirms morality and plays the flute...what? Is that really — a pessimist?
Friedrich Nietzsche

Crises tend to generate apocalyptic dreams and nightmares.
Benjamin Noys

The revival of overtly dystopian aesthetics on the dance floor coincides with mainstream culture's recent infatuation with 80s and 90s cyberpunk. Remakes of *Ghost in the Shell*, *Blade Runner* and AAA series like *Altered Carbon* and *Westworld* claim to be pertinent commentaries on our dark 2017/18 mesh of political chaos, Silicon Valley betrayals and revelations of mass surveillance. Yet in Hollywood, the future doesn't even sound as a warning. Instead, it is shown to us as a money-making tapping into the fantasy of how much worse *and exciting* the future can in fact get. Today, cyberpunk is a revenant corpse promising us speedy and exciting obliteration. The 'punk' is gone. In its place *cyber-nihilism*. This chapter highlights two sides of crisis: one which inspires the creation of art as a warning, and the other side, which fails to produce energy for change, instead petering out to become an all-encompassing dysphoria. Here, what might be called 'cosmic pessimism'[2] circles back into a magical belief in nihilism, nothing, simply doom. The future is a grey mess. A common response to hollow times is to become hollow yourself. But like the saddest philosophers out there, Arthur Schopenhauer and Emile Cioran, total pessimists still find it hard to give up on music. Be it in the playing of the flute after a good dinner, or the blasting of deconstructed dance music in the club, pessimism can remain expressive. In Greek tragedy the flute is the symbol for solitude and grief. In the club, deconstructed music becomes a similar signifier for bodily and sensorial isolation. Is there a way to repurpose these tears, or is loneliness symptomatic of political inaction?

Chino Amobi's *Paradiso* beckons us into a city of enchanted destruction I unpack where its energies thrive and where they flatten out. I discuss the exit strategies these energies may embody, and more broadly I question what has been left out from these imaginings of the future — how the sounds we might make (or not make) may indeed curse future becoming. This chapter wriggles and orientates itself around the unearthing of not just 90s pop culture, but also the bringing up of that decade's associated philosophical movements. At the turn of the new millennia, machinic futures were in vogue. However, retro-transhumanism comes back in 2018, not as a philosophical-scientific conundrum, but as an occult desire.

i) Malediction and Cyber-Nihilism

To speak badly of the future has consequences. If the voice in harmony is sacred, the hate-filled voice is destructive. Maledictions — magical curses — have a really non-magical *causal* power to them. In philosophies of horror, like those expressed by the nefarious philosopher Nick Land and the remnants of his cult-like following, badly privileged 'causality' is the platform which gives agency to darkly speculative arguments. In Land's reasoning, any action becomes an event with concrete ramifications. The smallest change is still a change. One thing causes another thing to happen. More than a butterfly's wings causing a cyclone, writing a word and having it read can influence future politics. Making a sound and having it heard can cause a chain of possible events. Land calls this *hyperstition*. This is superstition, but 'real', a performative attempt to change the future through speculation alone. Musicologist/occultist Eldritch Priest describes this best:

> Something is therefore 'hyperstitional' when causal links are made between a fiction's semiotic field (which includes the special case of 'art') and the real's effective terrain. This 'fiction making itself real' can be understood as a form of classic occult causation, or, if you want to invoke Land's terms, a case of cybernetic action wherein 'reality' and 'fiction' are both elements of a closed signalling loop that feeds change back into a system to regulate its constraints, potentials, and tolerances.[3]

In these affective loops, hyperstition makes Chaos Magic real. It rationalises the way thinking and sharing and believing in a meme can cause it to change the future. From a personal stand point, I found resonance while reading Nick Land's collection *Fanged Noumena,* as it coincided with the heightened cyberpunk movement in the music venues I was visiting, and the spiralling meltdown I was witnessing gaining momentum online. I began to see evidence of hyperstition all around me. Suddenly music, theory and fiction gained radical new importance. The politics of even abstract music was affirmed to me. That notion of us living in the *wrong timeline* began to influence the coincidental connections I was drawing and my own desires to make art or write about art which *actually* mattered. *Elon Musk played Star-Fox on his Super Nintendo and thus dreamt of building spaceships; Marx read Robinson Crusoe and thus conceptualised theories of the bourgeois economic man; Obama heard Dylan's song Hattie Carrol and was inspired to enter politics; voters in the American election saw a cartoon frog and thus became neo-Nazis...*But of course, the level of distance and speculation between one thing causing another thing to happen is more accurately described as conspiratorial apophenic thinking. *Nick Land's Twitter avatar — a hand holding a bloody heart — hyperstitionally causes him to have a massive heart embolism.* In conspiracy, like Chaos Magic, people gather desperately trying to bring something fictional into reality.

Other similar theories of causality are found in Kodwo Eshun's interpretation of Sun Ra's *Myth Science*; in the rigorous 'speculative materialism' of Quentin Meillasoux's *After Finitude*; and in Timothy Morton and Graham Harman's Object-Oriented-Ontology. These are philosophies which try to re-enchant our scientifically de-enchanted world. In philosophies like these, the awareness of your infinitesimal existence gains meaning: your online posts can be seen as newly powerful and the oceanic ripples of everything you do become a galvanising mesh of possibilities. These are philosophies which inspire political action, both good and bad.

In my prologue I posed a sequence of cursed questions, let me rephrase them: if we believe in *hyperstition,* then should we really be saying bad things about the future? If we believe in causality, should we be imagining and representing the future with dystopian aesthetics? Are we chanting a malediction for the future? I think it is indisputable that the things we do and say cause changes around us, no matter how small. What brings me to raise these questions in the first place are a series of really small things coming together to create a whole artistic movement. A snowball effect. A couple of dark thoughts expressed on a page, and a few devastatingly seductive pieces of deconstructed music which significantly wrap the future around them.

One such dark thought which can speak badly of the future is *Unconditional Accelerationism* and its offshoot — 'cyber-nihilism'. To further scrutinise Nick Land, I should comment on his unique materialist position, namely, philosophy as destruction, not salvation.[4] This thinking has inspired both right and left-wing interpretations. In 2008, Mark Fisher (who was an ex-student and colleague of Land at Warwick University's *Cybernetic Culture Research Unit*), coined the term 'Left-Landianism'. The idea was to treat Land's burning call to accelerate the forces of capital and remove the anti-human sentiment to which it was originally tied. Passed around online, this would inspire Benjamin Noys to formulate a critical term for this ideology: *Accelerationism.* The criti-cool use of Noys's term became its own violent embolism, living torrid for only a moment, before becoming just as quickly scorched and withered. Left-Accelerationists like Alex Williams and Nick Srnicek described a radical and seductive pathway to revolution: tap into the Crisis Energy of capitalism, they said, and accelerate its forces until it eats itself up. Reach a post-capitalist society through capital's own methods of relentless progression. Demand full-automation, robotic labour and a liberated future *for* human-beings.

To avoid adding more repetition to the already oversaturated theory-landscape of accelerationist essays and critiques, I'll mainly draw attention to its application in the club scene. In the renaissance of fast, deconstructed dance music, Accelerationism of course had immediate purchase. The revival of CCRU thought by the Left also dug up all the cyberpunk references, transhumanist ideals and neologisms that were being passed around in the 90s. Post-War dance music has strong ties to futurism, so without much effort the club space suddenly had a new left-wing politics with which it could associate itself. Unfortunately, the foundation of this movement couldn't escape Nick Land's legacy. For a time, in every gallery bookshop I visited there were copies of *Fanged Noumena*...and then suddenly they were gone. Apparently, no one had checked what Land was up to recently, and his new, not just unsavoury, but dangerous political associations with the extreme and fascist right-wing became an inescapable black hole for the movement. The seduction of a new Left which was finally acknowledging technology (a creatively imagined future even) seemed to become extinguished (if revolving-door journals like *Eflux* are any indication). Accelerationism went through its cycles of defiance and critique so quickly that it became old before it was mainstream-new. Its legacy remains to be seen, but it may have completely died off before it had a chance to inspire a positive real-world movement.[5]

Sadly, however, Accelerationism's corpse lives on in right-wing niches, and in some misguided club cultures. Neoreactionaries and to a lesser extent the Alt-Right (or perhaps the 'New-Right' with a politics directed towards the 'far' future) are still moderate Accelerationists. In their political fantasies, the processes of capital are exaggerated in efforts to fragment the state. Their future society is one ruled by profit. CEOs are the new authoritarian dictators and nation states are disbanded to make way for mega-corporations. Yet what makes these doctrines only moderately accelerationist is their preserving of the Human, the reproduction of traditional gender relations and a cognitive outlook of a 1930s yesteryear. In the mega-corp future, the fantasy goes: white males sit atop the food-chain, women claw onto them for protection in this fragmented violent world, our blue marble globe now over-used and grey, made parched in the wake of old-school valour and value and Enlightenment rationality and big, really big, guns. The once exhilarating, dystopian hyper-capitalist fantasy found in 90s SF and genres of furious dance music has become inseparable from the imaginary found in the New-Right and NRx.

Writing of our time of crisis, Benjamin Noys contends: 'Apocalyptic desires are ambiguous: at once consolatory fantasies, deferred hopes, and, potentially, spurs to radical re-orderings.'⁶ In the chaos of dystopia (or the stratification of feudalism), the fantasy of a distinctly white male Hollywood heroism emerges. A future transhumanist American Dream. A prayer that techno-enhancement will grant the body unbridled rationality. *Picture for a second, Fallout 3: a lonely masculine survivor wanders the decomposing landscape — dust becoming beautiful in the nitro-sunset, a female-form on the horizon silhouetted for rescue.* Forget the emboldening of identity politics in experimental techno-futures, right-wing Accelerationism paradoxically twists transhumanism into a cis-gender unifying process, a last-ditch hope that the 'traditional' male–female dynamic will re-emerge under conditions of apocalypse and the survival of the fittest.

Is our world today so entirely de-enchanted and stripped that even apocalypse can stand in for the magical enchantment we so crave? In Unconditional Accelerationism, it isn't so much a desire to make the world magical, or a desire to reclaim an agency perceived to be lost to the purported 'Social Justice Warriors' and their identity politics, instead these *real bad-kid* Accelerationists take aim at the world from a more rudimentary angle — they argue humanity as a concept is simply too fucked up to be saved.

The end point towards which they speed is the dissolution of the human being to a technological artificial intelligence god. Inspired directly by Nick Land, this 'God' is that of 'the singularity': the very moment when technology surpasses human intelligence and becomes conscious itself. To believe in this AI God is to hope for an intelligence which is more than the sum of all of human consciousness, a *more-ness* as well as an otherness. In this SF trope, the AI God (labelled *Gnon* by Land to give it a cool occult edge) will no doubt strive to destroy the flesh-stain which is humanity. Thus, both Land himself, and his unconditional accelerationist followers, argue that the Left cannot truly embrace progress, for progress ends ultimately in death. The end of humanity and its obliteration is seen as the way out — and in the end, death speaks to these particular believers.

In broader circles, this worship has been given a fitting name — Silicon Valley *Digitalism.* Discussing Silicon Valley in *Das Magazin*, William Gibson exclaims: 'The evangelical fever is fascinating...These people are atheists, they don't have religion, but the mechanism is the same. God comes and saves us all. Just that in their case God is technology.'[7]

If this sounds too much like good vs evil, it is because these movements position themselves in hypothetical extremes. In contrast to passive nihilism, Unconditional Accelerationists (or what we could label instead cyber-nihilists) express an active rebranding of the philosophy. Sadness, anxiety and pessimism are never acknowledged for the in-the-worldness they can bring us. Instead, this brand of nihilism reconfigures these dysphoric feelings into action. They become energised as feelings for an exit-from-the-world. The theorist 'N1x' (whose Twitter avatar is an edited image of Nick Land made female) describes passive nihilism as 'cold, endothermic, life-denying', and active nihilism as 'hot, exothermic, life-affirming'.[8] From the perceived maelstrom, N1x penned the *Cyber-Nihilist Manifesto*. N1x makes clear that nihilism isn't an identity, it's a condition. While I disagree with this description, even if we take it as some kind of atmospheric all-around-us 'condition', nihilism undergoes a paradoxical change, that is, it begins to *act* towards something — to say 'yes' to being annihilated by capital.

> To make nihilism cybernetic is to bring the anti-praxis of nihilism — pure negation — into the digital age. The burden of pure negation is not put on the individual or the affinity group, but rather is captured in protocols that can propagate themselves through memes, infecting other people and subsuming them into the hivemind. The more people it infects, the more rigorously it is exposed to fitness tests and refined...Cyber-nihilism, as a post-humanist position, isn't interested in whether or not homo-sapiens or any other living biological life-forms can survive this transition. It recognizes that Nature is neither static nor kind, and that our subjective experience need not be tied to a particular physical form... Cyber-nihilism therefore welcomes the alienating influence of technology so often derided by primitivists and denied or ignored by anarcho-transhumanists. Let ourselves be alienated from our Selves.[9]

In this active heat, nihilism paradoxically becomes its own belief system. N1x's manifesto is at odds with some of Land's other writing (especially his reactionary desire to escape hegemony and the belief systems of democracy). Following from the desire to surpass Nature, cyber-nihilism acts out its negation through technology which always says 'no' against the organic body. To avoid this endless 'no' becoming a 'yes' and thereby undermining its entire intention, the human decision-making in the aesthetics of this ideology is relegated as much as possible to algorithmic intelligence. Stochastic processes come into play once more. N1x contends: 'The more that pure negation can be done entirely without user input, the more effective it is, the more it can clear away human command-control systems and hegemonies, and the more it thereby comes to both make space for itself and own itself.' The fundament of this aesthetic remains modernist in its intentions — to reach an objective 'no-ness'.

I introduce cyber-nihilism because I believe it is not only highly reflective of the music this chapter goes on to discuss, but that it is also actively supported by distinct musical structures. As will be made clear, cyber-aesthetics rely on algorithmic fragmentation and machine-learning for their forces of outsideness. But *before they reach that outside*, in the conclusion of the *Cyber-Nihilist Manifesto*, N1x makes the (ironically) fatal admission: 'We don't hope for a better world for ourselves, after all. We only ask for one that we can leave without regrets.' In this statement of *hope*, the entire doctrine collapses under its own internal contradictions. For to live without regrets is one of the most Human of desires imaginable. When the light is switched on the cyber-nihilist is revealed to be farcical as simply a hedonist in a 90s rave. The spirits of the singularity scream out in dance music — music which still cannot be tossed away, no matter the movement's efforts to be above human expression. The pessimist still plays the flute. The sound can't toss the feeling. I hear a glib robot voice proclaim: 'there's a void where there should be ecstasy'. What comes screaming back to us is the old-school Jungle track, the *More Brilliant than the Sun*, the 90s folding back onto the present — reanimated and critically weak.

ii) Zoom Zoom Fragmentation as Progress?

In 1998 Kodwo Eshun wrote the highly influential *More Brilliant than the Sun: Adventures in Sonic Fiction*. His unrelenting prose captured an epoch of future-oriented music, namely 90s machinemusic, Drum and Bass, Jungle, cosmic Jazz, and Techno. Within this text Eshun espoused a cultural reading strongly tied to Warwick University's CCRU. Eshun's iconoclastic music became the aesthetic inseparable from the influence of this university department and the florid thought of Nick Land.[10] This was a music expressing the anti-human sentiment of collapse — viral techno-pathogens, alchemical consciousness enhancement, stimulant transcendence on the dance floor. Notably, *More Brilliant* was more than just a side-note to the work of CCRU. It was a text bristling with new ideas, proselytising neologisms and an aperture blade which framed an emerging history of Afrofuturism — the struggle to not only rethink sound, the dance floor and the social apparatuses which mediated that era's listening, but also an attempt to reconfigure the Human more broadly within the transparent flat-culture of the machine.

Written during the first peak of mainstream transhumanism, *More Brilliant* discussed the sonic manifestation of William Gibson's cyberpunk: a 'sky the colour of detuned television'; *Wintermute* and rouge artificial intelligence systems; *Terminator* and *Blade Runner;* Japanese anime reaching Western eyes in *Ghost in the Shell, Akira* and *Neon-Genesis Evangelion.* In the Drum and Bass subcultures of 'Darkside' and 'Jungle', listeners often heard quotes from these popular transhumanist sources interspersed throughout the music. On the track 'Lord of the Null Lines', by Hyper on Experience, the British duo quote the dystopian thriller *Predator 2* ('Fuckin' Voodoo Magic Man') and a *Diva on Downtime* ('There is a void where there should be ecstasy.') This is exactly the music of Land's shamanistic Nietzsche.[11] The void *is* the stand in for ecstasy. A magical nihilism prefaced by unbridled destructive hedonism.

The sound of old machines is wrapped in the significance of metal. In the 90s futurist imaginary, the machine is packaged with almost the same referents as those expressed by the 1920s Italian Futurists. The Techno producer mashes samples as if an old figure lit by forge-fire, beating out shapes in hot metal. Metal sounds not as precious earth, but broken earth. Its properties of fired smoothness, shininess, tensile strength become blood on a blade, brutality and hardness. The nuance of the sound is trapped in a nostalgic industrial past — a sonority of the Fordist factory — the same sound-tracking of molten Soviet steel heard in Dziga Vertov's first sound film, *Enthusiasm: The Symphony of Donbass*. Western society is no longer Fordist, and the most important machines today aren't *just* metal. The Cloud is a soft and gooey amalgamation, its efficiency is like liquid. In the millennial social media assemblage, the sound of that CCRU aesthetic loses its forces of representation. That steely dystopia which once sounded so imaginative in the 90s, today is far less dystopian than present material crises. When metal stands in for a kitsch nihilistic anti-humanism it invariably gets worse. Pessimism, in the dark, functions as a particular kind of earth moving depression towards flatness. Narcissistic and misanthropic movement on the dance floor in high drama always moves downwards to that flat subterranean sheet of volcanic black glass we call meaningless hedonism. In the bottomless, wall-less cave that once fed a vast reservoir on the surface — the water in the well is slick — a rink of heartless and dated ice.[12]

'Impending human extinction becomes accessible as a dance floor'[13]

Warp forward, and today we find a re-appropriation of 90s transhumanism. In my opinion, the previously discussed duo, Amnesia Scanner, share some of the strongest ties to CCRU. Amnesia Scanner's initial releases attached music to videos of Boston Dynamic's uncanny walking robots: wobbling bodies referencing a nostalgic futurism found in turn-of-the-century sci-fi Hollywood. In other examples, mangled humanoids in a rendered 3D environment move around the camera, fleeing or perhaps dancing within a post-apocalyptic industrial setting. Seeing them in performance, Amnesia Scanner place two rotating projectors on stage with blood-red lights blinking in time with the syllables of the fragmented voices found in the music. It is an image reminiscent of Hal 9000's flashing red light. A swathe of colour beamed out of the projector scans the audience like *Total Recall*. This aesthetic is brilliant like Eshun's future *sun*, but also profoundly disturbing. Each time I've seen them perform I've been lost to my surroundings — made an amnesiac to the present.

The emergence of Amnesia Scanner's aesthetic (sometimes referred to as neo-futurism[14]) found its success in the appropriation and exacerbation of 90s transhumanism, all within a lens of ironic lightly fetishised nostalgia. However, the irony and sincerity here are dangerously close. In presentation, Amnesia Scanner and Eshun's 90s music share perhaps too many similarities. Due to this reliance on the past, their future vision is undermined. Benjamin Noys's analysis of what he considers the 'paradoxical velocity' of Accelerationism and the imaginative failure of 90s dance music applies to much of the music of Amnesia Scanner:

> Contemporary Accelerationism modulates this schema. It concludes that we have been robbed of our future by an inertial and crisis-ridden neoliberalism that has rescinded the dynamism of capitalism for the opaque mechanisms of speculative finance. What we don't manufacture any more is the future. Instead we dwell in a generalised nostalgia, with even dance music, the signature aesthetic form of Accelerationism, failing the accelerative/inventive test.[15]

Future critical purchase is often made forceless when it stays entirely stuck in the nostalgia of the past. When listening to 90s dance music there is an incredible stasis on the dance floor, an embodiment in the 'now' enacted from the intensity of low-frequency rumbles and sensory overload. This music's static neoliberalism concludes that to access the future we need more of the same.[16] There is a distinct lack of self-awareness in a genre which keeps plundering more of the same images from stale SF, as well as its exaggerating of pre-existing musical structures. The now-ness of an overwhelming performance and the reliance on the past become at once *too* manifest — they block the future. These references are revenant. In today's club re-appropriation, the reliance on drives of 'malign hedonism' (following Noys) keep the venue's walls unchanged from the 90s rave, a space which was rapidly reterritorialised into a commercial venue for temporary escape. In this escape, capitalism found a new and highly useful process: a brief release of spirit, to prolong the acceptance of other oppressions.

This isn't to say that in the revival of 'accelerationist aesthetics' there have been no changes. There have been many beautiful and vibrant ramifications from the rehashing of the past. Amnesia Scanner's music is in many ways awe inspiring. Compositionally, those structures present in 90s futurist music have been exaggerated and taken to their logical conclusions. The already fragmented Amen beat of Jungle has become so deconstructed that its reconfigurations have allowed it to exit Drum and Bass entirely. In contrast to the basic tenant of machinemusic (to reconfigure a singular rhythmic pattern in evolving and disjointed ways), today's deconstructed aesthetic paves the way for a rhythmic diaspora, speeds, rhythmic groupings and styles blurring in never consistent or linear directions. The rhythmic origin rarely matters for the end result. The surprise comes from a fresh juxtaposition not from a fresh reconfiguration. In the extreme manipulation of samples and emotional signifiers, what is new in the accelerationist aesthetics of today is the fragmentation of style itself. Hence, the recent trends in experimental electronic music are simultaneously easy and hard to group together. The only stylistic consistency in much of this music is its emphasis on referential discontinuity. Most strikingly, fragmentation here is not simply a narrative method (as in postmodern pastiche); instead, fragmentation supplies a supposed politics of progress.

In Amnesia Scanner's *AS EP*, the style jumps between Nu-Metal and Cyber-Eurotrash, each shift equally jarring and emotionally comforting — alienating and then reassuring. Similarly, Chino Amobi's highly fragmented *Paradiso* has us suspended in transition, from Robocop club, to Havana Lounge, to deconstructed machinemusic, to trance hip-hop, to hindustani vocaloid, and then back all over again. A voice calls out: 'obliteration, radical zero, night, organ plate, bleeding, wheeling, negative flame, something foul, mute, death'. Helicopters circle the mess, sirens, gun pops, earthgrey-quakes, a circus theme plays:

> Welcome to the un-holy city, Paradiso. There is simply no void anymore, since everything has been designed to lead into here...witness...the maroon oil fields at the coast...the lunatics, glowing messages inscribed into the side of their skulls...you begin to glimpse blackness, like none you have ever seen, and wonder for a moment whether this blackness is inside your head or outside, which makes no difference once it begins to compose the outlines of this un-holy city you are about to enter.

Before critiquing the implications of fragmented music, it is important to first consider fragmentation as an empathetic act, and as a structure of solidarity within the music of artists already treated as *other* due to their skin colour. In the work of Chino Amobi, as well as *Hyperdub's* Klein and *Halcyon Veil's* Mhysa, these music makers could be considered the next generation of leading afrofuturists following Kodwo Eshun's *More Brilliant than the Sun*. In that image and thought of the void, perhaps one can find both a source of expression and a form of collective reassurance in a 2018 which still sets out in many ways to make non-white skin colour void-like. For theorist and activist Denise Ferreira da Silva, an open question of metaphor is asked: what if blackness is like a rarefied material, a 'substance without form', as if thinking through blackness presents that quantum unreality of a blackhole which impossibly devours matter? Blackness seems to present a value akin to negative-life, as da Silva finds, in 'the production of a racial subject destined to obliteration… the call for Black Lives (to) Matter hides the question it answers: Why don't black lives matter?'[17]

In the already dehumanised, in the un-life and Thingness attributed to being black, theorist Aria Dean writes of an 'acclerationism which already exists within the territory of blackness'.[18] Here the normalised experience of racially motivated everyday violence encourages one to question that future we travel towards when it appears mostly within the vision of white theorists. Kodwo Eshun explains, 'You get this sense that most African-Americans owe nothing to the status of the human.'[19] In this, profound solace and solidarity can go hand in hand with either a deconstruction of ideas of humanness, or the accelerationist's AI solution to move beyond humanity entirely. Here, Accelerationism is not so much a way out, as it is for Anglo Nick Land; instead, this political-philosophy is a mirror which is held up to an already outsideness.

Afrofuturists and white futurists play at a range of progressive club nights which have emerged over the past few years around the world. While I have been living in Amsterdam, the club-night called Progress Bar has been an inspiration. Now in its second year, Progress Bar hires a range of producers (many of whom I have discussed above) to perform and hold talks at the venue. In Los Angeles, Club Chai is another futurist club-night expressing similar values, and equivalent rhetorics of 'progress' can be found in festivals like *CTM*, *Rewire*, *Today's Art* and *Unsound*. Club Chai's first compilation record, *Club Chai Vol. 1*, is an excellent summary of this movement. A dominant technique in these spaces is to present sound as a cut up, stretched, shrunk or fragmented and granulated substance.[20] The micro manipulation of musical time becomes a representational and phenomenological tool. Granulation (the cutting up of a single sound into many tiny grains) holds onto the original philosophical importance for its inventor, Xenakis, to transcend the culturally determined 'human' through the Enlightenment project's quest to find the smallest micro building blocks of our reality. Equally, granulation gains new representational qualities, becoming the sound-par-excellence and materiality of a machinic future. In granulation we hear 'progress': old-school 90s molecular technology, nano-production, self-reproducing particalised machines. A future where nanomachines run amok consuming everything until the world is left as a chemical sludge afterwake, a grey goo.[21] Granulated sound often becomes its own slimy afterwake: cut up and re-arrange a sound too finely and it becomes akin to white noise.

At Progress Bar, I think of this quote from a CCRU classic, *Swarmmachines*, and wonder what has changed since the late 90s:

> Jungle functions as a particle accelerator, seismic bass frequencies engineering a cellular drone which immerses the body in intensity at the molecular level...rewinds and reloads conventional time into silicon blips of speed...It's not just music. Jungle is the abstract diagram of planetary inhuman becoming.[22]

Despite how inspirational I have found the music of Progress Bar, if you replace 'Jungle' with 'Progress' there is the disturbing feeling that the whole premise of the event begins to resonate in a stale, if not problematic way. CCRU's description fits much of Progress Bar's music perfectly. In its accuracy I wonder whether the signification of low rumble and micro-time can refer to anything else but 'planetary inhuman becoming'? Of course, working against this inhuman becoming is the experience that too much fragmentation can actually become bizarrely romantic. Other elements of the progressive club emphasise a disparate and intense raw affect. Love, friendship and kinship sound out within despair and hopelessness. When *Club Chai Vol.1* slips into a moment of Soul slow-dance, the effect is enhanced. The presentation of a 'pure inside' is stark in contrast to the storm which brackets it musically.

Consider the importance of speed. These artists don't shy away from the commodity-time of replacement culture, or the fragmented experience of having your time defined by the framing speed of an internet connection. Instead, they subvert it from within. Rather than presenting a critique through denial, this music assimilates 'network time'[23], hyperspeed and fragmentation, thereby exacerbating its effects. It tries to outpace 'network time'. On this, philosopher Patricia MacCormac writes: '...futurity, time and acceleration can constitute a demand for the *next* that outruns capital's consumption of the now'.[24] This music is fast: high bpm's of 140-200 affirm the importance of speed to this music, as does the resurgence of the 90s Dutch hardcore style of *Gabba*. With speed comes the feeling of an 'escape velocity', the sense that the music is about to run away from our ear (or from systematic society). Micro fluctuations in tempo reflect the ever-changing perception of time while browsing the web, the blindingly fast live-stream chat-box, the outpacing of 4chan's continual progress to death-by-page-10 — a speeding towards oblivion. In these tempi fluctuations, pulse gains the feeling of a potential unravelling. In Amnesia Scanner's 2017 release *AS Truth,* fast sport cars rev their engines continuously throughout the album. I also think of Charlie XCX's hit *Vroom Vroom* and the birth of crypto-rich Ferrari drivers. Speed is equally old-school Wall-Street — speed is capital — but is it critiqued? And how does it function as 'progress' when the wider politics of the event is held under the rubric of being a critique of capitalism?

Accelerationism rests upon the assumption that movement = progress; that speed = progress. These assumptions, imprudent and dominant imaginings of progress, can be traced back to the prominence of the industrial revolution in modern thinking (its own machinic spectre). The common assumption is that the industrial revolution marked the 'great advancement' of humanity. Problematically, what is mistaken here is a concept of radical change for an idea of scalability. Most of the 'progress' of the industrial revolution was in fact a movement of expansion and scalability. Most of the products of this period were not radically new, just produced in previously unfathomable quantities. In this, 'progress' becomes equated with corporate expansion. I am inspired by Anna Tsing, who urges us to turn our attention to the non-scalable.[25] I would argue that a true conception of progress relates to new objects, structures and ideas which are resoundingly non-scalable. Consider music of speed: does making the same melody faster constitute an advancement of musical language? Consider fragmentation: does the act of fragmenting *more* represent progress, or simply another form of scalability — the expansion of divisive thinking? Diversity is different from division. Diverse ideas, both musical and not, mark radical difference and new forms of thought. Fragmentation is a splitting up of the same into smaller parts of the same.

Progress as synonymous with scalability becomes a race against the physical properties of the universe. In a cosmos considered *terra nullius*, the expanse of capital positions itself against a world left barren and depleted. Capital tries to decouple itself from Nature. Capital tries to decouple progress from the natural limits of its holding pen. Here, Accelerationism becomes tied to a wider *Prometheanism*. From those mystical waters, from the godly gift of fire, Ray Brassier argues that Prometheanism is simply 'the claim that there is no reason to assume a predetermined limit to what we can achieve or to the ways in which we can transform ourselves and our world'.[26] Despite all the promising 'promethean' thinking which has emerged from the Left (see Helen Hester, Xenofeminism, Alex Williams and Nick Srnicek's work) Brassier's claim that there is 'no *reason*' to assume a limit is flatly wrong. There are plenty of reasons. The environment and our care for it is one of the most dominant reasons. Why assume there is no limit when assumptions like these lead to the overconsumption of the planet? Ideas of limitlessness turn out time and time again to reproduce the logic of neoliberalism.

Returning to music and club nights, perhaps we should question those promethean ideas of music and culture which are present in their DNA. To be fair, Progress Bar has in its second year drastically changed its press releases and accompanying imagery. What started as an accelerationist party (progress is still in the title) has manoeuvred its politics towards compassion and togetherness. Still, something feels hollow about this change in the accompanying language. The following rhetoric still hangs over the event: 'to understand crisis you must hear crisis'; 'to understand racism you must hear sonic alienation'; 'to hear progress — divide'; 'to be empathetic to the void, enter it yourself'. These methods of consciousness raising feel outdated and are even built upon a dubious history of political double negatives. Unable to produce a positive outcome, this reasoning instead offers a praxis which enhances our normalisation of the bad. The mechanics of fragmented and deconstructed music are actually metaphors for the exact opposite of progress; they are analogous to an anti-praxis. What's more, I would suggest that in progressive club nights it is not really the music, but everything around it which raises the political awareness. It is the solidarity in loneliness, the kinship within a fragmented dark room, the gathering together in outsideness which provides the greatest aesthetic answer to issues of empathy and understanding.

So, of this music I ask: what does fragmentation achieve if it is tasked with a political praxis? As with cyber-nihilism, fragmentation in a musical structure is to in some sense say 'no' to structure itself. It is to be in a constant state of negation. At a superficial level, to write fragmented music is to align your creation with an anti-humanism. While discussing a politics for the future, Nick Land writes: 'the only thing I would impose is fragmentation'.[27] Land prays to the free-market forces of capital, and to a fragmentation which promotes experimentation and technological divisiveness. Placed in market competition, the rationale is that we supposedly *speed* up our path towards the singularity and hence towards dissolution. Fragmentation is that thought and image of breaking through a brittle surface. It is a shattering rather than a clean cut. The fragmentation of a dropped ceramic on the floor ends in a mathematically predictable, but experientially unknown pattern. In the physical world, to fragment is to undermine the clear intention behind a separation or break. In the realm of ideas, it indicates a confusion of thinking.

In all of this posturing, Land is famous for aligning fragmentation and his wider belief with a self-described 'anti-praxis'. Following Land, Unconditional Accelerationists also describe their belief as a form of anti-praxis. To partake in anti-praxis is to promote a 'passiveness' towards all efforts to radically change human society. Basically, 'stand-by and watch as we "inevitably" progress towards that AI god which is so very determined to arise from the goo of capital'. In many ways the 'inevitability' of this future is at odds with the act of creative hyperstition. A critique of 'anti-praxis' can be found by simply turning to the original and positive Frankfurt School version. In what is also applicable to the thought of Marx, Georg Lukács describes praxis as a 'revolutionary act of self-consciousness'.[28] History can be changed in the very act of trying to *understand* history. The axiom follows: the proletariat can transform society and humanity by understanding their role in society, and thus, use this understanding to transform their conditions. Land must accept an unavoidable contradiction: in the very act of trying to formalise 'anti-praxis' the accelerationist comes to understand their own conditions and thus can never be said to enact that supposedly blessed political passiveness. In a beautifully crafted blog post, *Faster Daddy: A Tale of N Accelerationisms*, the anonymous writer relates the rejection of political action and activism with 'a kind of "dreaming" where Accelerationism opens up a frontier space for hallucinating the post-Human possibilities of hyper-modernity'.[29] I find these descriptions of 'dreaming' and 'hallucination' an extremely pertinent diagnosis of Accelerationism. *Faster Daddy's* summation is that:

> ...it is clear that Unconditional Accelerationism is, at bottom, a duplicitous and deceitful position, one that attempts to hide behind the process its identity as an ideological party vanguard of lecturers at Anglo Universities. At best the Unconditional position amounts to an abrogation of responsibility, a denial by the dreamers of their own active role in mysteriously enacting the dream.[30]

It is this old-school understanding of praxis and the revolutionary potential in 'dreaming' which leads me to fear for even those musics which deny their politics. Many producers, DJs and composers react badly when questioned about the meaning of their music. The statement: 'I make music for the sake of music and the crowd' can easily stand in for the passive accelerationist's claim that they simply 'dream' and 'hallucinate' about the future. To deny politics by citing 'music for the sake of music', quickly becomes a problematic and hollow response. As I'm now quite deep into an analysis of a world on the edge of transition, I hope that the potential in all sound to help us 'understand' becomes clearer and more forcefully supported.

The total fragmentation of a musical form and structure is an act which presents a strong image of that world towards which we transition, a world made confused, made not inhuman but unhuman. To write *purely* fragmented music is to reflect a cyber-nihilism where fragmentation is *everything*.

On the dance floor, dystopian music could be what Ngai calls a 'noncathartic aesthetic': 'art that produces and foregrounds a failure of emotional release (and does so as a kind of politics)'.[31] To fragment and always say 'no' to what came before is in many ways a sentiment of disenchantment. These structures are fear inducing, because despite their potential to help us elucidate and dream of a future world, in their innately disenchanting qualities, they encourage inaction. To hear the dark does not energise and unleash activism; instead, the release comes through embodied movement on the dance floor. The dark is thus revelled in — celebrated even.

Those who remain stuck *entirely* in the seduction of fragmented quakes end up attracting believers from both sides of politics. Jungle became the soundtrack to Unconditional Accelerationism in the same way neofuturist music of 2018 and beyond can easily become the soundtrack for new fascisms. From dark thoughts we get dark sounds. Although good news and happy music are equally responsible for propping up the system, a persistent diet of grim and alienating sound does not automatically produce action to end an alienating system. On the contrary, the premise of reflection as political action becomes counterproductive when you *only* reflect darkness by making dark music. Here, as a music maker you are not just reflecting the unease of marginalised people in an oppressive society, you are *also* reflecting the very ideology which wants to keep these people marginalised in the first place. It seems like this is sadly forgotten in the curation of festivals devoted to crisis and turmoil. However, I don't want my critique to encourage the feeling that all is lost for political art. In what follows, I hope to strengthen my analysis, as many of the artists I discuss *do* move beyond *just* a simple reflection of the turmoil of today.

iii) Crisis is an Energy

This is major shit we're dealing with here, Yag mate. I've been nibbling at crisis theory for arsing years. In a nutshell: I'm saying it's in the nature of things to enter crisis, as part of what they are. Things turn themselves inside out by virtue of being things, understand? The force that pushes the unified field on is Crisis Energy. Stuff like potential energy, that's one aspect of Crisis Energy, one tiny partial manifestation. Now, if you could tap the reserves of Crisis Energy in any given situation, you're talking about enormous power. Some situations are more crisis-ridden or -prone than others, yes, but the point of crisis theory is that things are in crisis just as part of being. There's loads of sodding Crisis Energy flowing around all the time, but we haven't yet learnt how to tap it efficiently. Instead it bursts over unreliably and uncontrollably every so often. Terrible waste.
China Miéville, Perdido Street Station

Behind the molar surface of China Miéville's reimagined metropolis, New Crobuzon, we can read of a warbling potentiality. Crisis Energy. Miéville reflects the unstable forces underpinning capitalism. His metropolis (and reality) is one where the conflicting magical, physical and social forces of a city bubble outward, stretching their boundaries thin like the effervescing contents behind the membrane of a cell wall. Weird fiction specialist Carl Freedman describes Crisis Energy as, 'a certain ontological instability at the very centre of reality. The core of Being itself tends towards hybridity.'[32] I would also describe this core as onto*genetically* unstable. In the space between the rachitic forces of New Crobuzon, meshes of flesh-like material and ideas grow and mutate. Inspired by Deleuze and Guattari,

Crisis Energy speaks not only of the dividing and territorialising effects of accumulation culture, but also of a future critical point — of the very real potential that these engorging materials will collapse the system from within — that capitalism will consume itself.

This force, this energy which is felt in unstable times, is that which not only underpins Accelerationism structurally, but also emotionally. Feelings of crisis inspire dystopian thinking. Feelings of crisis also inspire utopian thinking. What if music of crisis, that is all that has been discussed previously, was not conceived of as *just* a mirror and coping mechanism for the disturbing political, technological and ecological catastrophe we feel looming towards us on the horizon? What if crisis music could instead function as a critical hammer, and an inspired act of future world-building?

Crisis and 'criticism' are already etymologically linked. In their roots, 'judgement', 'reason', and 'reflection' interleave with a use in early medicine to infer the 'critical turning point' of an illness, and more suggestively, crisis as a 'decisive point in time'.[33] Through this, those who channel future crisis into their work lay claim to a deep criticism of the present. Works of crisis are some of the most politically powerful. They funnel the pressures of the jaded atmosphere, capturing and passing judgement upon a decisive moment in time. Crisis is always in a relationship with permanence. It underwrites the edge of a transitionary structure, a movement towards something better, or perhaps worse, and it forms an opposition to what was once structurally *normal*. Crisis is metaphorically flexible. For Marx and Engels, it symbolises a key moment in the cycle of capitalist economics — the moment when the ordinary contradictions of the market (the 'normal' balance of production and consumption) reaches a point of abnormality and overproduction. In this conception, the potential for revolution is hemmed within the innate nature of capitalism to inevitably enter crisis. Here the term describes a transitional period to a *better* world. Engels writes in a letter to Marx, 'The crisis will make me feel as good as a swim in the ocean.'[34] Contrast this to eschatological crisis, and the word implies the transition towards a dystopia, or worse, an apocalypse. In either its utopian or dystopian form, crisis has a futurity. It brings the future into consideration and it allows its agency to loom over us.

The energies of crisis play out in opposites. In mood, some are inspired with a dark excitement and passion for change. Others are depleted, sapped, disillusioned. This balance is often strongly linked to the timescale upon which our fears for a transitionary world play out. In the long-term, the knowledge of mass surveillance, global warming, automation and a geological and sociologically fragmenting world not only inspires pessimism — it inspires *horror*. Eugene Thacker describes the horrors of philosophy as pertaining to an increasingly unthinkable world, 'a world of planetary, tectonic shifts, and the furtive, always-looming threat of extinction'.[35] Not to downplay crises of the past, but the *now-ness* of our contemporary crisis plays out in the timescale of planetary extinction: the timescale of the human no longer being simply human and of organic life transitioning to a fully digital existence. And in this, it is clear how our exponential advancements in technology, and the subtle increase of daily oppressions, can easily inspire someone to philosophise from the perspective of planetary destruction, rather than from a perspective of planetary salvation. Even concepts like the Anthropocene intuit an end point to the habitable world. If musicologists posited Death Metal as an old-school nihilistic genre of music, I would make the argument that dystopian music aligns itself with philosophical horror. However, unlike what Eugene Thacker might term 'cosmic pessimism' — the unrelenting feeling of being 'doomed' — Crisis Energy does have the ability to shrug off the doom. It can operate with a political force behind it. To destroy is also a political act. Crisis can of course lead to pessimism and nihilism, but when it doesn't, it becomes meaning-inducing in both directions: to do better, or to make worse.

It is the feeling of a crisis on a distant horizon in which I am most interested. I think, when sincere, the potential energy within long-term transitions enhances revolutionary thinking. In Miéville's nearly collapsing city, the Crisis Energy is found in the very potential of a 'collapse'. In many ways the music I discussed is an expression of the feeling of the fall. It revels in the implosion, but at the same time, the energy generated by the feeling of the fall can (within long-term timeframes) also enhance revolutionary thinking. The added importance artists feel in light of looming future catastrophe is a speculative drive.

My prior analysis of deconstructed and fragmented music ignores a whole host of structural and affectual ramifications for these formal decisions. For instance, consider that the simple act of deconstructing a sound also implies the creation of a new and magical set of frames for listening. The work which is imbued with crisis is felt to be so because of a fine balance between denying and reassuring our listening expectations. In the creation of these frames (ie, the frame of shock when a consistent beat unexpectedly changes) the work begins to become full of new potentialities and tensions. *The potential for a better future.* When we as listeners are placed at the edge of the unknown, our desiring ears, in response, construct imaginative answers. Consider further, that when a piece of music denies our listening expectations through structural crisis, the work *also* has the potential to bring us together once that crisis ends. Music as a shared sensibility can momentarily disturb us, all in an effort to subsequently nurture and support us. These moments are as Brandon LaBelle might say, 'expressions of critical and creative togetherness'.[36] Unknowables abet energy. Potentials abet energy. In contrast, normalcy and the forces of hypernormalisation deplete the energies behind movements of change. Music which embodies crisis can reinvigorate us, but it needs to support its turmoil with a greater narrative.

Through Miéville's speculative city (so close, yet so alien to our own), we observe this fictional 'Crisis Energy' not just through its direct description, but through all the formal qualities of the work of literature: its structure, the characterisation, the tone and imagery, the poetics of the language itself. This totality of aesthetic experience brings us outside the text to an observation of Miéville's creative processes. While reading, we consider our own world and city, the world the writer sits in while they write, and the crisis-ridden energy which fuels their imagination. In music and listening, I see the same experience occurring. In the club and in the rarefied conceptual album, music of this loose genre I describe has indeed sounded like the city of New Crobuzon — collapsing and eating itself from within.

But as an emotional *fuel* and a resultant structure in recent electronic music, and for all its double-edged nature, when crisis doesn't peter out into pessimism, crisis can become a force of potent optimism and power.

iv) Exit Music 1

So, the fundamental question arises: 'how to be a futurist, but not a fascist?'
Anonymous

To find ways out, is to let the outside in.
Nick Land

As a form of conclusion to all that has so far been discussed, I propose to share some examples of what I consider to be *Exit Musics*.

To Mark Fisher, who gave life to and nurtured many of my

thoughts, and who died while I was finishing revisions to this book, an 'outside', of him, and of all of the musicians and artists, and fellow listeners and dancers and revellers, haunts this discussion of future-oriented music. To be an accelerationist, to be a Neoreactionary, or an Afrofuturist or a Marxist is to long for an exit: to desire an outside to the present. For some, as with Fisher, that exit was made closer than most in his fight with an unforgiving depression. I thank him, whom I never met or had the chance to talk to, and I thank those who blog in memory of him, especially the writer Xenogoth and their philosophising of the 'outside', which crystallised some of my own ideas of what it can mean 'to exit'.[37]

Fisher provokingly claimed that contemporary music (by this he meant music post 2005) was hauntological — playing out in an exhausted future, stuck in a cycle. His claim that we were in the midst of a 'slow cancellation of the future' arose from a perceived lack of imaginative potential in both music subcultures and society in general. His was a two-fold prescriptive: a capitalism which made alternatives seemingly impossible to imagine; and a future which was thus haunted and disappearing.

Living through and growing up in a time vibrantly alive with sub-cultural movements, especially those surrounding the birth of punk, it is understandable that Fisher looked at the more muted musical landscape of today, and viewed it as politically uninspiring. In contrast to the twentieth century, perhaps it is uninspiring. But for me, and those who have nothing (in living memory) with which to compare this music, there is the undeniable feeling that a future is still alive and imaginatively being birthed from current music scenes, and, importantly, that these imaginings are becoming livelier with every passing year. Those musics which I consider to not be hauntological, to not be trapped in a 'capitalist realism', are those which present that ethereal feeling and narrative of an 'outside', and moreover point to an exit to today's oppressions.

What has preceded the desire to enchant the world, either through annihilation or through pessimism or through the capturing of crisis, can be rephrased as a desire to exit, and to be *outside* reality in its most radical sense. I have hinted at those problematic instances when music momentarily becomes too caught in its processes of reflection. I could clarify this thought by saying that trouble arises when music is 'all voice and no exit', or all representation and no imagination. This is not an inference to fragmentary patchwork. To be outside, rather, is in its most simple and hard to define sense, to imagine a future that breaks free of present political trajectories. If I had the space here, I would love to trace a history, as Fisher has done, of those luminous exit strategies found throughout the history of art and literature. Or to trace, following Herbert Marcuse, those moments when the exit strategies of a sub-culture get folded back into the fabric of capitalism and thus made mute. Instead, let me point to a few moments when music manages to succeed in its egress. Fisher once used the word 'egress' in place of 'exit'. Egress, coming from nautical use, is an exit to the great depths of the ocean, or in astronomy, an exit to the vast cosmos. Thus, to egress seems more fitting in the following descriptions I will make of music which presents in the most magical, vast, deep and enchanting ways — a future way out.

My first example is from Holly Herndon and Mat Dryhurst. Their work will feature heavily in the second half of this book, and it is founded upon a deeply felt artistic drive to enact change. In interview, Herndon states more clearly than any artist discussed in this book what it might mean to 'imagine an exit'.[38] Her music functions as an active attempt to bring us towards not just any future, but a distinctly utopian and 'together' envisioning of one.

How do we escape the accelerating momentum, how do we exit before everything is consumed by the system? In Herndon's music we hear an exit. Alienate us, fragment, deterritorialise us, but then *show* us an outside. This strategy of alienation and then reassurance is a narrative which pulls us through sound towards an optimistic conclusion. Her voice is rearranged and made particulate, but it always emerges at the end whole again — *as one* — crystal clear in its message. Hers is a judicious music. Assiduous in its structure and made of a material which has been thoroughly questioned. Herndon's track, 'An Exit', inspired the title of this part of the chapter. It opens with dripping liquid and then the sound of a granulated whip:

> Day after day, if you were to say what could we be with will and belief? What could we be, if we were to leave? When there is nothing to gain, when there is nothing to lose. If I knew the way, would you go? Would you, would you go? You, you, you, you, you, go, go would you, would you, would, you?

Belief manifests in her voice with a fulcrum in causality — the very same as those who believe in hyperstition. Here, by contrast, is a tasking of the powers of speculation, of a standing over the future (as in the etymology of superstition) and placing in it a hope and want for wholeness as opposed to fragmentation. Wholeness appears at odds with ideas of outsideness, especially today, where the inside is the un-whole part of our political system. What we live within is a space which continually rips apart. The outside is the space for togetherness. Wholeness is so foreign to us that it is almost made unimaginable. Instead of the neologisms and unspeakable future of Nick Land, Herndon's causality steps in via a singing voice, a wishing voice. In some circumstances we should not shy away from this romanticism, the voice in prayer, the sacred element, a hope for change.

When I talked of machine-learning, what I failed to mention was that even in commercial creative practice, the algorithm functions within completely different use-value guidelines. Those qualities cultivated by economic power relations (efficiency, scalability, precision) are often ignored by artists in favour of ambiguity, inefficiency and rarity. In these circumstances, one would hope that the inhuman neural-net is no longer an economic actor. Instead, that the inhuman is to be appreciated for its modes of being. In Herndon's latest work, she along with her choir and collaborator Mat Dryhurst, have attempted to circumvent these issues of economic and artistic ownership by giving communal 'birth' to an AI child. Calling their inhuman child *Spawn*, the collective means of 'training' an algorithm poses important questions. Here the training was largely done via Herndon's voice in song, speech and play. In April 2018, there were a series of scheduled 'training sessions' with *Spawn* and a public audience. While talking with Herndon, I was most interested by her description of the training as a form of 'play'. Here the concept of play, which will become a crucial topic for the second half of my book, informs the creation and freeing of an inhuman rationality through that most honest of formal interactions: playfulness.

In concert at CTM festival, I see Herndon preview new music and the results of training *Spawn*. A pregnant woman sits on the side of the stage. The performance opens with her 2014 track *Chorus*, sung now with a choir instead of one lone and cut-up voice. The metaphor is not lost when the pregnant woman suddenly moves to the stage to sing an exquisite solo. Marking this event, Herndon uses a different microphone and begins to sing into it, triggering what I can only guess is the sound of *Spawn* reacting. The emerging inhuman voice of *Spawn* is simultaneously so un-voice like that I am momentarily confused. It giggles, it roars almost like a big cat, it sounds suddenly akin to an entire percussion section of an orchestra. Yet in all samples it is somehow also child-like, and low-fi, perhaps a digital equivalent of early twentieth-century attempts to record the voice in wax. I immediately think of Jeff VanderMeer's incredible novel *Borne*, and its protagonist, a non-human creature which learns via the sanctuary and luxury of play in a post-apocalyptic world. *Spawn* is in this sense like *Borne*. A non-voice, which through play (and the sanctuary of its creator's non-commercial creativity) has amplified a set of unconscious or taken-for-granted latent states of human to human *humanness*. This isn't just a vibe of a human, the algorithm's training via play and the inherent improvisation of the activity results in a more-than-human — an inhuman joy.

Finding resonance with Left-Accelerationism, one could hope that these investigations into inhuman machine-intelligence may have positive ramifications for the future. A machine trained and influenced through the inherently political act of communal singing, and given the most honest and playful sets of data to analyse, calls to being a future where machines might have a far more compassionate view of the earth and its creatures than we do.

Chino Amobi's *Paradiso* may appear hostile in its acts of representation, yet within its dystopian imagination and relentless fragmentation there are a few glittery moments. As with Herndon's music, these moments illuminate a narrative of possible hope filled exits.

Among the angelic voices in 'Floating World Pt2' a voice calls out via megaphone to the survivors:

The night is filled with the cries of dispossession
Dispossessed children in search of paradise
A sign of unresolved ambition
Drives the pinwheel on and on

When memory bears witness to
The innocents consumed in dying rage
The way lies through our love
The way lies through our love
There can be no other means to the end.

In interview, Amobi talks of his desire to express 'an optimism in the face of dire circumstances'. Continuing, he argues that music is 'making a point of showing care or empathy in a space that can seem like a void. Empathy through the matrix'.[39] These desires can be heard in *Paradiso*. In my experience, hearing the album performed live, in the crowd, I experienced this shared empathy.

Finally, in dark sound, like that of Amnesia Scanner, it is easy to overlook the very medium of abstract expression, as musc itself can be that *outside.* Although I have argued that Amnesia Scanner's catastrophic music can align it with a cyber-nihilism, this does not make the music *intrinsically* problematic. The point is not to present an aggrandising argument that ignores the other dimensions of the work, including the embodied aliveness and joy of its affects. Every time I listen to *AS EP* the originality of its construction, the energy of its crises remind me of the potential inadequacies of ascribing a politics to abstract expression. This energy is already an outsideness. I worry when music evokes an unspeakable haunted future. All the same, when I am totally lost within its grasp the music requires me to take responsibility for my own imagination, to learn to speak again.

In Kodwo Eshun's memorial lecture for Mark Fisher, he captured more clearly than anything I had previously heard or read all those exits which permeate thought of the future. Despite all their conflicting promises, antagonistic alliances and factions, Eshun points to what unifies and what charges their forces of resistance:

> Those of us who are unable to reconcile themselves to their existence, those of us whose dissatisfaction and disaffection, whose discontent and whose anger, and whose despair overwhelms them and exceeds them, and who find themselves

seeking means and methods for nominating themselves, for electing themselves to become parts of movements and scenes that exist somewhere between seminars and subcultures, study groups and hangouts, reading groups drawn together by the impulse to fashion a vocabulary — by a target, by a yearning, by an imperative to consent — 'to consent not to be a single being' [Edouard Glissant].[40]

In resistance, Eshun evokes the inverse of discontent — joy — and a joy which must be protected by practising it. He proceeds to list to exhaustion all the sub-cultural movements inspired by CCRU: the *xenofeminists,* the *cyber-nihilists,* the *unconditional accelerationists,* the *afrofuturists*, to name a few, and in turn these future 'exits' and the collective joys that they undeniably share and practice:

...each of these neologisms are actually forms of life. Each of them is the names of and for aesthetico-political positions that operate by disagreements and differentiations, that make claims that must be argued. Each of these is not so much a term, as a war of an over interpretation, a stance that aims to intervene in cultural politics, that fashions itself to articulate a discontent, to focus despair and depression into theories to live by, theories that are embodied, theories that live in us and through us and with us and on us.[41]

In this sparkling elegy which seemed to open up endlessly in defiance of a full stop, Eshun performed his own dismantling of those future visions which seek to work against 'joy' and thrive primarily in despair. In the very act of creative thought, even the nihilist performs a life-giving and affirming process. In a collective mourning of our reality, those who speculate towards an 'outside' come together. In crisis, when the future collapses onto the present and the border between life and death fades, survival is made ambiguous, and the future becomes a vector to invest in and to dream an exit upon.

Part 2
Flooded World

Flooded World Prologue

In the dream from which he'd wakened he had wandered in a cave where the child led him by the hand. Their light playing over the wet flowstone walls. Like pilgrims in a fable swallowed up and lost among the inward parts of some gigantic beast. Deep stone flues where the water dripped and sang. Tolling in the silence the minutes of the earth and the hours and the days of it and the years without cease. Until they stood in a great stone room where lay a black and ancient lake. And on the far shore a creature that raised its dripping mouth from the rimstone pool and stared into the light with eyes dead white and sightless as the eggs of spiders. It swung its head low over the water as if to take the scent of what it could not see. Crouching there pale and naked and translucent, its alabaster bones cast up in shadow on the rocks behind it. Its bowels, its beating heart. The brain that pulsed in a dull glass bell. It swung its head from side to side and then gave out a low moan and turned and lurched away and loped soundlessly into the dark.

Cormac McCarthy, The Road

Cormac McCarthy's *The Road* opens with the indeterminate hum of a creature's rank and dripping mouth. This hum is the lingering moment before silence, the sound of a nervous system in an anechoic chamber, the slow disintegration of McCarthy's writing, the 'autistic blackness' of the future. There is a sense that the world is a chamber which is slowly collapsing. The air is being sucked from it, along with everything else: affect, culture, sound and life. In this deforming void, McCarthy's characters understand a different ontological time. Their existence is like McCarthy's language — a glacial melt towards stillness, a single indefinitely oscillating sine-tone, and then finally — muteness. By using stationary nouns as verbs (which exist outside of the present, past and future) we gain a new understanding of the stillness of this post-apocalyptic world. McCarthy's language alienates us from a historical understanding of literature. It separates us from the traditional regulation of punctuation, from the cultural connotations of meter, and from structure's capacity to implicate meaning. McCarthy has constructed for us a type of anechoic chamber in which to read his novel. In this soundless chasm his writing references its own erosion. It divorces its relationship to us, yet at the same time merges to form the low pitch sound of our own nervous systems: the hum of a dripping mouth in a cave.

In the image of the far far future and the far far past, the earth is swallowed by water. Humans live in caves heaving rocks together in the dust, carving holes into bone to form rudimentary technologies of culture. When the survivor of the calamity, or the early ancestor of today, blows through their flute-like instrument made from an extinct animal's limb-bone, the future and the past in image and sound form an arch. As with a frail aged person who becomes like a baby in their worn-out body and child-like cognition, our atmospheric warming and technological exploitations point to a far future which has become as lifeless as the very birth of planet earth: a torn rock floating in space, and then endless rain and flooded soil. In sci-fi, there is a trope of the far future inspired by Einstein's omen: 'I know not with what weapons World War III will be fought, but World War IV will be fought with sticks and stones.' Too much progress seems to unravel progress. Thus, in this cyclical imagining of past and future, Part 2 of this book addresses a music that embodies a time perhaps 100,000 years ahead of us: a post-climate-change world; a flooded imaginary; a flooded body — a future made past and child-like.

The extract taken as this chapter's epigraph deserves examination, not just for *The Road's* post-apocalyptic barrenness, but because it places youth and age in such a cyclical relationship. McCarthy starts *The Road* twice: firstly, in a dream-like fantasy where the Child leads the Man; and secondly in a woken world where the Man leads the Child. The novel thus progresses in these interrelated realities. The Child and Man form an allegory for our own journey towards the future. Will we be led by a Man into potential destruction, or will it be the other way around, a Child leading us into a future of hope and togetherness? In our own descriptions of a flooded world, and music's representation of such a place, can we evoke that 'child-to-come'[1] to inform the politics of our speculation with an optimism and new-birth? In an overturning of Enlightenment logic, can we describe what-is-to-come with unique reversals? Animals evolving from humans; the sky falling to create the world not destroy it; or silence functioning not as fear but as hope.

In the sea and the sky and the buried earth are warnings. Still, in their cloudy and dirty movements are also seeds for imaginative reversals. In *Look Above the Sky is Falling: Humanity before and after the End of the World,* theorist and artist Pedro Neves Marques writes:

> Many Amerindians believe that animals have descended from humans rather than humans from animals. Within these cosmogonies, in the beginning everything was human. Then the world ended and from that cataclysm the many species, forests, rivers, stars, and minerals were formed... There are only some of us who, despite our technologies and sciences, cannot sense the disguised humanity of others. The Yanomami believe that the sky fell on earth and that it had a forest on its back. For the Yanomami, according to their shaman Davi Kopenawa, the sky is in fact repeatedly falling, redistributing this common humanity at each fall. Each falling sky, which is to say each forest, sets in motion a process of sedimentation, metamorphosing some entities while suddenly burying others and transforming them into

spirits—perhaps into oil or coal spirits, which wouldn't be far from the geological explanation of these materials' origins, or into gold, lithium, or any other of the many rare minerals that energize the earth's technosphere. [2]

Reading of non-Western conceptions of ecology inspires the reconsideration of long hold biases. These Amerindian myths support the recurring cross-cultural loops which see the far future as somehow equivalent to the far past. In the spirits of the sky, and within the minerals and oil and coal of the earth, an animism (the belief that non-human objects are also animated by a life-force) implores us to rethink our relationship to these materials. In this second half of the book, I will write of Oil Music, a music which I describe to be akin to that aliveness (energy) superstitiously believed to be within oil. However, alongside myths of *aliveness*, oil is also that which has irrevocably destroyed the planet. In the burning of these supposed spirits of the earth, we prepare our world to be flooded and to return to its pre-life proto-form. The sounds of liquids, both oily and not, will become a key point of discussion, as will the mutant life-forms imagined to have evolved to survive the atmospheric boiling of the planet. Climate Change is the fundamental crisis which threatens all life on earth. From my discussion of music which has a tension functioning in the timescale of planetary destruction, I introduce a parallel imagining, one which considers a world post-crisis: a world of rising seas and floating plastics washed up on the shoreline. In the analysis that follows, it is not just the planet which offers mangled vocalisations; the remains of the Human call out as well.

Within a Cagean avant-garde tradition, the human (and the voice) is treated as McCarthy treats language: it is stretched out in time, eroded, alienated. It begins in a human larynx and disappears in a poetic black cave. Importantly, this voice still maintains its original humanity. It dissipates contorted yet graceful in the air. For this modernist tradition, muteness does not represent a post-apocalyptic nightmare: it represents liberation. There is a great freedom in silence. Emancipatory listening. An alienation from one's own language is an alienation from the destructive predilections of history. There is beauty in timelessness, a spirituality to be found in the stretching of a vowel, in the warbled phonetics of speech.

Douglas Kahn's *Noise Water Meat* traces an intricate history of the voice in sounding media. The materialism within his text is a fundamental inspiration for this section of my book. Kahn is a sonic egalitarian: he finds the voice not just in sonic art, but in mythology, literature and in the private soundings of a bicameral mind.[3] When Cage stood in an anechoic chamber searching for the absolute, Kahn heard a third sound: a heartbeat, a nervous system and then Cage's internal voice rattling around his head, questioning the reality of his listening. Kahn's sonic history hears creatures and mutant voices, meaty and fleshy sounds, screams and terror and calls for political action, orgasm and analogue hum, instruments mimicking speech, speech mimicking animal, voice becoming the sound of dropped bombs, or the intermittent buzz of a taped phone connection in Cold War Europe. It is a history demarcated by the unprecedented destruction of flesh, Nature, the atom and a fear for a non-existent future. His tracing reacts to a fear of rationalised humanity. There is a desire for the human voice to be lost in abstractions, to be liberated in its expression, to find a new de-instrumentalised humanity. In Cathy Berberian's mouth noises one hears a pleasure in escaping language. In Laurie Anderson's *Oh Superman*, there is a sombre excitement in the digitalisation of the voice, the voice is exploring new edges of thought. Semantic liberation: language-less liberation stands in for Superman.

Importantly, however, Kahn's sonic history ends in 1999. It ends at the precipice of the internet. Compare the water and meat sounds of post-war Europe to today, and we find a voice which speaks logarithmic and logorrheic utterances. Mouth sounds cycle around their pink cavity forcing their way out. There is horror in disappearance. There is a fear of muteness. The voice would rather rip its way out of the throat mangled, slimy and contorted than disappear entirely. The glacial melt towards silence exchanges tranquillity for trauma. Avoid atrophy, fill the ear with digital noise. A ceaseless dripping.

In what follows, I trace not just the imagining of a planetary future flooded and mangled, but also the expression of a bodily future gooey and chimeric. The chapter *Chimeric Flesh and the Hyper-Child* discusses the bonded together nature of sound as a chimeric material of two or more hybrid parts. It introduces bodily fluid, goo and slime as fundamental signifiers of a far future gone wrong, but also as intimate referents of a humanness still intact. These materials are thought through Julia Kristeva's theory of the Abject. Focusing on the mouth sounds of a voice unable to remain silent, the significance of a particular kind of hyper-childlike vocal processing will become a key issue for discussion. In the words this hyper-child speaks we gain a deeper understanding of the Cloud's para-language. We can begin to theorise the way online speech informs an oppressive 'listening to the weather' 'Ky' or non 'Ky' atmosphere. What's more, liquid is a substance in a state somewhere between stability and chaos. In this, it stands as a perfect material metaphor for the music to be discussed.

In contrast to the first half of this book, there is the sense that the following music is 'dark' in a completely different way. Or even that it might be 'light' in comparison. Technology is still a shadow behind these representations, but these sounds seem to be heard in an open, life affirming and almost 'organic' space. What follows is way-more-alive and way-less-machine-like than the music I previously discussed. This is a music bursting with an organismic vitality: sound leaking bodily oils; sound which is materially fluid; sound as warning; sound as enchanted whispering.

Chapter 4

Oil Music

Performing under the moniker AGF, I see composer and 'sound sculptress' Antye Greie-Ripatti play in Berlin to a packed out Berghain. She begins with a tribute to Ursula Le Guin, and concludes by prefacing her last track with the statement: 'This is music for 100,000 years in the future.' In the middle of her performance we stop, perform a deep listening exercise reminiscent of the late Pauline Oliveros, and are requested to consider ourselves as a joint organism of the club ecosystem — a poly-hybrid ecology.

AGF's musical and extra-musical language is expressed in a poetic register. As listeners in a live performance and bodies in a purposefully alienating concrete space, the call to hear sound and feel yourself moving in a landscape of far-future imagination is an experience necessary for the reconditioning of the dance floor and a fresh politicising of the affects it can evoke. AGF's earlier work, which was more industrial and flecked with the timbres of machines, gives way to the 2017 release *Solidicity*, an album that much 'wetter, 'ecological' and full of the calls and cries of creatures. The opening track is a vibrant harmonisation of the sound of a mosquito. Objects rattle, are blown about in an unmade wind, 'the internet of things' around us becoming its own future jungle. At some level it is easy to focus on AGF's network of referential sounds. Among the insects, a swarm of migrating Finnish swans can be heard coexisting with sonifications from mycelium fungi and critters of the forest. Still, around these field recordings there is a musical structure and instrumental material reminiscent of much more than the changing ecologies of today. Without reference, the bird-voices of swans and the movement of their many entwined wings sound profoundly alien. It is the track 'WATER-ROR' which confirms my assumptions. This is music for a flooded world. These are the sounds of creatures made *other* in the changing landscape; this is music which has a materiality best likened to a liquid.

The regurgitating patterns of moving fluids and the breakbeat deconstructions of percussive sounds are not just found in the work of AGF, but in the work of possibly hundreds of experimental electronic musicians today. Indeed, artists previously mentioned such as Holly Herndon, Chino Amobi and Amnesia Scanner also express similar materialities of sound. However, this is not just sonic wetness, this is music inferring a thick and black and multi-referential substance. I call it Oil Music.

The idea of representing a far-off future relies on sound which functions as a metaphorical speculation. Thus, I impose my own metaphor of oil to help explain the way this music presents its future imaginary. Oil Music pertains to all the non-linguistic and instrumental components of this music. I use the metaphor for the following reasons:

Oil is in many mythologies, alive.

Oil is produced from the decomposition of prior ecological eras.

Oil is the primary component of plastic.

Oil fuels capitalism.

Oil destroys the world.

Oil and its music is in a cyclical relationship with its own materiality: it is at once an expression of environmental destruction, and at the same time, an expression of human progress and the *construction* of new environments.

Oil is political.

Australian environmentalist John Wiseman writes: 'There is an increasing recognition that the biggest roadblocks preventing [successful environmental policies] are political, social and cultural, rather than scientific and technological.'[1] Taking up Wiseman's claim, Bogna Konior describes the heightened importance placed in art to help us grapple with our transitionary world:

> The Anthropocene configures multiple ways for artists to travel into this newly estranged territory that we once called 'the environment.' Like the mutated daisies growing near Fukushima or...the previously barren landscape of Broken Hill in Australia, the arts feed off the speculative radiation and unexpected changes that the current (intellectual) climate allows...This speculative drive is weaving an aesthetic and thematic alliance between academia and the arts, clocking in at the denial of 'humanity' as a productive term. Artists who seek to move focus beyond the immediate human everyday, extending it into the animal, vegetal, mineral, machinic and cosmic are reaching towards post-humanist theory...If there is a unifying tendency to much of 'Anthropocenic' art it is the task of fictionalising nature, of making it less familiar and less human; a desire to leave humanism behind and move 'towards an open field of naturecultures, infrastructure assemblages, and other newly contested territory'.[2]

Oil Music, according to my conception, follows what Konior describes as 'anthropecenic art', that is, art which performs a *fictionalisation* of nature. Considering the prevalence of liquidity in both sound and structure, it would be easy to relate this music to what Zygmunt Bauman calls 'liquid modernity'. Indeed, using Bauman's conceptualisation, the Cloud might be aptly described as a space par excellence where one could notice a movement from a previous 'solid modernity' to the fluidness of today's internet. In other words, constant mobility and change of identity, of *bodies* not as pilgrims searching for a better home, but as experiential tourists. However, while Bauman's analysis is highly relevant, it also conforms to a certain 'realism' in aesthetic practice, which in many ways is absent in the music discussed in this chapter. Instead, Oil Music's narrative relates to a different form of liquidity: a making unfamiliar of the bodies and identities we notice flowing around us, and a speculation and fictionalisation of the environments of today, projected onto tomorrow.

Performing another cycle where past and future meet up is the recent emergence of flattening new materialist philosophies such as object-oriented-ontology (OOO). In Morton and Harman's seductive writing, the hierarchies between objects are levelled. Our own conscious experience of standing upon a patch of dirt is considered no more important, or meaningful, than the experience of the dirt itself having the force of a foot pressed upon it.[3] In this way OOO ties in loosely* with ideas that all matter might possess an experiential 'consciousness', a *panpsychism*, or what might be called *animism*. Animism considers the rock around us as alive, that oil is alive and that matter is animated and might be able to *think*. I am not directly interested in animism itself, but I am interested in the magical thinking which has looped back to ancient human understandings of the material world. In the face of environmental catastrophe, we have had a mythological renaissance. Ideas once rejected by post-industrial rationality are being reinvestigated to help us understand how our ancestors actually *cared for and had compassion* for the world around them. What's more, as we are on the cusp of the bio-technological augmentation of the human, might we create forms of human consciousness in a post-human world which are so alien that they are totally unrecognisable? Might we need to consider all matter as conscious, in order to be able to care for those around us which may have become more liquid than flesh, more earth than organic body? Music is its own aesthetic animism. It animates the world and the air and future speculation. With this in mind, I will turn to the animation of oil, which has become forged into the plastic objects left littered around us. Through a selection of insightful artistic projects, I will strive to reconsider the nostalgic ghosts of consumerism and the discarded technologies of the early internet born from an oily past. Where I once insisted that a reality thought to be *wrong* might inspire political inaction, I now twist this claim, and instead consider how *fictionalised* worlds might be sources of political inspiration.

i) Cellophane Ghost Nets

Plastic's impact on the environment has been well documented. The recorded number of creatures displaced or killed by its presence is so large that it becomes almost unintelligible. An estimated 1 *billion* sea mammals and birds die every year ingesting translucent materials hidden in the water.[4] As a substance responsible for the unbridled destruction of ocean life, oil is sucked up in great seaward steel rigs and comes back to doubly haunt those very same waters in its processed plastic form. *The Great Pacific Garbage Patch*, also known as the *Pacific Trash Vortex*, is more than mere philosophical horror. Plastics drawn there by ocean currents have amassed to cover (in some estimates) an area of 1.6 million square kilometres, or one-sixth of the United States. In the cycle of black oil-leaks —> processed substrates into the shiny containers for modern consumerism —> discarded waste —> deathly marine ingestion —> and our own consumption of contaminated fish: those thousands of plastic micro-particles hidden in our food turn our own bodies into the haunted carriers of capitalist promoted non-human species destruction.

The term 'Ghost Net' once described forgotten fishing lines and nets which had been discarded and left to pollute the oceans. Floating invisible, all manner of exquisite marine life was prey to be strangled in a wiry death. Today, a Ghost Net is rarely a single object. Instead, it is a floating amalgamation of plastic bottles, shopping bags, mass-produced children's toys, phone cases and laptop components still carrying trace amounts of rare earth. To fly or swim into a Ghost Net is to experience one of the most disturbing physical consequences of human progress. In art which captures the plastic death-mesh of consumerist objects, like in Japanese musician Nyoi Plunger's album *Toiret Status* or in the music video to Holly Herndon's *Chorus*, sound performs a bathetic elegy to the sea.

Herndon's 2014 genre defining track *Chorus* was accompanied by a 3D rendered Akihiko Taniguchi video. We see a panning camera emerge from video-processing software to slip through the very surface of a computer screen. Once outside, the video consists of movements around a series of intimate and surveilled bedrooms. These spaces, rendered from scanned webcam low-res images, melt and contort in a plastic materiality. In a similar way, Herndon's voice emerges in a plastic sheen, somehow self-aware of its own processed materiality — performing its own *sousveillance* of a manufactured larynx. Herndon cuts into her voice so that the plosives and opening consonants of words are left out. We thus enter her voice in the middle of a word, thrown into its insides without warning. The disruption of time is exacerbated by these 'middle entrances'. Words become almost understandable, but not quite.

Turning to the method of musical construction, Dryhurst and Herndon's technique of 'Net Concrete' is almost more 'field recording' than a 'representation' of what it is like to hear and experience the Cloud. Net Concrete is a direct sonification of the chaos, crisis and paradoxical liquidity of online experience, but it is also a capturing and making alien of those most common online sounds: the ding of a social media alert; an hour's web browsing and skype conference call recorded and then compressed into a tiny percussive hit; a contact or coil microphone placed within the actual hardware of a laptop, recording the machinic warbling of its circuitry. Besides aural images of two fingers gliding across wall-to-wall glass surfaces, or the represented sound of a blindingly glossy bust of plastic, the sonic presence of Net Concrete injects a brittle tension into this music. This is music that could shatter into fragments at any moment.

Oil Music is a fitting term here because these composed sounds go through rapid changes from liquids to brittle yet equally bendy solids. In its plastic form, the material of these sounds is at its most haunting. Plasticity infers an almost oxymoronic substance which can bend and stretch, yet still snap at any moment. The language of a plastic sound is for me an audible glimmering, an audible bubbling, gurgling, fizzing, bubble-gum flavoured popping. The colour is pink. The design is the perfectly rendered image of a shiny 3D geometric shape. I think of the effect of a plastic sound as a 'bathetic elegy'. Plastic is so cheerful, lively and giddy that it is actually hauntingly sad. A ghost of childhood ignorant bliss. That development of impossibly thin and stretchy plastic, called cellophane, is responsible for enchanting so many childhoods with the glow of coloured light. In the 1940s, Susan Freinkel writes: 'The word "cellophane" was designated the third most beautiful word in the English language, right behind "mother" and "memory".'⁵ Plastic holds onto the life and death cycle of its oily proto-form. Like the Lacanian notion of desire always moving towards the object *a*, we are enchanted by that which might destroy us.

The record label Orange Milk has released the most profound demonstrations of a 'plastic music' which maintains a criticism of its own materiality. Label founder Keith Rankin (known as 'Giant Claw') has perfected plasticity as a compositional method. His latest album, *Soft Channel,* is an exquisite and moving dedication to the dissonance of consumerism. *Soft Channel* functions for itself, like what in film is known as a *soundtrack dissonance*: the juxtaposition of opposite 'moods' in music and image. An example which immediately comes to mind is Werner Herzog's iconic *Lessons of Darkness*. Beneath or perhaps overlaying the devastation wrought by the first Gulf War, Herzog plays the prelude from Wagner's twinkling, albeit tonally complex, *Parsifal*. In other scenes, Prokofiev's sonata for two violins accompanies Saddam Hussein's torture instruments. Perhaps most pertinent of all is the dissonance between the seemingly eternally burning oil fields of Kuwait — oil spilled across a landscape where no grass will ever grow, blackly reflecting the sun, 'attempting to disguise itself as water in a lake' — first accompanied by *Siegfried's Funeral March* from *Götterdämmerung* and then in a reprise by Verdi's *Messa da Requiem*. The music begins sombrely but as we fly further over the fire which seems to endlessly shoot right into the clouds, the music becomes grand, angelic, uplifting — joyous even. The devastation wrought upon the earth by burning oil is sound-tracked in total dissonance with its visual effect. Some might argue this is an aestheticisation of war in the worst way possible. Instead, I see it as an enhancement of war's terrors via a sonic alienation in line with the critical arguments of Brechtian theatre.

In *Soft Channel*, Keith Rankin performs a subtler dissonance with the material of his music. Here, the consistency of the album's compositional method (flurries of sound interspersed with silence) work to perform a critique via the music's relentless energy. These unforgivingly restless joys work to highlight those special moments when the music is sombre. If only for a second the burst of a minor sonority figures the entire album with a haunting of its own construction. Speed and vitality contradict sorrow and work to emphasise its sentiment.

In many Orange Milk releases, this materiality is expressed through the use of crude synths from plastic's consumerist heyday, the 80s. I sometimes imagine that music absorbs the consumerism of the era in which it was produced. Indeed, in the 80s, newly produced synthesisers sound-tracked much of the advertising industry. But it goes deeper than this. Perhaps the sound of a Roland Juno embodies rather than soundtracks plastic. Bendy, brittle, wobbly and multi-coloured, the vibrato wheel morphs musical substance in minute folds of neon candy. A pitch bend becomes the curvature of a Pepsi bottle. Today plastic also infers a certain poor quality. It's colourful but cheap; 80s Midi Sound is as plastic as it gets. James Ferraro's 2011 album *Far Side Virtual* is a Midi-orchestral masterpiece. Different companies like Yamaha and Roland raced to create an industry standard for the synthesis of orchestral instruments. The dream was to play and arrange your own orchestra from the comfort of the home — horns, strings, wood blocks, timpani all sounding in magnificent hyper-reality from one's lonely bedroom. However, back then, the actuality of the technology was that it produced an almost obscenely bad replication. Strings sounded like plastic wires, horns were more car-like than trumpet-esque. General Midi Sound 2 was a collection of hollow one-dimensional toy-instruments. Constructed predominantly from General Midi Sound, Ferraro took the junkspace of yesteryear and turned these poor orchestral imitations into something exquisitely beautiful. In his genius, Ferraro revels in *poor* replication. But importantly, as a listener, the total midi absorption in *Far Side Virtual* doesn't sound wrong or laughable. Instead, the virtual loses its virtuality, it slowly becomes real, subtle, honest, haunting.

Ferraro's work loops back to my earlier discussion of royalty-free music and the somatic neoliberal self. In his music, plastic timbres coincide with blocks of superficial emotion and mood. As a commentary on a culture of instrumentalised sound and mood manipulation, the album *Human Story 3: 10 Songs for Humanity* includes a synthesised voice orating poetry for our somatic bodies. At opportune moments in the music the voice says words like: *'Starbucks', 'Yoga', 'Health-food', 'Ikea'.* Glib orchestral bells accompany these statements. No follow-up sentence is ever provided. These isolated words, totally mundane in their sounding, somehow capture neoliberalism better than most works of theory. Occasionally a choir will emerge from the texture to harmonise one of these signifiers in an angelic echo.

In the simplicity of this spoken list, like striking off words from a productivity app, I'm reminded of the experimental poem by Robert Fitterman called 'Directory'. Fitterman simply took an unnamed mall directory and wrote it down anew on the page.

Macy's
Circuit City
Payless ShoeSource
Sears
Kay Jewelers
GNC
LensCrafters
Coach
H&M
RadioShack
Gymboree

The Body Shop
Eddie Bauer
Crabtree & Evelyn
Gymboree
Foot Locker...[6]

And it goes on. Hearing a recomposing of royalty-free music makes it poetic and devastating in unintentional ways. Through what might be considered an ironic critique of sweet music, Ferraro's total exaggeration of tone and signification actually pushes it into an ethereal state. It floats above our despicable culture of self-improvement, becoming its own unique space to inhabit. From the ether, from sweetness and the aliveness of music, certain internet-born genres ignite optimism through their utopian use values. Vaporwave is one such genre. In 2009 Daniel Lopatin (now known as *Oneohtrix Point Never*) posted on the YouTube channel 'Sunsetcorp' a looping deconstruction of the chorus of Fleetwood Mac's 'Only Over You'. Entitled 'Angel', the hallmarks of Vaporwave were founded in the repeating lyric, 'I miss you when you're gone, Angel please don't go.' As a genre, Vaporwave became defined by the repeating of isolated fragments of 80s and 90s pop (cheesy and poignant), commercial television soundbites and esoteric Japanese BGM and Jazz. Invoking a haunting of ghosts trapped in machines of the past, Vaporwave re-coded the broken remnants of past consumer culture. In this imaginative landscape, music cycles on defunct cassette tapes, morphing at ever-changing tempos cut and spliced poorly together. It calls out from a parallel lost-technological history. Early Tron-like, Gibson-esque visions of the internet are expressed in matrices of grid lines and the floating 3D shapes of a 90s daytime infomercial. A plug yourself in through the back of your neck aesthetic. The purgatory of an imagined lost server — a space in sparkling permafrost — crude sensory consumerism interleaved with fragments of bygone internet utopias like *Geocities*.

The title of the seminal release 'Memory Vague Full DVD' captures the sad history of Vaporwave. As a genre it opaques and dissipates as soon as it is breathed. Grafton Tanner authored one of the only books on the rise and decline of this online artefact. He opens *Babbling Corpse: Vaporwave and the Commodification of Ghosts* with an acknowledgement of his failure to capture adequately the complexity of a culture lost to dead forum threads, now mostly reduced to the vagaries of human memory.[7] I can make a similar admission. What once felt so vital is now buried within our haggard and faulty memories, lost to the cyclical-graveyard of the internet. When I first heard 'Memory Vague' it called to mind David Foster Wallace's mysterious videotape in *Infinite Jest*, simply known as 'the Entertainment'. Here, the viewer is compelled to watch endlessly, unable to eat or drink until death via dehydration. In the Vaporwave community talking about the ethereal, embodied, haunting affects of the genre became a trope of its own. Exquisite YouTube commentaries propagate the trace remains of this dead genre. Users once wrote odes to their transcendental listening experience — the same sonic fragment of past-consumerism stretched and shrunk seemed to elicit a mood and affect which was undeniably gravitational. I remember first hearing Sunsetcorp's 'There's nobody here' and reflecting that I'd never felt such musically inspired isolation. Listening, I was suddenly on a moving train, globules of rain dripping down the glass. I was in a nostalgic recreation of an 80s metropolis, faceless people on the street. I was a ghost, I was a nobody. I was in the green rice fields, Walkman in my ears, the ether streaming in.

In image, cadaveric body parts accompany Vaporwave releases. Disembodied hands press and repress play on a VHS-machine, holding forever-old remotes. Close-ups of 80s advertisement faces slowly blink, block emotions captured and repeating until they become unbearably weighty. In similar disembodied ways, the online community self-cycled and transformed in its listening and re-creation processes. New Vaporwave often became direct interpretations of past Vaporwave. Cadaveric anonymous accounts spawned all over YouTube. Early pioneers like Daniel Lopatin and Romana Xavier had many aliases: 'Chuck Person', 'Macintosh Plus', 'Vektroid', 'Virtual Information Desk', 'PrismCorp Virtual Enterprises'; and other pivotal avatars of unknown artists like 'Saint Pepsi', 'Internet Club' and 'NMESH'. Through this anonymity, songs and fragments could be looped around in relational ways. Anyone with an internet connection could make Vaporwave, which only required knowledge of rudimentary production techniques: slowing-down, speeding-up, cutting and pasting.

Accordingly, Vaporwave was plastic like no other genre

before it. It was malleable, it was simple yet life transforming. Like plastic, it turned up ghostly on the shore of the browser. It swam in its own kitschness, and talking about it required the highest romantic sentiment. To speak of it on forums evoked mood as if looking through cellophane. It needed a language of material metaphors.

ii) Virtual Ambience for the End of the World

In the late 2000s Daniel Lopatin became known as 'Oneohtrix Point Never'. A string of releases during this fertile period included his highly influential *Betrayed in the Octagon* and *Zones Without People*. In both albums, Lopatin learned from and twisted the language of Vaporwave, recomposing the synthetic bird chirps, the Silicon Valley infomercial soundtracks of 'new age' synths and the floating arpeggios of Japanese Background Music. In the refinement of his musical language, this 80s/90s past was no longer only sampled. Instead, it was recreated anew, as if existing in a parallel reality. While philosophically kitsch, in 2009, this evolution of Lopatin's musical language might have been theorised as a movement from 'simulation' to 'simulacrum'. The album is without spoken or sung text, yet it emphasises that which it lacks, a human presence. We can hear the space carved out where a person might stand.

In these nostalgic re-compositions, many sounds, like those from 'new age' music, changed signifiers. What was once the sonic referent for a 'spiritual opening of the mind's eye', became 'an entering into a lost and siphoned-off digital memory'. *Betrayed in the Octagon*'s swathe of grainy synth provided the ambience for an alternate end to our millennial cyber-age. All the affect of Vaporwave was still there — the loneliness, the haunting, the faulty memory, the tears for material suffering — yet in the creative act of composing something afresh, these referential sounds felt so much more real, so much more sincere, dislodged towards a virtual world, itself a virtual elegy for the destruction of earth.

Like an 'Ecco Jam' (a term once used to describe a Vaporwave compilation), *Zones Without People* bounces ideas around internally. In the echoes of its relationship to the past, and its own compositional structure, this release manages to close us off in the alternate history of its construction. This music is both a hauntological lament to a bygone era, and also a fervent reminder of an outside ecology on the verge of becoming lost, a reminder of an 80s daytime-television future within which we could become irreversibly trapped. The virtual, along with its references to the early internet and the world of videogames, could also be understood as a space outside of past, present and future. To enter a virtual space is to have one foot in our own reality and another in a reality made temporally and spatially *other*. In this way, music like *Zones Without People* constructs a parallel space to experience an alternate history, or to watch from afar the kind of destruction we might inflict upon the planet.

Music makes virtual space via a twisted nostalgia and poetic purchase. To acknowledge the aphorism: *music takes me to another world*, is to confirm a range of affect creating phenomena. In the recognisable melody ingrained into us by the history of Western harmony, or the referential timbre of an 80s synth, we are often caught between forces of nostalgia and new creation. Nostalgia is an easy and powerful transporter. When felt, we rocket back in time. However, when placed in contrast with 'newness', or more importantly, *'corruption'*, this feeling and longing for the past draws us into another timeline. Even though it is so hard to define, I would still argue that there is a distinct feeling when one hears a composition which verges on the *border* of nostalgia, or when a piece paints a twisted or corrupted image of the past. In the almost-past not quite right, or an almost-future not quite believable, we experience the work in a virtual space. This is the manifestation of the slow cancellation of the future.

Besides the already discussed nostalgia of midi sound, both

Lopatin and Ferraro frequently use the synthesis technique of *physical modelling* to make real instruments virtual. The name of this technique hints at the process: a physical object (be it a string, or drum, or object which could make a sound via the passing of wind through it) is mathematically modelled so that it can be 'played' virtually within software. Many composers ignore the range of exciting possibilities for unearthly long horns, or strings the width and material of sky-scrappers. Instead, the technique is used commonly to simulate real instruments. The quality of the mathematical representation varies greatly. Hyper-real imitations of instruments and the rooms they sound within are nearly impossible to perfectly model. Lopatin often seems to use crude simulations, especially of strings and semi-acoustic guitars. These virtual instruments sound 'fake' but work perfectly to draw our ear into that parallel virtual timeline. A cello is bowed, but something is amiss. A flute blows, but the vibrato is a little too even. Physical modelling is responsible for the orchestral version of the uncanny valley — something is *almost* human, but not quite. *Digital artefacts are lodged into the wood of a Stradivarius.*

* * *

So far I have discussed musical representations of a parallel history, but I turn now to artistic projects which rather than represent, appear to live within and come from unreal spaces. While researching this chapter, I found a lively sub-community on YouTube creating ambient 'field recordings' from different videogames. The first video I encountered came from *Dark Souls*, a 2011 RPG set in a post-apocalyptic fantasy world.[8] My memory of the game related to its horror and profound difficulty: clawed abominations hiding behind corners; a near impossible boss made out of sewn together limbs; the particular warning bells of another human player 'invading' your world in an attempt to hunt you down. In this reality, cruelly invented, I had never before noticed the ambient sounds of just standing still, or of moving but not fighting. The action always took precedence. Revisiting these worlds now through this YouTube sub-community, I find that the ambience is calming — a physically modelled wind (even while indoors) soothes the tension. Within are the sounds of moist footsteps on puddles, the shuffling of a skeleton's bones behind a wall, the cry of a beast somewhere many hours away.

Besides *Dark Souls*, I stumbled across a series of 'virtual field recordings' from the 2007 masterpiece *Bioshock*.[9] This game's alternate history is set in a city called *Rapture*. The city is a failed utopian project preserved in the era when it was constructed, a haunted 1940s. Its billionaire creator, inspired by Ayn Rand, imagined an underwater paradise away from 'the human parasites of the earth above'. In the ambience of this flooded world, audio director Emily Ridgeway pieced together a total recreation of a late 30s /early 40s soundscape. Among the bubbles of passing water, Blues plays from old transistor radios in empty hotel lobbies. The Art Deco decor is almost period perfect, minus the fishbowl windows and the marine life swimming outside. There is a warmth and eeriness in this setting. Liquids seem to warp most sounds made by the character you control. The horrors which hide behind closed doors are audibly wet, or electrified by deteriorating power lines. In the alternate history of *Rapture*, a virtual history, we extrapolate this flooded world to a description of the near future we head towards. Here, humanity forced to either adapt houses for rising sea-levels, or abandon land all together for underwater life.

Fredric Jameson's famous critique of postmodern nostalgia was that it supposedly produced political inaction in its fetishisation of the past. In fragmented, stylised and colonised references, a thoroughly neoliberal repackaging of the past is argued to lead to a suppression of historical time. Jameson considers this type of nostalgia as a negative promoter of a flat 'perpetual present'.[10] While Vaporwave may fit Jameson's description of 'postmodern pastiche' perfectly, I'd argue that the later work of Daniel Lopatin, and a game like Bioshock, is empowered by the instrumentalisation of nostalgia. In virtual space-based mediums nostalgia functions entirely differently. Pastiche, and its criticisms, disappear through the ambience enacted in the creation of an entire inhabitable world. Bioshock's *Rapture* employs the manufactured nostalgia of a bygone 40s-60s in order to critique this period as the birth of a neoliberal utopianism. In this drowned city, the story describes a failed consumerist utopia which collapses under the freedom to augment the self in limitless ways. Set in an unreal past, we play Bioshock in the present, and yet like all good sci-fi, this story speaks to our future. In fact, by appropriating the aesthetics of the past towards such a critical goal, Jameson might agree that Bioshock is satiric rather than nostalgic.

Within these ambient virtual spaces, sound undergoes new compositional and material changes. The most dominant experience of hearing sound in a videogame environment is that the movement of the game and your character constantly modulates it. In realistic simulations, if a car drives past your character the sound undergoes a Doppler Shift like it would in real life. The pitch dips due to speed. Likewise, sound sources can be placed behind objects, softly resonating until the player reveals them. A distant waterfall will become deafening when underneath it. Diving beneath liquid will muffle the world outside.

Footsteps, or the squelching movements of whatever body you control, are by far the most common sources of virtual sound. The London-based record label *Quantum Natives* specialises in music which is either produced through game development software, or which exists purely in a videogame context. Talking with one of the label's founders, James B Stringer, aka Brood

Ma, I learn about the software *FMOD Studio* which can be used in tandem with popular game development engines like *Unreal Engine* and *Unity*. Experimenting with the software reveals it to be an easy to use physical modelling engine, capable of simulating distances between sound sources, the material of their construction, the amplitude changes undergone via the muffling of a closed door, and a range of other manipulations like the Doppler Effect produced due to the unique physics of a moving sound wave. The ease of creation, and the rising prominence and availability of virtual reality experiences call to being a world where virtual works of art can produce the embodied critiques of the present, and imaginative speculation towards the future we desperately require. When videogame realism becomes trite, projects like *Quantum Natives* and Clifford Sage's *Recsund* inform an expanded use of these engines to produce unreal and fictionalised worlds. The environment, not flat but 3D, can now be imagined in polyvalent ways. Footsteps of a character needn't sound like leather on gravel, they can sound in infinitely unreal materials, and can be modulated based on the physical properties of a world which does not adhere to the constraints of earthly physics.

David Kanaga's videogame opera *Oikospiel: A Dog Opera* inspired this entire chapter. Here the footsteps (or paw steps) of the dog you control continually trigger some of the most engaging and arresting sounds of any artistic project I have experienced. Sometimes a jump of your dog avatar launches you far into the atmosphere, the sound of wind passing, only to have you fall back to the earth with the triggered sound of an orotund bass drum. In *Oikospiel,* Kanaga has created a profound and fiercely important landmark. I think it is the first to truly redefine the musical experience of the twenty-first century.

Kanaga explains that 'games are a conversation between space and time'.[11] Focusing on that beautiful notion of 'play', his thesis is simple: 'Games are formalised play.' While music can be theorised as a game itself (see Xenakis' *Duel and Strategie* or John Zorn's *Cobra*, as well as that rich history of structural 'games' in the Wandelweiser contemporary classical movement) we find new modes of expression when the videogame itself is an instrument. Where Xenakis expressed musical games as a series of rule-bound experiments directed always towards an end goal, Kanaga considers the game as an open-ended structure which is not necessarily goal oriented. What's more, when each element of play within a game results in a different sounding state, Euclidian space and time becomes the very 'exoskeleton' for a new instrument. In this way, the musicality of a game is akin to that utopian moment of simply *playing* in pure improvisation your bedroom guitar, or cello, or midi-drum set or the sound producing walls and surfaces of your bedroom objects themselves. Kanaga even writes of the earth as an instrument of play:

> A bouncing ball drops, bounces, rises, and repeats, and we hear the gradual accelerando of successive bounces speeding up to a buzz, illustrating the loss of potential energy and corresponding diminution of vertical height caused by each bounce. The Earth's gravity plays this piece with the material of the ball. Play is causal influence.[12]

Besides looking towards the ecology of the earth itself as a guide for artistic practice, Kanaga ends his 2014 lecture *Music Object, Substance, Organism* with a hint towards another fruitful and important place of inspiration: non-human bodies. The lecture slides suddenly devolve into videos of cats and dolphins and wolves playing joyously in their respective elements: sea, forest, snow, kitchen.

To simplify what is a complex story, Oikospiel's looping narrative occurs in a reality where dogs are charged with the creation of works of art. More specifically, a cruel producer sometimes called David Koch (named after the billionaire Koch Brothers who sponsor the Republican Party), or a self-referential 'DK' for David Kanaga, has employed a team of these artistic dogs to create the very opera you play. In this meta-narrative, the minds and hearts of these canine labourers have an installed OS (Oik operating system) rendering their dog forms simultaneously software, hardware, creativity itself and bodies for platform oppression. Accessing the contents page, one finds that Act V is called 'Neo Lib / Dream Machines'. I think this best describes the opera. Through a world where ANCAP flags fly above oil fields, and tech CEOs clash with animal slaves attempting to rise up and unionise, Kanaga's work presents a unique critique of the immaterial and material dominations of our present political system.

The environment of this world, and the very way in which you engage with its setting, functions as both the object and the means of critique. Your first on-screen instructions notify you that your own mouse movements control the 'wind power' of the ever-present turbines which dot this inventive reality. By the end of the game I had forgotten this simple mechanic and it felt like the circling of my finger on the mousepad was itself spinning the vinyl record of this soundscape. You power the sound with your own movements. The world itself is its own instrument.

Divided up into contrasting scenes and acts, the game is labyrinthine, varied and full of exquisite music. Characters speak to you in timed speech bubbles which link words with musical rhythm. Every scene replayed offers a different re-composition of the material. By interacting relationally with the game, I was caught between an appreciation of Kanaga's wild music and an appreciation of my own dog-movements and artistic voice. Many of the scenes appear in mundane office environments. Your dog character shrinks down to become the size of a mouse icon, and you can run across the tabletop interacting with sheet music and the computer screen itself. These moments place multiple instances of sound generation on top of each other. In one scene set in a Desktop environment running OSX, you can open files and play this familiar interface like an instrument. Cycling between the speeds of playback of Celine Dion's *My Heart Will Go On*, I simultaneously ran across the note heads of a Wagner score which sounded in time with my crossings — that is, out of metric time — in what I can only describe as Oik time: the time it takes for a dog to run across a piece of paper.

Following Kanaga on Twitter, I was interested to see him share the score of R Murray Schafer's opera *The Princess of the Stars*. The Canadian composer and theorist most famous for his invention of the term 'soundscape' produced many graphic scores which echoed his ardent environmentalism. *The Princess of the Stars* includes pieces like 'Wolf's Aria', which is notated as a series of flowing note heads that emerge from the mouth of an illustrated wolf, curling gracefully around the page. Each piece of the opera is visually exquisite, and relationally aesthetic in the indeterminacy of its graphic notation. I reference this because Kanaga's work is a making virtual of graphic notation. Interactive videogame music is the evolution of a history of indeterminate composition. In certain scenes of Oikospiel I found myself moving my mouse as if to strum a lyre, or in more abstract ways pressing the W, A, S, D keys to arrange the silhouettes of animals against the setting sun. Given a waypoint marker and a new map to explore, a play through of a scene felt like the bracketed beginning and ending of a score. If Schafer would play Oikospiel, he would find the hyper-realisation of his soundscape project: not just work which functions as a recording and composing of the indeterminate world outside, but instead, a work which is a composing of *the very world* itself in sound.

The title, Oikospiel, references both the OS of a machine, the domesticity of the home and also 'oikos' as the ancient Greek demarcation of the 'eco' of ecology and economics. Aside from functioning as an innovative musical instrument, the game is also highly political. Wind turbines feature, as do oil rigs, black liquids, spilt shipping containers and huddled animal survivors in a world on the edge of environmental catastrophe. The player quickly learns that the opera's narrative functions on many levels. It is simultaneously a retelling of the Greek tragedy of Orpheus and Eurydice, an uprising of dog labourers as they strive to unionise, and a conspiracy where those ever-present wind turbines are revealed to be in fact powered by oil, spinning endlessly to falsely appease those who wish for environmental sustainability. In interview Kanaga expands on this:

> ...the labor themes have a more hidden presence in the wind turbines and oil pumps — because these are signs of objects which do WORK, and generate POWER (work through time). So I wanted to examine economic functions amidst the ecological backdrop — and also, the ecological aspects of the economic foreground (...the 'brand ecosystem', or the 'asset store ecosystem'). [13]

When considering the actual construction of Kanaga's world, its ecology is both a reference to, and constructed out of, what is called the 'asset store' in videogame engines like Unity. In these online marketplaces, creators can buy pre-made objects and packages (an elephant, a tree, a house, a city) which can be used by amateur game makers. Some of these 'game assets' are special works of art in themselves. However, the vast majority are made by amateur developers for a quick buck. They cover uninspiring collections of common real-world objects, and are mostly unprofessional in their detailing. Kanaga's game is made almost entirely out of these objects. It is both a junk space, as Rem Koolhaas might imagine, and more than the sum of its junk objects. Surfaces clip, your dog falls through or within what once appeared as solid, and the animations of characters are endearingly poor. Yet the term endearing describes it best. This world is a beautiful mess.

In one moment the world dissolves and I fall through the sky to land upon the back of the earth: a giant score of Tristan und Isolde. The famous chords begin to play. I'm reminded of Lars Von Triers 'Melancholia' which seemed to endlessly repeat the opening overture as a giant asteroid plummeted towards our home planet. Back in the game, the first chord lingers as I stay unmoving. I flick my mouse sounding the next chord and remember it as a harmonic progression which nearly redefined Western Romanticism. The movement of my dog avatar plays through the score until I realise that the paper is in fact deep below me, sunk beneath an ocean which I float upon. With the music still sounding in warped and stretched ways, back and forth, I try and swim down beneath the waves towards it. When I reach the seafloor, I realise that the note heads aren't pen on paper, instead they are great black squiggles of oil leaking from the earth. All around me are the legs of oil rigs pumping the score for its natural worth...Many scenes later in a house in the year 2090, a CNBC news cast is playing on a TV, it's describing the advancement of trees upon the arctic circle due to global warming, a man on a couch curses the TV presenter as being a 'climate change cuck' — the climate scepticism placed in dramatic contrast to all I have experienced in this future world so far. To write glibly like the game seems to require of me, I've become one with the wind turbines, one with the hearts and minds of the dog actors, I'm as much a part of Oik OS as them.

The sound of water mixed with the ominous *Tristan und Isolde* reminded me of my own physical body, the liquids it produces and the fallibility of our flesh as part of a greater ecosystem. Trying to come to terms with Oikospiel's simultaneously dead, yet so alive world, I found resonance in Gean Moreno's explanation of the prevalence of 'images of a dead world' in art today:

For capitalism to sustain itself, to reproduce indefinitely, it needs to incrementally gobble up more and more...Extinctions are drawn to it like filaments to a magnet. The imperative to grow and the need for unrestricted license to devastate are two sides of the same coin — not only mutually dependent but structurally essential. Yet, however deplorable, growth and devastation can be aesthetically generative: they set us on a course toward imagining what the world will look like as it slides toward the inorganic. By constantly invading and liquidating resource-rich contexts, capitalism encourages images that project what will inevitably be left in its wake: a dead world...a planetary condition: the globe as a rotating, dead lithosphere, coated in a fine dust of decomposing once-organic particles. Individual patches of dead world synthesised into a continuous crust.[14]

Adding to Moreno's analysis, I could include the importance of sounds of a dead world. In granulation, in the un-aliveness of physical modelling, in fragmented vocal manipulation or the unhuman stretching of voices in Vaporwave, we hear a representation not just of a post-climate change world decomposing and dusty, but also of a privileging of that aliveness it once had. Musical dust is everywhere in this music. In the tiny clicks and manipulations of white noise we hear the remnants of a lost world. Thinking about all these ambient sounds of wind and rain and dust, I wonder whether this material presents 'weather', the atmosphere, as a monster which is simultaneously an independent political actor, and also an object so big and omnipresent that it becomes itself instrumentalised.

Weather and the environment is represented in these works of art as a hybrid material, its significance is bonded to a place outside of human-time scales. Yet when fictionalised, in an unreal world, the enormity of our ambient timescales can be put in perspective. Fictionalising our ecological home can help us understand the catastrophes we inflict upon it. In this chapter I have hoped to further my discussion of music which criticises current future trajectories. These tales, imaginative and moving fictions, can be augmented by compositional decisions. Oil music is a material decision, and its metaphors speak as a warning yet also as a coming together. In the virtual, we live out a space torn-down and exposed in environmental disaster, boxes, plaster, intimate bedroom objects, all the trash found in the asset store of a game engine thrown around in a caustic wind. In Vaporwave the rendered sound of birds and liquid, the physical modelling simulating reality, calls to mind a future where we can *only* experience Nature digitally. We hear a future sublime in the sounds of a rendered bird. We hear the simulated ocean which will one day consume us. Returning to Douglas Kahn's pre-twenty-first century sonic history, water appeared in modernism as the space for real soundings of liquid. Cage's *Water Music* 'really splashes' on stage. The difference of hearing water digitally enacted is the gap it poses between life and our ears. A gap which creates a haunting lack, a horror which immediately associates the water with time. Unlike Cage's music which ripples in the present, Oil Music ripples in the future. What's more, in these works, we inhabit an alien body and an alien world. Becoming alien, becoming the instrument for the sound of weather, creates something else. Empathy. Care.

Chapter 5

Chimeric Flesh and the Hyper-Child

A Concern Troll's willingness to identify as such affords a position discrete from those who are externally determined by HATERS or and skulk cross depleted, burbles X into a glass. The more common 'Socially Censured Trolls'. Devised, I would say, by this bleak and hard patio of government, in whose interest and under whose proptotic glass eyes our anger SUNKS like a wooden stilted village into virtual or parabolic mire, where slights and tar are only ever between individuals and singularly resolvable according to same. A ritual method involving the invention of a one-off monster for the sole purpose of its on-off, symbolic beheading. A chimera, X crossed with X. The hind legs of mother, the face of legitimacy, ect.

Trussed to a very real spare room in a very real undisclosed location render farm: buckets, cabling, chased silver, rapiers; a kerosene level of drunkenness maintained for neither action and so, unable to live with the discovery, I go the fuck seek assisted suicide at a government clinic called, genially enough, 'Home'.
Ed Atkins, A Primer for Cadavers

Ed Atkins writes prose-poetry of a hybrid world. In writing he presents a hybrid linguistic style, a chimeric language of his own. His images are never singular. They mesh together, tail to tail, in lieu of that famous Woolfian style — a stream of words. The breakdown of poetry into prose is the 'deliquescence of lineation'[1] — it is the linguistic manifestation of rising sea consuming land. To loop back to Part 1 of *Hearing the Cloud*, I find an equally apt description of the materiality of chimeric flesh in China Miéville's bubbling crisis-ridden city. The energies at play produce 'a certain ontological instability at the very centre of reality'. The core of Being itself smushed, as it were, between contradictory forces, tending towards hybridity because *to fuse* is the only way out of this mess. This chapter discusses those sounds forced into fleshy fusions. Energies of crisis produce music which fuses as an exit strategy. Spoken online words and musically uttered sounds break out into unlikely combination: part coping mechanism, part act of political resistance, and part sellable-spreadable aesthetic in the service of a malleable smiling pop idol.

Donna Haraway made famous the analogy of a chimera. In *A Cyborg Manifesto*, the image of the mythical-biological-machine fusion was central to her descriptions of a radical post-human feminism. To describe the materiality of the following sound, I use the image of a chimera in praise of Haraway, and avoid other analogies such as viruses, mutants or monsters which often have immediately negative connotations. The word 'chimera' has a rich etymology commonly used to describe the fusion of different animals to form a fearsome creature in Greek mythology. Equally, Mount Chimera in Lycia, Turkey, is a location where ancient-era volcanic vents once emitted burning methane thought to be a metamorphic force. In genetics, a chimeric organism, or a chimerism, is a singular organism formed from multiple zygotes. The results can be an animal with multiple gender organs, or one with two sets of DNA trying desperately to be one. Moreover, in the word chimera we hear the hard 'c' of chameleon, camouflage, identity-manipulating and fluid pigment-distorting skin. This term is not about a being mutated away from some 'pure perfect state', rather it is about the original already-born hybrid. This term reflects the bonded together nature of all post-internet experience. An idea fused to flesh, a cultural artefact welded to a body, a sound meshed to a representation.

Thirty-four years later, Haraway writes of the Chthulucene. Her rewording of the Anthropocene is inspired by endangered Californian spiders, named, as if to hint at that famous cryptid chimeric beast, the Cthulhu. Haraway's future, and post-humanism, has evolved to discuss a world on the edge of a great flood. To evoke a chimera today is to rest upon that mythical mountain in Turkey waiting for god's liquid judgement — all the animals and critters and non-human entities of the forest piled into our Ark of theory.

Today, in language alone, the titles of albums and songs and the librettos of radio-operas give adequate foreshadowing of this world. Iranian composer Ash Koosha's 2017 release is simply called *Chimera*, and a few years earlier Venezuelan producer Arca released his seminal album, *Mutant*. In 2016 Sean L Bowie burst onto the scene going under the moniker Yves Tumor, a name close enough to out of control flesh. Yves Tumor's self-described 'dystopian' *Serpent Music* encourages the most common image of a chimera: a half-snake, half-goat, half-lion, the mythical beast killed by Bellerophon who rode the equally chimeric winged horse Pegasus. One chimera slaying another.

Material traits can be noted in the *flesh* of the instrumentation and voices of this music, specifically, disintegration and decay, slime and bodily fluid. These artists continue a cybernetic tradition while also projecting a great scepticism towards any idea of the absolute. There is no coincidence in all these recent artistic obsessions with becoming mutant and becoming abject. The Cloud is a disgusting place. It makes culture fragmented, it trolls, it makes agency hybrid. In considering what kind of child-to-come might be born to save our future, often all that comes to mind is a being born both corrupt and parasitic. In this imagery, I question whether modernist transcendence appears either a fiction, or only attainable in an inhuman reality? Perhaps the absolute can be found, but only in mechanical or fragmented flesh, in the grotesque objectivity of a sentient algorithm, or in the sublimity of the abject. Therefore, this music becomes the space for a different kind of nihilistic exploration. A perverse dark will emerges from an accelerationist's flirting with this very dissolution of subjectivity. This music is in part an exploration of a human meltdown: the sublime in melting flesh.

Many artists today voice a speculation founded in part upon this dark (yet animated) sonic materialism. The voice is dissolved into bites of information. Granulation reorders and retimes fragments of vocal data. Phonemes become clicks, vowels become atmospheres to inhabit. Speech calls out from unreal and constantly changing spaces. Importantly, it keeps calling out. It is ceaseless, and in its endless rearrangements the voice takes on other materials and becomes a chimerism. To call again on Douglas Kahn's twentieth-century sonic history, his 'mutant creature' is like the one depicted in McCarthy's *The Road*: an alabaster white, glowing imaginary fantasy, still in the shape of a beastly animal drinking water after a killing. For artists today, the present is more imaginative than fantasy. Their music's chimera is a creature of welded together ideas. Penderecki turned violins into the screams of the victims of Hiroshima. Today, screams emerge from the tiny speakers in the back of a children's toy. This music moves beyond a twentieth-century idea of catastrophic flesh — burnt flesh fused to a brick wall in Hiroshima; flesh fused to Agent Orange (Anderson sings: '*So hold me, in your petrochemical arms.*') Instead, flesh is now bonded to a speculative future, it is fused to a hyper-real wall, a pop-cultural device, a hyper-real slime, a Japanese Tamagotchi.

i) The Hyper-Child

On YouTube a man syringes semen into an unfertilised chicken egg. He is attempting to create life. To create a chimeric child for himself — a Homunculus. In early videos we see the Russian vlog-scientist known as Korney experimenting feverishly. In full hazmat suit he wanders a room filled with containers of broken eggs and other vats overflowing with purplish egg slime. No child has been born. His breathing sounds laboured behind the gasmask. He tries another method. After 40 days of egg incubation he again turns on his video camera. We are greeted by an ascetic table and a down-lit hand holding an egg. The Band-Aid he had placed over the shell's syringe-wound has become black and mouldy. In translated Russian, Korney explains: 'A Homunculus is an artificial being' inspired by the medieval treatises of Paracelsus. He cracks the egg and more of this green muck fills a plastic reliquary. The once yellow yoke of the egg is gone. With tweezers he searches in the mess. He finds life. A creature is pulled from the goo. It is dull alabaster. It resembles primordial life. Its head twitches as it is held upside down in tongs. Slowly it raises its body and its gaping mouth stares directly into the camera.

25 Million Views.

Korney keeps alive his artificial child in a foggy aquarium. He feeds his Homunculus the protein powder he himself takes after working out in the gym. In front of millions of online viewers, he raises his very own chimera. Vlogging throughout the process, we follow as the creature grows, tripling in size, and more disturbingly, as it develops a tubular red tongue which emerges from its mouth cavity.

After requesting that his viewers name the creature, the online community overwhelmingly decides on a name: Pikachu.

Flesh becomes fused with children's videogame imagination.[2]

* * *

Korney's (fake) child darkly resonates with the visual language of Oneohtrix Point Never and his frequent collaborator Jon Rafman. The video clip for the track *Sticky Drama* encompasses all the materials this chapter will analyse: slime, gore, bodily fluid, fusion. As the lead single from the album *Garden of Delete*, Jon Rafman set the visual tone, filming 35 children violently Live Action Role Playing, stabbing, killing and dismembering each other. In Rafman's imagination data has become corrupted, childhood innocence is a fallacy, and memory is recalled in damaged VHS vision. The two music videos for *Sticky Drama* follow a libidinal quest to find a flesh-fused toy Tamagotchi. Its plastic housing and tiny rectangular screen appear enveloped by out-of-control tumours. Around the Tamagotchi a great battle is waged between rebel and imperial forces. Dressed like cyber outcasts in an apocalyptic fantasy, all the child-actors brandish space age weapons. Cultural signifiers are fused with costumes comprising a lattice of styles. Skin is melting, kids are reduced to pink dehumanised flesh-piles. Gun wounds leak neon green Nickelodeon Slime and children speak through videogame text boxes — RPG narrative strings where up-down options decide the morality of your character. The protagonist of the video has mutated boils on his young face. A cyber-princess dances on her bed in a dress made entirely of CD-ROMs. She is the keeper, or the prisoner of the conflict — to assimilate the knowledge of the Tamagotchi. At a key moment in the music video the toy creature's screen flashes time-warp neon. In an attempt to speak, a particalised laughter, half child, half cyber-nightmare enters the mix. [3]

This voice of the chimeric Tamagotchi is the very first sound heard on *Garden of Delete*. Signalling the importance of the voice, the opening track, *Intro*, is comprised entirely of distorted mouth sounds. A click, and then out of silence comes the unaccompanied sound of a baby's spectral giggling. In Lopatin's *Garden*, children — the cultural embodiment of purity and innocence — are already born corrupted. At birth the baby's first cry is a biological act of survival, an attempt to fill their small lungs with air. Yet here we interpret this cry as suffering, a sonic injustice, a being ripped from the purity and safety of the womb into cold space. In Cormac McCarthy's post-apocalyptic vision, a child is born pure into a disintegrating world, wandering the scarred earth as a symbol of the last vestige of hope. In contrast, the child in *Garden of Delete* is itself born disintegrating and hopeless. One imagines the baby as faulty code typed into existence. Instead of crying out, it laughs in terror. The child is a trapped icon in the screen of an addictive toy. *Clip the device onto your belt, shake your device, level up your creature inside those plastic walls.*

Lopatin and Rafman's obsession with distorted child-like voices and bodies finds critical purchase through its twisted nostalgia. Along with the green slime of 90s Nickelodeon daytime TV, those famous proto-digital devices which you'd clip on to your school backpack (like the Tamagotchi, or the Digimon and Pokemon spinoff toys) informed one of the first widespread instances of a crossover between real and virtual environments. Each of these plastic housings contained your very own pet creature which you could raise and diligently care for. I remember bringing my Digimon to school, pulling it secretly out of my pocket during class to press a few buttons and feed it, digitally pat it, level it up, evolve it and battle it with my friends. These virtual companions were a highly addictive and lucrative phenomenon. With estimated sales reaching over 70 million, the Tamagotchi not only became a pop icon, but even won its inventor, Aki Maita, an (Ig) Nobel Prize in economics. Lopatin and Rafman react to the present-day influence of the Tamagotchi. The success of virtual pets is strongly tied to the emergence of virtual partners, assistants and also virtual pop idols. *Alone in a tiny one-room sleeping compartment, hatch your very own companion out of a virtual toy egg.* Today in Japan, an unlikely reality has come to be where one of the most popular 'virtual creatures' to care for and hold in your pocket, is a pop singer called Hatsune Miku.

The forever 16-year-old Hatsune Miku is internationally famous as being one of the first virtual mega pop-stars. Despite existing as a hologram on stage, her very real performances have sold out concert halls packed with hundreds of thousands of adoring fans. Miku is equal parts software, hardware, singer, idol, brand and an empty shell for misplaced desires. Aside from being the lead star of shows, operas and hugely popular music videos, she is also a creature to be cared for within videogames like *Hatsune Miku Project Mirai DX*. While these rhythm games are largely focused on pressing buttons in time with different songs, arguably the real draw is to hold Miku in your portable device and to continually interact with her within what is also a *slice of life* simulation. In the 'Home' of the portable videogame you can care for Miku, dress her up, decorate the kitchen, interact with her friends and feed her. You become responsible for her virtual life — you shape it.

The name of the pop star is significant, translating as: 'first sound' (Hatsune) of the 'future' (Miku). The 'Miku', in this case, is the holographic body of a 16-year-old school girl. She embodies her name. She is a software marvel in vocal synthesis, and also forever innocent. As described in Hiroshi Aoyagi's *Islands of Eight Million Smiles*, a history of Japanese pop idols largely points towards the total construction and maintenance of contrived and fictional pop narratives.[4] J-Pop idols in the 1990s and 2000s had their lives and personalities defined by male producers and executive board members. The producer behind the scenes wrote in the human backstory, manufactured controversy when necessary and employed movie-esque narratives to attract admirers. On the surface, Hatsune Miku appears equally contrived. Produced by the company *Crypton Future Media,* Miku has been given the body of a school girl in an oblique attempt to fit into an *otaku* culture favouring *kawaii* (cute) bodies. Much has been written about the maintenance of sexual politics in Japan through the depictions of animated women like Hatsune Miku. Her body encourages real women to be treated conservatively in line with gender-stereotypes and fantasies of ideal bodies. In this case, the ideal is what theorist Yuji Sone describes as *shōjo*, a Meiji era word used to describe a female in a definitionaly liminal state between the legal age of marriage and the onset moment of her own fertility. *Shōjo* are women who are by definition, sexually unobtainable. They are innocent, virginal and desired in part because their bodies are prohibited. Sone describes Hatsune Miku as unobtainable 'by virtue of her virtual form', and as 'a contemporary version of the shōjo, a product of Meiji modernisation'.[5]

In all portrayals of Miku, she holds onto her school girl innocence. However, what differentiates her body from the J-Pop idols of the 90s is that her very body is the *only* consistent thing in her produced narrative. Miku is famous for updating the J-Pop success formula for the new millennia. Her personality, her backstory, her actions and her desires and wants and flaws are *all* user-generated. Hatsune Miku can be anything you want her to be. Aside from *Crypton Future Media*'s copyright claims, and initial artistic direction over their pop idol, Miku has largely been opened up to the public. She has thousands of fan-made backstories and her personality can conflict in radically oppositional ways. She can be incongruous, one moment appearing in a fan-made music video sweetly frolicking in a space-themed galaxy, and in another she can appear dressed in black playing a dominating villain in cyber-dystopian conflict, electro-bullets flying around her singing form.

The idol is chimeric. The idol is also an externalisation of the somatic self. In her unobtainability, the neoliberal pressure to control all manifestations of one's desires creates a paradoxical situation, namely, to control one's desires necessitates actually *manufacturing* them into a virtual body. Users who generate the music and videos for Miku are in some critical Japanese circles considered to be 'obsessed' and 'in love' with their very own creations. This culture of manufactured desire leaks over into the West with niche parts of 4chan dedicating their threads to sharing pictures and the backstories of their 'Waifu pillows' (images of animated idols printed out onto life-size pillows to sleep with at night).

Hatsune Miku's famous voice is equally malleable. Created from sample-based synthesis from recordings of Japanese actress Fujita Saki, Crypton Future Media utilised Yamaha's *Vocaloid Synthesis Technology* (known as Vocaloid 2 'V2' and then later generations of the software as 'V3', 'V4') to produce their pop idol. Miku's original voice and identity are found in a set of default parameters and samples within this consumer software. What's more, Yamaha's *Vocaloid* is a relatively easy program to use. A user simply picks their virtual singer (a voice library pack), inputs midi notes into a piano roll and then finally writes any lyric they desire, with each syllable of a word matched to a note. The process enables an isolated bedroom producer to literally play with a voice, to gain a new voice, a new identity to speak through and a body which can be programmed to respond to these externalised desires.

In *Vocaloid 3* you can select six slightly different voice library versions of Hatsune Miku. Like royalty-free moods, these six versions of Miku are described as '*Original*: clear and cute; *Sweet*: gentle and light; *Dark*: calm and sentimental; *Soft*: soft with a sense of unity; and *Solid*: energetic.' Each category of Miku is also attached to a recommended 'genre' of music. For example, *Sweet* Miku is recommended for 'French-pop, ballads and electronica', at a tempo of '55-155bpm' and a register of 'F2-D4'.[6] Users can modify Miku's voice in many other ways outside of these presets, bending her voice to become guttural and aggressive, or instead choosing to enhance its pure and child-like quality. The samples by voice actress Fujita Saki might be the only immutable timbral quality of the virtual pop idol. In other words, new pop economic success is found in malleability and the encouragement of user generated content. Miku absorbs the atmospheres of wider online culture and literally distils these affects within her voice. Japanese sharing platform *Niconico* (formally known as *Nico Dōga)* once dominated the sharing of Vocaloid tracks and fanart. Today, fan interaction has become exceptionally popular on YouTube. The Japanese virtual pop star has inspired the rise of equally neoliberal virtual 'taste-makers' on Instagram and Facebook.

ii) A Slimy Coming of Age

THE CHILD is a kind of archive. Like an archive, it anticipates the future from a moment in the present. It is the archive of past and present that we send into the future as a guarantor of our continuity, of our immortality, of our extension into a time we cannot foresee. But where the archive implies a time that is always already past, the child enfolds futurity even as it incorporates us as the past. We invest in the child the way we would invest in an archive, sending it into the future just as we do our collections of ourselves. But the child is no dead letter it will continue to write us anew, to renew us, even as it promises the continuity of the same.
Veronica Hollinger, Make This a Different Future.

Despite the malleability of Hatsune Miku's vocal chords, she is most famously rendered with a certain child-like quality to her voice. For artistic creator Hiroyuki Ito, it was a necessity for this voice to be considered a 'Lolita Voice' (young, cute and innocent). She is attributed with an almost unwavering pureness. The child voice made virtual — the hyper-child — is a powerful indication of a disturbed culture which requires idols to be so angelic and perfect that they are airbrushed all the way back into adolescence. Hatsune Miku has been profoundly influential for a range of experimental musicians. I introduced her through a discussion of Oneohtrix Point Never, but the influence goes in the opposite direction. Daniel Lopatin is famous for his use of 'chip-speech' (a proto-vocaloid). Early Vaporwave once reacted against the 'smoothness' of commercial capitalism. It functioned in the uneven cuts and abruptness of its harsh editing. Now, in the liquidity and plastic sheen of what has evolved from the movement's legacy, one can witness a different material reference to the hyper-reality of online life. What once was a genre critical of the over-produced, commercial, hyper-perfectionism of late-capitalist sound, today assimilates these production techniques into its oeuvre. There is new cinematic grandeur found in glossy production techniques which appear within the guise of experimental music. Objects appear too smooth, hyper-real. Since the death of critical Vaporwave, it is clear that there has been a significant material movement or shift. Vaporwave's 'ghost in the machine' is reframed as a ghost of the future. What once was a haunted past is now presented as a haunted hyper-real future.

Born from this plastic future are the voices of plastic children. The track 'Child of Rage' on *Garden of Delete* opens with the hollow voice of a young boy interviewed about the violence he expresses towards his brother John. Amnesia Scanner's 'AS Atlas' samples a haunting child-like voice repeating the Japanese word 'basho', which translates as 'place', repeated until it becomes placeless. In turn a boy's voice opens 'AS Angels Rig Hook', *a violent industrial attack mixed with a squelching moist sound — machine and biology. It builds, sounding at first like breathing ventilation systems and then like the rumbling disintegration of a mechanical and intricate object, until finally, the voice bursts through the texture:* 'Where is my mind?' he asks. Within this simple question lies a rhetoric present in all these artists' music — an open-ended plea from the next generation who will inhabit our endangered world. The Cloud hangs over creating chaos out of singular ideas. It is a space within which to lose your mind, a space to continually reconfigure messy fusions of a remembered childhood.

In the experimental music I have discussed, a conflicting materiality is found within the implied innocence heard in a child's voice. For example, Amnesia Scanner distort it. They reach into the spectrum of the waveform and twist it, dragging down partials until those which remain are made hybrid — chimeric. Thus, we hear what we once associate with innocence, manipulated. A disturbed innocence. The child is born conflated. Another word for a ghost is a spectre. As with current twenty-first century thought, a spectre also haunts these child vocalisations.

The manipulation of the spectrogram infers a manipulation of what could be considered the spectre of a sound. Timothy Morton notes, 'spectre is a word made "spectral", by its own definition, since it wavers between appearance and being. It could mean apparition, but it could also mean horrifying object, or it could mean illusion, or it could mean the shadow of a thing.'[7] The compositional investigations made in the 70s by Gérard Grisey and Tristan Murail have formed what is now known as Spectral Music. Discoveries in mathematics and music granted composers the ability to find a range of 'hidden' 'spectral' notes which make up the totality of any sound. Often forming a natural harmonic scale, these 'hidden' spectres of the fundamental pitch, (technically called 'partials') conform to the physics of strings rather than the culture of Western tuning systems. They are found through mathematical calculation based on the frequency of the root-note, but are more easily understood by looking digitally at a spectrogram of a recorded sound. A spectrogram looks like a series of differently shaded lines. In this type of graph, those pitches which resonate more are visually made prominent. A spectrogram also shows that which is above or below the limits of our biological hearing. In this way, it both describes a ghostly technique and reveals the ghosts hiding unheard in all we experience.

A common effect in vocal processing is what is called 'spectral manipulation'. With software that can create or infer from spectrograms, a user can literally grab those 'hidden' sounds in the waveform and bring them down into human hearing. The free software *Spear* is an exciting example of this. Within *Spear* the user can even draw shapes and interact with these spectres in visual-audible ways. Removing the 'hidden' partials of a sound often produces a pure note verging on a sine-tone. The more you remove, the 'simpler' the sound becomes. The popular technique of 'auto-tune' relies on spectral manipulation to greatly narrow the range of partials in a voice. In a similar way, spectral manipulation gives the voice that digital, cyber materiality. The making chimeric of a voice is supported via the mixing and contortion of those qualities which hide inaudibly within it, or through a determined stripping away of those parts of a sound which supposedly taint its original purity.

The making child-like out of an adult voice is a process of shifting the fundamental pitch upwards, and twisting the upper partials of its sound. The great prevalence of this effect across musical genres, spells the emergence of a hyper-child-like voice. Another way of describing this unique vocal treatment would be a hyper-pop voice. Here the voice is welded to the artefact of *contorted pop innocence*. It is a process which emphasises innocence, purity and, importantly, commerciality.

In 2013, prior to *Garden of Delete*, a song entitled *BIPP* emerged online. It was posted by a mysterious artist called *Sophie*. There was fierce speculation about the artist, as the voice sounded almost perfectly child-like, uncannily so. *BIPP* arguably ushered in a new genre of music. Along with *Sophie*, the British label PC MUSIC (and its host of artists) embraced a new commercial and corporate aesthetic. Their distinct style functions as a soundtrack for online consumerism: sparkling, angelic, airbrushed music. PC Music quickly became highly polemical. At its inception, these British producers were creating ground-breaking polished sound. In their exaggeration, or performative affirmation, this over-polished sound functioned as an ironic critique of consumerism. *Sophie* was the moniker of a London (now LA)-based producer) known today as Sophie Xeon. Her then voice emerged in 2013 childlike through digital treatment. *Sophie* and *PC Music* re-contextualised the innocence of childhood to an emphasised place within capitalism's enclosure. Predictably perhaps, the rise and critical collapse of the genre came with the 2014 track 'Lemonade'. Capitalism assimilated hyper-pop, hyper-normalising it so that it became just that — normal — regular pop. 'Lemonade's' aesthetic was so perfectly commercial that it was used by McDonald's in a TV advertisement. The original irony was lost to horrific appropriation.

Today the meteoric rise and fall of PC Music has led to a number of sincere pop collaborations. The high/low divide between art music has long been completely eroded. Moreover, in those years since *Sophie*, the hyper-child, as pop star, has become highly influential for even more popular billboard music. PC Music's vocal techniques are clearly inspired by J-Pop and Hatsune Miku. Perhaps they are also inspired by an unlikely pair of Norwegian high-schoolers who invented a sub-culture called 'Nightcore'. The myth goes: tasked by their school with the assignment of making music, Thomas S Nilse and Steffen Ojala Søderholm simply increased the speed of some of their favourite Trance and Eurodance music. Despite how simple the process was, the result was emotionally powerful. Many years later this high-school project sparked an enormous internet phenomenon.

Far from the imagination of these teenagers, today you can search for nearly any popular song on YouTube with the preface 'Nightcore', and find an altered version of the song. Nightcore as a phenomenon is so widespread that it has potentially sparked the re-interpretation of the largest amount of music in human history. In a Nightcore version of a song, the music is typically sped-up by around 25 per cent, and through this process the vocals and entire harmonic content of the song are also pitched-up. Finally, and perhaps most importantly, an objectified female anime avatar is placed as a cover image on the YouTube video. Nightcore can actually be made relationally within the mechanisms of the YouTube webpage: simply click x1.25 speed on the video-player and you have created a basic Nightcore version of any song. The medium of YouTube contains the tools. Any fan can experience the energy and amplification of Nightcore. This is utopian exchange value: listener and creator as one.

In a relationship to the past nostalgic trace of your favourite song, hearing it anew, sped-up with a now innocent and feminised vocal, clearly enhances emotional memory. Speed, acceleration and feminisation meet. The trace — the memory re-enacted sped-up and energised — calls to being a slow and monochrome past and a highly-saturated effervescent present. I'd argue that Nightcore's recent prevalence in gallery art and experimental club practice taps into a similar ethereal experience of Vaporwave's 'memory vague'. This is music doubly powerful when revived from a nearly-forgotten past of teen-existential crisis. The private listening experience, where music once lifted you out of interiority and into an autonomous selfhood, combines in vital ways within the rehearing process.

On YouTube and Twitch, Nightcore live radio stations play a 24/7 stream of sped-up, pitched-up pop. In the real-time comment sections, users live out their sonic experience in role-play. Inspired by *Nico Nico Dōga*, comments appear permanently rendered to the screen at the moment a user posts them, thus establishing a powerful sense of communality in the medium itself. In many ways it is profoundly moving to be a part of this community. People in spread out geographies privately listen to the same live music. Through this anonymous sharing, the individual can enact fantasies within the comment window, role-playing as an invented self, making friends and lovers. What's more, through the sweetness of the music, the comments are almost uniformly optimistic, caring and supportive. In contrast to Vaporwave where irony often critiques the hollowness of royalty-free commercial musics of the past and present, Nightcore seems to sincerely participate in the consumerism, yet does so through its total unbridled love for the music itself. In the Nightcore community there is an assiduous appreciation for the purity, innocence and sweet qualities of music. Nightcore isn't critical, yet it manages to reclaim old signifiers of sweetness: wholesome hearing, assiduous listening.

Despite all of its utopian potential, Nightcore also feeds

into a darker online politics. The perceived 'softness' and 'innocence' of the community has become a popular target for outside bullying. Strangely, in this case, the community seems to have rubbed-off onto the bullies. Certain teens (and disgruntled adults) who view Nightcore and secretly enjoy the kawaii aesthetics of anime, have found inspiration in the treatment and portrayal of 'ideal' female animated bodies. The chimeric Nightcore voice has become the ironic soundtrack for a contradictory rhetoric of reactionary masculinity. There is a particularly eerie phenomenon on Twitter, where outwardly and proudly racist and fascist accounts seem to regularly have anime avatars. Anarchist William Gillis' article, *Authoritarians and the Ideology of Love*, (previously titled 'why do so many fascist Twitter accounts have anime avatars?') provides a pertinent diagnosis of this unexpected link in pop culture:

> The racism of young white men in the west often takes the form of projecting all the uncontrollable fearful rage and pain you feel, all the brutality and nihilism, onto an animalised other. Self-recognition deferred. The middle class white boys in basements howling for the heads of feminists, posting guides for getting away with rape, and shooting up churches? This tornado of raw scar tissue is not primal. It's not some kind of genetic destiny that rules us like puppets. It's ideological. A worldview beaten into us. Sure there's sexual frustration, but mostly it's emotional-mutilation alongside a model of How Things Work that carries such stakes we can never risk breaking from it. The more society hurts young boys and the more we hurt ourselves the more we desperately hunger for what it promises, following its instructions and hurting ourselves all the more. Success, power, toughness, the softest boys become the hungriest for the currencies we are told might buy back what the world has stolen from us.[8]

The 'Lolita Voice', cute and young, sounds out in transgressive dissonance particularly when it is forced to accompany adult and violent themed lyrics. Vocaloid technology enables would-be fascist users to co-opt animated bodies with their own messages. The desire to be both politically 'hard' and ironically 'soft' at the very same time is itself a chimerism. The meshing of contradictory pulls due to the pressures of mainstream narratives within coming-of-age masculinity forces its way out through the unlikely combination of a feminised cute voice as loud-speaker for the uncompromising harsh world-views of misplaced teen angst. In experimental practice, as in Oneohtrix Point Never and Amnesia Scanner, to employ the voice of a child but then to make it ugly, aggressive and horrific is also an expression of *fusion as a way out*. By combining contrasting signifiers this fusion is equally an expression of crisis, and a Crisis Energy which is intended as criticism. Take artists like FKA Twigs and Arca. In their work, the sexual norms and pressures of an oppressive mainstream culture are expressed through visuals which subvert the culture through exaggeration. Depictions of fleshy, wobbly and disfigured babies dance erotically on camera. Hyper-rendered plastic innocent bodies collapse and reform, like liquid, dancing on screen to critique the slow collapse of the future. The slow cancellation of Mark Fisher's future can be reinterpreted to be the collapsing of an air-filled plastic bag: as the content escapes, each side gradually sticks together.

* * *

Lopatin and Rafman found critical inspiration in the coming-of-age pre-pubescent energies of openly racist spaces like 4chan. In interview, Lopatin refers to Julia Kristeva to provide a support for his critical perspective which often borders disturbingly close to a transgressive fascination with this culture. Another way to conceive of a chimera is to conceive of outer and inner drives in disconnect. Julia Kristeva's *Powers Of Horror* explores the complex interplay between a repulsion and a desire for the abject. Her contention rests on the horrific discovery that our own body is in fact sickly and repulsive; that we have a body which is beyond, or in excess of, 'clean and proper'. Using the image of the skin which forms on a glass of old milk, Kristeva outlines a theory of outside and inside, of an 'I and the other'. When we loath a food to the point of nausea, we experience a complex realisation that the abject food isn't actually an 'other' in direct relation to 'us', but simply an 'object'. Therefore, instead of pushing the bad food away, we turn inward, and as Kristeva writes, 'I expel *myself*, I spit *myself out*, I abject *myself* within the same motion through which "I" claim to establish *myself*.'[9] In her example of an abject milky membrane we glimpse a representation of our own fallible skin. Skin 'thin as a sheet of cigarette paper', easily torn on a sharp surface, leaking out our bodily fluid and at the same time letting in the pathogens of the outside world. Kristeva's Human is defined not only by its constantly leaking, extricating, crusty and pus-ridden body, but also by its perverse and ever-ready awareness to find symbolic company among those decaying non-human surfaces which remind us of our own.

The prevalence of the abject in online communities like 4chan can outwardly be attributed to a protective mechanism which walls off the community from so-called 'normie' outsiders. In *Attaining the Ninth Square: Cybertextuality, Gamification and Memory on 4chan*, Vyshali Manivannan notes that, 'seemingly misogynistic phrases...gore, and deviant pornography, is a two-fold proscriptive designed as an alternate barrier to entry. First, it identifies new users as those expressing offence and excludes them because they are unable to perceive the self-awareness and irony inherent in the use of slurs.'[10] However, by attributing culturally-charged-gore and racial slur to irony, Manivannan simplifies a deeply ingrained anti-politically-correct and gendered rhetoric found in the culture. The culture is itself an initiation ceremony whereby all users learn to appreciate self-debasement and debasing others. The supposed catharsis of anonymously sharing your 'beta' inner turmoil in self-help threads on /r9k/ is simultaneously a perverse satisfaction found in the inevitable group deprecation which normally follows. 'Softness', to be a beta male, is an expression of a fascination with the abject. As with Kristeva's glass of milk, the community in totality acts like the object which reminds us of our own fallible body. 4chan's obsession with the abject expresses a certain unhinged desire, the powers of horror Kristeva proclaims.

Another way of considering these 'powers of horror' is through the political lens of 'transgression'. In what has become widely contested, Angela Nagle diagnoses 4chan as a community which has reclaimed transgression from the Left and applied it to right-wing politics. The argument is that the bodily transgression, particularly around sexual liberation, has been appropriated from left-wing 60s counter culture. To *counter*, to transgress, to react against the cultural norm, is repurposed today as a method to reclaim a perceived-to-be-lost masculinity and old world order. Transgression relies on the maintaining of a cultural memory. Those who pass down stories of 'a before' play up the abject past of 4chan: the time when anon's doxxed 'femi-nazis' and convinced others to commit suicide. Passed down to the next generation, these stories are told like they were from a supposed 'golden age' where teen boys roamed free on the internet. Transgression is easily weaponised. Language is weaponised. Irony and humour is set to use in the creation of memes, music and video art. What becomes apparent is that in these histories of transgressive right-wing politics, there is always a reaction to a perceived 'feminisation of mainstream music or culture'. Their supposed indelible male world is 'reclaimed' by sharing frequent representations and reminders of that more sexless sickness: rotting food and meat, cadavers in film, bodily waste in a toilet.

Charles Manson, neo-fascist metal music and the late 80s industrial noise scene, can be seen as precursors to today's spheres of online life which have become centred around a detesting of all (particularly female) norms. Former member of the 80s noise band Whitehouse, transgressive extremist Peter Sotos, and porn-star James Gillis wrote the controversial text PURE FILTH. Their manifesto echoes within today's online culture:

> In our search for extremes, we are constantly bombarded with humanist, feminist and other equally asinine diatribes that writers employ to alleviate the strain on their 'conscience' or to try and seduce us into their maudlin world of false securities and self-contempt. PURE exists, then, for those who desire extremes and are tired of listening to, and/or acting like housepets.[11]

I would argue that today, whether artists like Lopatin or Rafman agree with it or not, the abject within their images and sounds has been adopted by right-wing communities because of a bizarre sense that gore and abject fluid are a distinctly 'male' and PURE indulgence. Today, reacting to a perceived 'feminisation of culture' is expressed through the making of supposedly 'male' music, 'un-normie music', where transgression is employed not just for the sake of transgression, but for the sake of reclaiming something 'dark and wrong', something seen to have been lost from their 'once masculine music scene'.

When I think of 'male music' it's hard to avoid thinking of the certain notoriety and fame Lopatin and Rafman gained through their interactions with 4chan. Anecdotally, a large section of the music board /mu/ still pedestals Lopatin's music. For the video collaboration, 'Still Life (Betamale)', they actually premiered the track on /mu/, choosing to directly interact with the community they reference. *Still Life (Betamale)* plays like a 'Worst Hits of the

Internet'. Images of sticky grime-filled keyboards coexist with fleshy shots of 'furry' pornography, bodily fluid, mud, blood. An overweight man with anime panties over his head places two guns to either side of his temples. The sound is transgressive as well. Of course, experimental practice has a long and problematic history with transgression as a form of aesthetic 'progress'. Nevertheless, it remains relevant to acknowledge that music like Lopatin's uses shock, contrast, pastiche, screams and significantly horrific sounds in a transgressive method which has strong parallels with the 80s noise music scene.

While Lopatin does not share the wider politics of 4chan, the critique of the culture present in his work is expressed in a way which easily borders on fascination, rather than negation. Lopatin's focus on those abject materials present in the community (sonic slime, gore and bodily fluid) is attributed to his reading of Kristeva. In interview he reflects:

For me her [Kristeva] whole thing in *Powers Of Horror* is that she's pointing out this amazing thing about society, which is that although we try to constantly cover up the things that we find grotesque — abjection, excrement, our organs, whatever — we tend to put those in a category of morbid things. They don't really necessarily have a productive place in society and yet we still have this thing that connects us, we still have this fascination with them. The example I always think about is when you blow your nose or sneeze and there's that moment where you kind of want to look at the napkin or you do – everybody does it. So in a lot of ways for me this record [Garden of Delete] is about that moment where you just look at the napkin and check it out for a second before you throw it in the trash. You're kind of told in various stages of your life that you shouldn't do that in different ways, but that primal feeling is who we are, it's what the universe is, it's a factor of life, and she just writes so poetically about that, the confusion between this ineffable, deeply expressive state that we're bound to...[12]

This 'ineffable, deeply expressive state' that Lopatin talks of sounds a lot like the sublime: an aesthetic awe in the recognition that we are all linked by an innate reaction towards the grotesque. This is a feeling of 'boundlessness' in the face of a greater and shared 'other'. But here, instead of a Kantian mountain range, the sublime is snot on a used tissue — ineffably beautiful bodily fluid which has escaped. In image, Rafman's LARP children bleed mucous. Accompanying the gore, Lopatin fills our ears with sonified slime. Three minutes into 'Sticky Drama' and the hybrid voices of the Tamagotchi and the child warriors have become meshed in a thick white noise liquid. Their vocal cords try to vibrate, but instead only gooey sound escapes: contorted, dribbling, sickly. As with the screams heard in the track 'Mutant Standard', other songs on *Garden of Delete* such as 'Animals', 'Freaky Eyes' and 'Ezra' combine this crisis signifier with varied material extensions. In 'Freaky Eyes' the scream becomes caught in detuned radio static and the beep of an unplugged life support system. 'Mutant Standard's' mouth sounds have a chimeric flesh reminiscent of a microphone placed deep inside the mouth cavity, saliva sloshing against the device's metal housing.

To put it another way, the voice is slime. Those images of Nickelodeon green slime relate to a more mainstream online obsession with the material. Slime, snot and bodily fluid are frequent subjects of viral YouTube videos where people pop pus-filled zits, or post compilations of 'try and look away' videos filled with disturbing leaking fluids. Kristeva's *unexpected* realisation that you too possess an abject body can be heard in the sound of bodily fluid. The pus-filled pimples on Ezra's (Lopatin's invented teen identity) face signify an internalised abject flesh which has made its way to the surface. The pure untainted skin of the face has been torn to let out a bodily yet surprisingly alien liquid. The abject emerges from the horrifying realisation that this liquid was within you all along, that your *inside* is rotten. Referencing Sartre, Timothy Morton refers to this realisation as the *stickiness* of objects: you thought you were interacting with an object from an outside position, yet suddenly you realise that you were inside the sticky jar of honey all along.

> 'The slimy is myself'. [Sartre] Viscosity for Sartre is how a hand feels when it plunges into a large jar of honey — it begins to dissolve…It is possible to imagine a sound so piercing that it could rearrange our inner structure and result in our death, and no doubt the Pentagon is now developing, and possibly even deploying, such sound weapons. When the inside of a thing coincides perfectly with its outside, that is called dissolution or death…A baby vomits curdled milk. She learns to distinguish between the vomit and the not-vomit, and comes to know the not-vomit as self. Every subject is formed at the expense of some viscous, slightly poisoned substance, possibly teeming with bacteria, rank with stomach acid. The parent scoops up the mucky milk in a tissue and flushes the wadded package down the toilet.[13]

Lopatin's fitting track name, 'Sticky Drama', pertains to this: children on the edge of puberty stab each other with rusty hooks, revealing each other's internal goo. This is a sticky 'coming of age' replete with these abject realisations. Importantly, the abject is placed in the middle of aggrandising accelerating music. Its placement inside a swarm of sound thus infers a certain sublimity as the ear searches for it in the background. Its horror serves to take us outside the frame of the instrumental music. As a form of alienation, hearing your own human voice distorted makes you aware of the very (soft) human behind the music's construction.

Importantly, there are attempts to reclaim slime from the boys. For instance, see VNS Matrix, who called for feminists to become 'mercenaries of slime'.[14] What's more, Slime ASMR, slime makeup tutorials and playful slime videos made by women express a profound and important notion of self-care. The reclaiming of the grotesque is seen most powerfully in women playing with slime, not for men, but for the other women who share their love and solidarity with the material. Even so, despite the lingering presence of a pre-pubescent male fascination, slime's prevalence on 4chan is more than sexual or psychoanalytic. It is ideological. Returning to William Gillis' essay, transgression and the finding of sublimity in the abject body is also a response to the neoliberal repositioning of male agency. Liking anime is a softness which stands in for a closed-off hardening to the outside world. In the fragmentation of identity groups, to be abject becomes a self-fulfilling prophecy for right-wing indoctrination. Those who are unable to find a place in a mainstream culture favouring sporty jocks over nerds become hardened together through the appreciation of a different kind of masculinity — one which stands in for physical prowess, and instead centres around the domination of animated women invented to serve. While not all anime is like this, the problematic treatment of women in otaku culture is a relatively new invention. Anime series like *Yuri on Ice* fight against this culture with radical portrayals of male identity which react against the divisive norm.

Certain artists repurpose the abject as a form of resistance. The female body is deemed abject in its own menstrual processes. Unlike a sickly male body, a leaking female body is not only chastened by patriarchal society for its innately damaged surface, but this non-sickness is trapped within a cyclical bind. To remove the abject, to chemically or surgically lessen the leaking of menstrual blood, is in some senses to defy one's own fertility. Yet, to be infertile (and 'clean') is to become equally abject in your alien inability to reproduce. What is more, to drip blood, but not from a wound, becomes a constant reminder of the supposed uncontrollability of the female body, deemed by wider patriarchal society to be in contrast to the virtuous male one. Kristeva explains thus, how only female blood is perceived as a pollutant:

> Why does *corporeal waste*, menstrual blood and excrement, or everything that is assimilated to them, from nail-parings to decay, represent — like a metaphor that would have become incarnate — the objective frailty of symbolic order?...Neither tears nor sperm, for instance, although they belong to borders of the body, have any polluting value. Excrement and its equivalents (decay, infection, disease, corpse, etc.) stand for the danger to identity that comes from without: the ego threatened by the non-ego, society threatened by its outside, life by death. Menstrual blood, on the contrary, stands for the danger issuing from within the identity (social or sexual); it threatens the relationship between the sexes within a social aggregate and, through internalization, the identity of each sex in the face of sexual difference.[15]

In music, Kristeva's words remind me of the politically-charged music of South-London artist Klein. 2017's *Tommy EP* had Klein lead the CCRU-linked label *Hyperdub* in a direction away from its accelerationist past. Klein's voice doesn't speed out, it crawls out over the top of the disjointed instrumentals of the record. Hers is a vocalisation which forgoes the shaping of words and seems to drip and stretch without digital gritty artefacts. It is sticky within the middle of the music. Friend and fellow musicologist Malte Kobel wrote a dedication to Klein's work, calling her creative practice an evocation of a voice becoming monstrous. This is a voice which begins whole, and then rips into itself to reveal a hidden goo. Reacting to a history and legacy of monstrous voices, such as Cathy Berberian's mouth sounds, Klein updates what a monster can be, rendering this violence within a certain sombre sentimentality. *Tommy EP* has subdued qualities; Klein's message arises softly and powerfully. In its vulnerability, the communal singing on this album slowly reflects upon those outside forces and ideologies which mis-figure togetherness into the cries of a monster.

Notably, *Tommy EP* begins with laughter and experimentation. Klein and her collaborators gather around the piano bouncing joyous singing back and forth between themselves. As Kobel describes, it's as if they are a group of kids inhaling helium together. The voices are digitally pitched higher, they begin in communality, tinged with childhood, an innocent chant which suddenly reveals its monstrous innards. The voices at once descend into horror. Klein's evocation of a simultaneously joyful yet compromised voice is an antidote to this cycle of patriarchal depredation. It is the profound expression of a freedom to become monstrous with one another, to explore the insides of each other's voice, and to be unafraid. Klein takes on Kristeva's powers of horror and utilises them for the purpose of societal change.

Hearing Klein in contrast to Lopatin's *Garden of Delete*, her child is forced into monstrosity by an implied societal mistreatment. Lopatin's critical failure arises from his reverse take: a child already born monstrous, and rendered horrific as an implied act of transgression. While *Garden of Delete* is a coming-of-age story, Lopatin's politics are so muddy that they unintentionally support what they intend to critique. The sombre end to this album is the perfect example. *No Good* is a lamenting ballad of horrific proportions. The child-like voice cries in A-Flat major, all words indistinguishable, just a trace of intelligibility left as we apophenically search for pop lyrics. In the climax, Lopatin fuses its mechanical innocence with the most powerful, extreme, yet paradoxically pure, square-wave synth heard on the album. It carves out your ear in its synthetic purity. This voice is the haunting echo of the entire work. It maintains both its representation towards a history of vocal synthesis, Hatsune

Miku, the cute schoolgirl, the uncanny of the robot, a warning, and at the same time also a celebration of this fusion within the voice. It cries in a new imagined intensity. When I look at the half-meat, half-Tamagotchi I see two bodies whose boundaries have been compromised through an exchange of energies. Childhood imagination as energy, commercial accumulation as *addictive toy energy* colliding and rendering inorganic and organic matter one. A hybrid thought. The human here is a virulent energy. The critique is subsumed under a fascination with childhood which appears as a spectre of a too-too rendered human.

Chapter 6

Whispered Honesty

This chapter questions the intention behind creating dystopian future-oriented music. In art as elsewhere, critique is mostly a matter of negation and opposition. Yet frequently today, critique functions also as a subversion of norms through exaggerated affirmation. Patrick Frank calls this 'performative affirmation'.[1] His term refers to artistic efforts which assimilate, then reproduce and heighten the destructive qualities of consumer capitalism. When a political ethos is present, as in much of the music my book has discussed, critique often emerges through this exact performative method. Pertaining to accelerationist aesthetics, there is the sense that an integration of the 'darkness' and crisis of the present and future is achieved through intensification rather than negation. This chapter takes issue with modes of critique built upon processes of exaggeration. Over-affirmation as a method often relies on ironic gesture. However, in our conflated post-Trump era, where the New/Alt-Right appear to control the intellectual and aesthetic rights to not just irony, but an exaggerated sincerity, how and where can irony function politically and speculatively in left-wing artistic efforts?

'Trumpwave' recently emerged as a genre born from Vaporwave. The haunting affect of Vaporwave's ghostly music is clearly seductive to a political movement which revels in dystopia, the golden years of the 90s and the sounds of the 90s: financial boom, pedestalled American Dreams and nuclear cisgender family relations. What's more, Vaporwave calls out from a parallel history, one not just stuck in the past, but also trapped in a collapsing version of history. Vaporwave critiques consumerism through revelling in the distorted past. The line between poetic-collapse and catastrophe runs thin. As I have previously argued, catastrophe can be read as a culturally-charged male wish. In this dystopian imaginary, the fantasy is that patriarchal relations between men and women will 're-emerge'. On the blog *Return of Kings,* which aims 'to usher in the return of masculine man in a world where men are increasingly punished', a post can be found entitled: 'Four Reasons Why The Collapse Will Be The Best Thing to Happen For Men'. The reasons listed include: 'the return of primal order', and in continuation, that 'there won't be feminist harpies demanding equality when strong men are needed to rebuild civilization'.[2] Imagining the future creates agency. If those attracted to the New/Alt-Right are people suffering from a perceived lack of agency, then revelling in darkness can become something that fills that void.

This chapter presents a final investigation into the problematic relationship some of the music I have discussed has with dystopia. This relationship is analysed from the perspective of the changing conditions of irony and sincerity. Whether these soundings are heard ironically or sincerely has significant ramifications for the praxis of this music. In title, Trumpwave may once have evoked a certain ironic response, to be interpreted as derisive or polysomic. However, in current political times this genre risks becoming newly sincere. The YouTube comments beneath Trumpwave have become polemical. There are those who misunderstand the irony and treat the music as a soundtrack for their love of Trump. Conversely, those in on the joke demonstrate the destructive hierarchies within this form of critique, they make music into something which divides, and they laugh at those perceived to be intellectually beneath them. In the hollow approbation of that which was once ironic — sincerity now becomes ghostly and critical irony becomes a haunted divisive form of consciousness raising.

A ghost is to the physical body what a whisper is to the regular speaking voice. The materiality of a whisper will be this chapter's entrance point into the Cloud's disappearing act, a space where ironic critique no longer functions as it was once intended.

i) The Gentle Rub of Designer Suit Material

Throughout Holly Herndon and Amnesia Scanner's work there are frequent examples of whispering voices. In 'AS ANGELS RIG HOOK', and 'AS TRUTH', Amnesia Scanner present narrative voices which gently sound behind a dense instrumental texture. These voices speak directly to you. In their quietness and gentleness, a powerful intimacy is presented. On headphones this effect is heightened significantly. The sound of a light whisper close to your ear is sensual, even erotic. Its material is somehow smooth yet broken. At that precipice between silent mouthing and the birth of a sound, the voice undergoes an almost vocal-fry. The vocal cords move together with barely enough energy to sustain the creation of a voice. Only plosives and the eeriness of sibilance escape. We strain to make out words from this broken soft mess. 'Autonomous Sensory Meridian Response' (ASMR) is the term which emerged around 2010 to describe this distinct feeling of light tingling on the skin, and mild, relaxing euphoria. ASMR occurs primarily when listening to the small soft sounds of mundane repetitive tasks. And anecdotally, this effect is most powerful in the sound of a gently whispering voice.

The emerging science behind this phenomenon was facilitated by the Cloud. It began in a range of niche health forums, but underwent a fecund rise many years later with viral YouTube channels like 'Gentle Whispering ASMR'. In what is now a multi-million-dollar industry, the most famous practitioner is the enigmatic Russian simply known as *Maria*. With iconic ASMR videos like '- -ASMR Gentlemen's Suit Fitting Session--', *6.3 million views*, and '~ Relaxing Fluffy Towels Folds ~', Maria sparked the birth of a highly profitable niche.[3] Other tropes in the genre include: 'girlfriend or boyfriend simulation', 'bedtime goodnight sweet dreams', and 'welcome home after a long-stressful day' videos. The phenomenon can also be seen as a facilitator for the bizarre success of one of YouTube's most profitable channels, 'DC Toy Collector DC', who makes content exclusively depicting a woman's hands soothingly unboxing children's toys.

This unexpected phenomenon reached critical heights through its distribution on 4chan and Reddit. Besides children engaging in that associated care and kindness of a soft motherly voice, ASMR videos draw a majority teen-male audience. While they often innocently provide deep relaxation, some users refer to the experience as an erotic 'audio-drug'. Today the audio-video genre has expanded to become a diverse and often parodied part of internet culture. On Twitch, under the IRL (in real life) category of live-streams, almost all of the videos are of women whispering into specialty binaural microphones which look like the shape of a human head. 'How are you doing, ok? Good?' We hear in the background of 'AS ANGELS RIG HOOK'. In 'AS TRUTH' we see hands unboxing ominous packages, the sound of torn cardboard tingly and spectral.

Despite all the sonic materials I have tried to discuss in this book, perhaps the material of a whisper is the most pertinent to a hearing of the Cloud. It seems a fitting sound with which to conclude this book. ASMR has spread to become a subcategory of many other internet phenomena. Those ambient videogame soundscapes I discussed also have an ASMR sub-community. Listening to a fire softly crackling in *Bioshock*'s underwater dystopia is bizarrely soothing. Slime ASMR is also a hugely popular phenomenon. Feminine hands squishing goo-filled children's toys, slime falling between extended fingers, or even the whispered creation of miniature slime foods in miniature kitchens — says much about the lure of a fetishised domesticity. Yet perhaps the most pertinent ASMR niche for my discussion is broadly known as 'Dystopian ASMR'. Here, a gentle voice narrates fantasies of destruction and male heroism.[4]

Holly Herndon's collaboration with Claire Tolan, 'Lonely at the Top', is an ASMR track at the climactic point of her album *Platform*. Herndon describes it as 'ASMR for the 1 Percent', yet speaks positively about the genre:

> ...these hyper-domestic sounds that people are sharing over the Internet are physically impacting and touching strangers. I find that really beautiful. Often people say, 'The Internet is separating us all and there's no real friendships anymore.' But ASMR shows that the Internet can actually help soothe people.[5]

Herndon touches on the other side of ASMR: it is for many people a profoundly important support mechanism. I have friends who now find it hard to get to sleep without listening to a soothing bedtime ASMR video. Despite Herndon's honesty about the beauty of ASMR, her collaboration 'Lonely at the Top' is in part a cutting jab at the stressful life of a CEO. With a title emphasising the loneliness of exploitation, we expect a sense of irony, but instead, we listen to a whispering which follows with a feeling of what could be described as haunted sincerity. Arguably, for many of us, we understand the context, we are self-aware about the secondary meaning of these words, their references to a sickly consumer ideology, their reference to a failed Occupy movement and the alienating pressures of work, still, the words don't *sound* ironic, they sound deeply sincere. The words still incite a physical affective response — sincerity embodied. Claire Tolan whispers,

> And from what you've told me, so many people depend on you. And it's not just because you're good at what you do, it's because you're a great person. And from what you've told me so many people in your position wouldn't act as generously as you do...You're giving the world your ideas...I don't know

what we'd do without you.

These words are directed straight at you, the listener. The patronising tone in Tolan's insistence of corporate success is lost to our own personal interpretation of the words and their ASMR effect on the physical body. 'You naturally attract possibility *kiss sound*.' The affect is complicated. From these soothing sounds the message may manifest in a secondary way: 'fix the future', 'attract the possibility', 'please take the opportunity to fix the future'.

In a spoken whisper, perhaps the physicality of the words overrides our immediate cognition of them. Or perhaps it is the opposite, that tingly feeling instead emphasising meaning. Leaning in close to tell someone something special infers added significance. In Dedekind Cut and Yves Tumor's collaboration, *Trump$ America*, the duo employs ASMR as a kind of praxis.[6] *Trump$ America* juxtaposes anxiety inducing music against a whispering voice. Contra jagged blasts of sound, a soft voice describes techniques for relaxation and staying calm. It could be read in the following way: the violent instrumental music is the state of America and the whispering instructions for survival are our method of resistance. Still, I cannot shake the feeling that I've got it completely wrong: the whispering is the sweet nothings of populist politics, and the instrumental music is the oppositional dissonance we require. I ponder this as I'm kindly instructed to blow cold air on my thumbs; sinking into relaxation, I feel good just like the voice asks of me. But is ASMR in danger of becoming the ghostly coping mechanism for labour exploitation? The body works a 10-hour shift, gets home exhausted and alone, creeps into bed and inserts earphones for its nightly 'ASMR wife simulation'.

ASMR presents an interesting case study in the tug of war between irony and sincerity. Imagine this: what you once may have considered a deeply ironic phrase, is now gently whispered in your ear. The other speaks with the faintest voice, almost on the verge of audibility. Their voice is coupled with the resulting delicate mouth sounds of a tongue forming syllables. You hear the lightness of a quick inhalation and you almost feel the warm air of the other's breath on the side of your face, their whispering just inches away from you. The cognitive brain still perceives irony in this semantic language, yet your physical body reacts to these whispered words sincerely. Your neck tingles, the hairs on your arms rise, you are overcome by a feeling of incredible stillness. Here we are presented with a dilemma, a question pertinent to online culture's collapsing border between sincerity and irony. How do we interpret whispered irony? Is this a situation where a certain primitive physical reaction simply overrides a cultural one? Or is this a more complex issue? Can sincerity and irony coexist simultaneously, or is it that 'sincerity eats irony'[7], as Timothy Morton states in *Hyperobjects: Philosophy and Ecology after the End of the World*. Does the expanding chaos and crisis of the Cloud therefore *consume* irony?

ii) Disappearing Irony

In what has become widely theorised, a post-ironic late capitalism has learned to neutralise ironic critique by simply incorporating its subversive power into its own methods of control. Today irony is clearly more advertising tool than an aesthetic technique of disruption. More disturbing is its use in communities like /pol/ on 4chan, which instrumentalise irony as a defence mechanism. By going meta, their *'post-post-post'* ironic humour and piercing self-awareness work to deny criticism. It is difficult to criticise an ideology which is already self-deprecating. In the mechanisms of abjection and transgression, one learns to become frighteningly self-aware and readily open to make stereotypes out of one's own body and social standing. But I wonder, when irony cannot function critically, perhaps it disappears entirely? Or perhaps, what was once ironic disappears in the face of crisis.

On 4chan, and all large social media platforms, the lightning fast movements of internet humour can be observed through an analogy to the stock market. In Reddit's r/MemeEconomy, users discuss buying, selling and investing in memes through a satirical meta-commentary on the rise and fall of certain trends in the community. The progress from underground to mainstream is widely considered to mark the death of a meme. As with economic supply and demand, the over-saturation of a meme quickly deflates its desirability. However, one method of bringing a meme back from the dead is to move vertically above the frame and re-appropriate it into a meta construction. Otherwise known as: 'how many layers of irony are you on'.

This meta-movement pertains to a traditional sense of irony whereby the humour is restored because the meme now re-establishes the gap between its surface meaning (how a 'normie' might interpret it) and its actuality (how the self-aware community understands it). Timothy Morton explains this 'gap':

Irony is the aesthetic exploitation of gaps...Irony is the echo of a mysterious presence. For there to be irony, something must already be there...Irony is the footprint of at least one other entity, an inner ripple, a vacuum fluctuation that indicates the distorting presence of other beings...Irony has lost its 'postmodern' (I would prefer to say 'late modern') edge, its T-shirt sloganeering. Irony has become the feeling of waking up inside a hyperobject, against which we are always in the wrong.[8]

What Morton infers when he talks of this 'presence (a haunting spectre) of other beings' is that irony rests on the realisation that the object, the piece of art or the meme is never entirely what it seems. It always has an extra dimension to it rippling beneath the surface. Unless the viewer or listener is aware of the *entirety* of the object (both its surface and the referential gap) then the irony is in danger of being lost. This extra dimension is maintained by our privileged understanding of the work's references. Ironic humour always arises at the expense of an ignorant other.

In Australia, billionaire mining mogul turned populist-politician Clive Palmer (the Trump of Australia) posted a series of self-deprecating memes of himself, mocking his own overweight figure and bizarrely poetic obsession with chocolate biscuits. When Palmer posted a superimposition of his face onto a Star Wars poster (featuring flying chocolate X-Wing Tim-Tams), one user's top-rated comment exclaimed: 'Abandon ship, he's become self-aware.' The greatest fear for meme-creators is that they will no longer exclusively be the self-aware ones, that their 'mysterious presence' beneath the surface of a meme (which echoes in the moment of creation) will be uncovered. It is through this exact cycle of movement, from self-aware to no-longer-exclusively-aware, that we can witness the destruction of traditional irony. Arguably, 'going meta' is no longer possible in an age of impending catastrophe and the growing homogenisation of online humour — the impending disappearance of self-aware uniqueness.

There is the sense that the exclusivity of the meta-irony found in cyberculture is becoming increasingly fleeting. A meme's economic life-cycle is becoming shorter and shorter as a consequence of the homogenisation and sheer scale of the internet. 'Network time' spreads and fragments a meme until it loses the origin that is required for the function of an ironic 'gap'. Within Vaporwave, and other artists' expressions of a neofuturist aesthetic, there once was a certain 'meta' appreciation to be found. Vaporwave reflected upon its own construction. Toto's *Africa*, for example, opened *Chuck Person's Ecco Jams Vol. 1* — slow and mournful in its rendition, fragmented and disorienting. After the release, *Africa* became a Vaporwave favourite, yet in its meta-state, appropriated again and again, it somehow regressed, becoming closer and closer to its original wholeness. From radical to mundane. Later releases in the community presented the song uncritically. This is reflective of both the vitality and the death-drives of the genre. In Vaporwave's assimilation into mainstream culture it has lost its criticality. It has become re-coded into a commercial shell of itself: users commenting A E S T H E T I C on 80s fetishised retro synth-pop. Today Vaporwave exists in fragmented and disturbingly stale and appropriated forms: Trumpwave, Simpsonswave, Fashwave® to name a few.

In *Haute Baroque Capitalism®*, Toby Shorin picks up on the bizarrely Vaporwave-esque, Baroque aesthetic of Trump's hotels and living spaces. Like a gremlin guarding his gold coins, Trump features in family portraits in a shining cave of his own creation: gold leaf everywhere, neoclassical pillars, ornamentation until you're sea-sick. There are clear ties between the neoclassicism of Trump Tower and other fascist aesthetics of the past. Shorin likens the architecture of too-much-money to Gean Moreno's descriptions of a capitalism which leaves in its wake an 'Alien monstrosity, an insatiable Thing that appropriates the energy of everything it touches and, in the process, propels the world towards the inorganic.'[9] While I agree, in some ways I simultaneously see the reverse: money, enormous money becoming an organic living organism, becoming ornamentation *alive* and grotesque on the sides of bulging skyscrapers. More interesting, perhaps, is Shorin's claim that if a movement like 'Baroque Capitalism' is taking hold in 2018, at least in architecture and design, it must have had inspiration from earlier movements like 2009 Vaporwave. That now famous A E S T H E T I C posted non-stop beneath any YouTube video remotely dealing with the internet, has become a design trope of floating Roman busts, Greek pillars and neon colouring. Importantly, it also contains a set of images which perhaps unconsciously reflect the underlying tension of environmental catastrophe. It is a flooded imagining. Water ripples everywhere. Old paintings and sculptures and signifiers of human progress float off-screen. In this aesthetic we find a sunken and drowned virtual landscape.

In a similar retro fascination, the design language and the typography of many recent neofuturist albums hark back to Gothic block lettering and equally ornamented and saturated visuals. What originally appears as ironic or satire, gets taken up a year later in capital's assimilated form. In the commercialisation of Vaporwave, instead of a ghost or spectre of the original, it feels like a solid remnant is instead spat out, made sticky and one-dimensional. Thinking of Accelerationism, which has attracted its own set of 'compelling visual metaphors', the desire to relentlessly evoke the cycles of capital makes Accelerationism's own visual, audible and corporeal structures just as sticky and one-dimensional. All that may be left of our understanding of this movement could be those dead and haunted visual metaphors. A series of words which can only be taken at face value: Speedy Speedy Zoom Zoom.

Today the re-appropriation found in the act of 'going meta' becomes ghostly. It disappears partly because appropriation is the norm. There is the sense that every time an ironic image is re-appropriated, a little more of its humour disappears, until finally the image is left as it is — taken at face value. The meta-irony of re-appropriating a song like *Africa* is lost, particularly in a world where Trump or Clive Palmer can channel this humour towards the creation of a right-wing catastrophic future. And in this catastrophe, the prevalence of memes in destructive circles paves the way for a sincere reaction to their content.

Throughout *Hearing the Cloud*, I have given a few examples of where irony is mistaken as sincerity. The passing of time tends to make us all unaware viewers or listeners. The degrading effects of time on our memory, distorting humour from just 3 or 4 years ago, can mean that the gap necessary for understanding becomes too large, or simply non-existent. PC Music, as a label, was seen to warp from an ironic affirmation of commercialism, to become just regular pop. Those who didn't 'get' the irony instead became sincerely inspired. In a similar way, 4chan's attempt to 'reclaim memes' through the forced pairing of a meme with the abject, has led to actual neo-nazis circulating images of frogs. With these motions we can see clear evidence of the conflation of irony and sincerity. A haunting absence, a ghostly presence exists where that which was ironic is now sincerely frightening. Anything which uses irony as a method of critique runs the risk of misrecognition.

At the inception of Vaporwave there was certain irony present in the gap between rendered nature and actual nature. The sound of soothing bird chirps from kitsch 90s meditation CDs functioned ironically. Today, an age of looming environmental crisis strips these sounds of their original irony. Where there once was humour there is now absence. A space is left behind for us to wonder. How can rendered birds and picturesque sparkling gardens function ironically in a world on the verge of impending ecological collapse? In the future, the sound of kitsch meditation CDs could *actually* be the media we share with children when describing to them the beauty of a pre-climate change world. Crisis creates sincerity. This destruction of irony through the sincerity of impending catastrophe is Morton's exact expression of 'waking up inside a hyperobject in which we were always in the wrong'. It is as if we were asleep when we heard this music ironically, and today we wake up to the haunting quality it always possessed. Where we once laughed a void appears. Now we stare in disbelief. The early music of Amnesia Scanner portrayed vaguely ironic representations of 90s cyberculture. One can hear this sincerely today. Having just lived through an American election partly won through algorithmic interference, one can hear the destructive potential in AI, machine-learning and algorithmic mass surveillance. In algorithmic music we become more attuned to its futurity and a potentiality that strips it of its ironic gap. Instead of the eco of 'mysterious presence' which defines ironic gesture, a futurity and speculation ripples.

In *a* connection to the future, that ironic disjuncture dissolves.

* * *

To return to those forms of enchantment which are either utilised by neoliberal capitalism as methods of control, or formalised within works of art as resistance, it is important to equally note that irony has a history of being a form of political resistance. During Soviet rule, a mode of Russian parody known as 'stiob' became popular as a method to subvert the state. Due to the very real fear of persecution, Soviet writers, performers and filmmakers who were critical of the state were forced to fit criticism into their work by having characters and plots performatively affirm the system just a little *too* much. Stiob became known for its exaggerated affirmation: a criticism bordering ever so slightly between sincerity and subtle ridicule. This collapsing border between sincerity and parody, or sincerity and irony, can be seen as an example of a formalised enchantment within the location of the act of criticism itself. By placing criticism in this liminal space between affirmation and ridicule, by making the viewer uncertain about a work's intentions, art becomes enchanted by critical *uncertainty*. In many of the works I have discussed, LEXACHAST, James Ferraro's work, Oneohtrix Point Never, kitsch synth lines, midi sound and referential 90s sonic materials can become a form of very subtle stiob. In performance, everyone might dance to the music sincerely, but the slight sense of uncertainty lingers.

Irony, in its bitterness, can function to combat feelings of powerlessness. To evoke (or invoke) ironic detachment as a method of coping with oppression is a technique of self-alienation. It's an act of disengagement, and a disguising of the miseries of individual suffering. While this disengagement has often been seen to lead to political inaction, at its core is a heightened sentiment. Feelings of powerlessness are important.

Feelings of detachment can be directed towards those systems of power which are to blame. I agree with Ngai's claim that, '[ugly feelings] can be conductive to producing ironic distance in a way that the grander and more prestigious passions, or even the moral emotions associated with sentimental literature, do not.'[10] Ugly feelings and anxieties are perhaps even more important because they produce ambiguity. Instead of creating a work of art that is starkly ironic, consider Donna Haraway's alternative in *A Cyborg Manifesto*: 'serious play'.[11] Humour can be playful, ambiguity can be playful — play opens up spaces for critique. Works and performances such as those I have discussed already function in an ambiguous space somewhere between honesty and playful negation. I would argue that the same applies for all great works of music. Instead of producing distance, play brings us close together — in proximity. To play with references is to unhinge them. Memes are playful. Memes can open up spaces for action when they are sincere in their playfulness.

Dutch design and theory collective Metahaven jumped on the political potential of memes years before the online mayhem of Trump. Their 2013 book *Can Jokes Bring Down Governments?* is at its most pertinent when it deals with the political potential found in play and 'nonsense'. Metahaven rest on Susan Stewart's *Nonsense*, as she describes a humour which manipulates everyday language into unreal contexts:

> Playing at fighting may be 'not fighting,' but it is not fighting on a different level of abstraction from other kinds of not fighting such as kissing, skipping rope, buying groceries, or singing 'Happy Birthday.' Play involves the manipulation of the conditions and contexts of messages and not simply a manipulation of the message itself. It is not, therefore, a shift within the domain of the everyday lifeworld: it is a shift to another domain of reality.[12]

Creating nonsense through the playfulness of a joke opens up humour to become a speculative device. Nonsense can be powerfully revealing. It is akin to the kind of fictionalisation of the environment presented by David Kanaga. Or equally, the making 'alternate' of the past in Daniel Lopatin's aural visions. Or even the making horrific of playful laughter in Klein's work. By contrast, irony cannot be nonsense. Irony functions always within the reality of that which it sends up. Nick Land tweets: 'The "neo-" in neoreaction, and perhaps even in neocameralism, means – roughly – "ironical".' Case in point: irony is in some senses the equivalent of Land's philosophising from the perspective of worldly destruction. Irony becomes the humour of catastrophe.

Epilogue: An Abandoned Oil Rig Stands in for the Garden of Eden

In all so far spoken or heard, typed and re-typed, the act of making fiction remains central. An act of world-building. An act of not just storytelling, but spinning tales about a future. This is the making of sci-fi out of the present, or the explaining why the present is already enchantingly sci-fi. The musical gestalt, the listening gestalt, is thus of a world which sonically emerges around our ears. What's left outside of that world is as important as what's inside it. Those artists who show exits know the limits of the worlds they make music in service of. They know what to say and what to leave silent, and they know where and how to provoke a listener to find an outside to the present.

An abandoned oil rig stands in for the Garden of Eden. A garden is a walled space with vegetation. It contains encrypted knowledge of good and evil. 777 terabytes of data contained in a single gram of DNA. Wiping a tear off your cheek. Salty.[1]

Jaakko Pallasvou's libretto for *AS ANGELS RIG HOOK* congeals Eden within the conflicting image of a deserted oil rig. In its abandonment we imagine both a restored future where our actions to save the environment have put a halt to the oil industry, or we see the opposite, the forbidden fruit grasped and an oil-dry desecrated world. In 2007, ThePirateBay attempted to buy the unused abandoned ocean structure known as Sealand (a micronation). Their hopes rested on the creation of a data paradise, a space free from surveillance, consumerism and a sanctuary for our online personas. In 2014, with an internet now understood and thoroughly determined by corporate desire, we saw instead that billionaires began to buy abandoned oil rigs in the Caribbean for designer resorts. The future's provenance is expressed inside this structure. It is a space to reclaim the future with data protection and the ability to digitally enact emancipatory politics, or in contrast, an oil rig is an ANCAP haven for new hyper-rich survivors of mainland disaster.

The Cloud appears to us with similar see-sawing future-oriented speculations. It's an insincerely encrypted space of good and evil, and everything viscous in-between. An abandoned oil rig stands in for the Garden of Eden, an abandoned paragraph (or book) of signifiers stands in for 5 years of exciting and dangerous music which haemorrhages its waveform in service of a future becoming. Bloody sound in a centrifuge. Hito Steyerl calls this spinning excess of sound and image in the age of digital surveillance a process of being 'represented to pieces'.[2] But un-wretched is the sound which over-represents in the service of togetherness. On 'Unequal', the third track of *Platform*, Holly Herndon sings (in counterpoint with Mat Dryhurst) a lamenting prayer for the future:

Honesty, sing prayer to save the human form. Dignity cannot be broken. Our language is power, the action we've chose. Refuse, repose. Honesty. Fight for each other. For one, as one. Why? Why are we unequal? Honest — Parity, why are we? To change the shape of our future, to be unafraid, to break away. Dignity, Identity, why are we? A louder fight, a harder fight. For one, as one.

In this clear semantic language, one doesn't hear the unspeakable, untranslatable imagining of a future. Instead one hears a 'Platform' to imagine the future. Metaphors are platforms for giving sound agency. In Herndon's sonic allusions, the future is thought out from within our own language. Verbs have nouns, the Human is affirmed not denied. There is clarity and sincerity. In a swell of instrumental chaos Herndon's particulate voice bounces underneath the main lyrical line, cut and fragmented into the middle of words, placing us unexpectedly within the processes of her voice. This is anastrophic music. Whatever chaos the Cloud inspires in us is clearly placed underneath the foregrounded clarity. The dislocation is secondary to a message for a future coming together. The foreground is whole, and it is as if we have overcome the fragmentation of the background — to become unified.

The underlying tension throughout this book has been a questioning of whether art should function as a critical hammer, or as a mirror. I've so far confronted music which reflects and exaggerates dystopia, that which performatively affirms, which relies misguidedly on irony, and revels rather than negates. At the same time, I hope that what has grown in the space around my confrontations is an understanding of what might be the potential musical antidote. I'll redouble on my message: imaginative, honest and playful speculation denies dystopia.

Earlier, I also touched on a few moments of *play* which I might clarify as a form of conclusion to all that has been discussed. David Kanaga's insistence that games are formalised play leads me to a possible conclusion: *play is formalised honesty.* Throughout, I've hinted at moments of formalised honesty which are found in the construction of the voice: be that in the playing with the innards of a vocaloid, the fictional creation of online identities, role-playing in the comment sections of virtual radio stations, formalised acts of uncertainty, play in non-linear games and play in the training of an inhuman machine-learned intelligence. But most importantly, it seems that the Cloud, in general, offers up a daily, moment-to-moment form of play which seems so so close to what might be called a 'utopian freedom *without necessity*'. Friedrich Schiller's *On the Aesthetic Education of Man*[3] suggests that play reconciles what he takes to be the two fundamental drives of social beings: a material drive and a formal drive. Play encompasses both a physicality and a formality. Play is both pleasure and reason. Hence, 'man only plays when he is in the fullest sense of the word a human being'.

Taking up Schiller, Herbert Marcuse proposes that play might be the primary feature for a future post-capitalist world free from alienated work. To play is to be liberated from necessity and from the alienating tendencies of goal-oriented labour. It is in play that we pick up and refigure an instrument's strings, when we produce, without necessity, a song. Everyday interactions in the Cloud seem to frequently border this fundamental freedom. We browse *sometimes* without compulsion or necessity, we often listen without necessity, at times we even interact with strangers on social media without material drive. Yet, streaming services threaten to co-opt play into somatic playlists. Necessity is introduced unnecessarily in the always-ticking-on-over to the next song. In a similar way, the over-representation of the future threatens to take the enjoyment of the dark, of dancing to fragmentation and destruction, and make marketed and actual versions of what we once played about in acts of resistance. When soft-drink companies write of deconstruction as progress, when the economics of platforms dictate form in aesthetics, I'm reminded that play is vulnerable, that liberation within a confined club space is easily repurposed, that new imagination is ruthlessly locked up as soon as it escapes a hopeful noggin. I started writing what would become this book at the end of 2016. Since then, there has been quite a shift away from those one-dimensional dystopias I initially aimed to question. In the past, Bjork was rarely 'dystopian', yet the title of her latest album, *Utopia*, captures this wider cultural change both crudely and perfectly. In the face of recent politics, the praxis of the experimental music scene has clearly reacted. *Sophie* moved on from a past reliance on irony, and emerged renewed to the world with a proud statement of identity in her beautifully honest track: 'It's Okay To Cry'. Perhaps inspired, if not a little too late by Holly Herndon's original 2014 message, a range of anastrophic musics came into being in 2017. Yves Tumor released *Experiencing the Deposit of Faith*: no serpents, no dystopia, instead gentleness and softness. Jlin and Errorsmith redoubled their efforts to make profoundly joyous and playful music. Félicia Atkinson and Mhysa took the spoken voice, the whispering voice and set it to work for an honest politics. And Daniel Lopatin even sings (albeit with CCRU lyrics) in a relatively unprocessed and perhaps *honest* way on the first single from his new 2018 album. To take what was discovered in the logorrheic over-abundant murk of the poorly-politicised club space, perhaps it is the right kind of sentimentality to claim that we, in the plural, can learn and *have* learned from these investigations. With these changes, we shore up new communalities for a fresh and radically imagined future. Among the sounds of the platforms which weigh upon our writing and listening, and within the lithe and grounded world around us, audible and political enchantment is so needed. The challenge is to protect and nurture this music.

Acknowledgements

For a period during the writing of this book, I was sat working in a one-room Berlin flat with my partner Alice. At night we'd play the 90s SNES game *Earthbound* in which a group of kids fight an alien force brainwashing the citizens of Earth into 'salarymen' tainted by corporate greed. The protagonist of the game is visited by a heroic figure who hands him a small device for recording the sound of these defeated alien invaders. At the moment of vanquishing one of these bosses, you'd step out into a beautiful sparkling vista and hear a melody on the wind. These tiny snippets of music somehow evoked that feeling of saving the world. You'd hold out your little recording device, or ear, and stand there enveloped in the sound. Just four note melodies. I began to think of this book as a similar recording device, and that I was searching for some kind of saviour in the music I laboured over and for some kind of way to express how it touched me. I'd like to thank and acknowledge Alice for her support, inspiration and a kindness which wrapped me up and protected me. In the same way, to all my friends who read my drafts and advised me and just talked with me, you were a frequent warmth and mesh of support at the back of my mind. Thank you Eli for your friendship and meticulous help. To John Romans for your copy-edit, to Tom Kemp for your wonderful cover images which I shall cherish, to Benjamin Noys for your moving dedication, and to the *Royal Conservatoire*, Samuel, and the teachers who guided and allowed me the space to formulate a prototype of these ideas into a Master's Thesis, thank you. Finally, to my parents and family who were a constant source of guidance, care and love, to Doug and Zero Books for taking a chance on a new author, and to all the artists who both made this music and took the time to talk to me about it, I thank you.

Notes

Mackerel Sky Prologue

1. Jane Bennett, *The Enchantment of Modern Life: Attachments, Crossings and Ethics* (Princeton and Oxford: Princeton University Press, 2001), 155.
2. Bennett, *Vibrant Matter: A Political Ecology of Things* (Durham and London: Duke University Press, 2010), 7.
3. See, Gerald Raunig, *A Thousand Machines*, Translated by Aileen Derieg (Cambridge MA: MIT Press, 2010).
4. Karl Marx, 'The Fragment on Machines' from *The Grundrisse: Foundations of the Critique of Political Philosophy*, Translated by Martin Nicolaus (London and New York: Penguin Classics, 1993), 706.
5. Francois J Bonnet, *Order of Sounds: A Sonorous Archipelago*, Translated by Robin Mackay (Windsor Quarry: Urbanomic, 2016), 7.
6. Lynne Segal Quoting Fredric Jameson, *Radical Happiness: Moments of Collective Joy* (London and New York: Verso, 2017), 157-158.
7. Seth Kim-Cohen, *In the Blink of an Ear: Toward a Non-Cochlear Sonic Art* (London: Continuum, 2009).

Chapter 1: Sweet Music

1. Sweet Music Lady, *About*, YouTube, accessed 22/12/2017, https://www.youtube.com/user/chedwinikei/about
2. Diedrich Diederichsen, 'Music-Immateriality-Value', *The Internet Does Not Exist*, Ed. Julieta Aranda, Anton Vidokle, Brian Kuan Wood, (Berlin: Sternberg Press, 2015), 111-112.
3. The 'Altwoke' quote, Kevin Kelly, *Invention and Discovery are the Same*, KK, accessed 20/12/2017, http://kk.org/thetechnium/invention-and-d/

4. Sianne Ngai, *Ugly Feelings* (Cambridge MA and London: Harvard University Press, 2005), 43.

5. Kant Bot, Twitter, accessed 11/11/2017 https://twitter.com/KANTBOT20K

6. Arctic Empire, *Epic Chillstep Collection 2015 [2 Hours]*, YouTube, accessed 16/11/2017, https://www.youtube.com/watch?v=fWRISvgAygU

7. Nikolas Rose, *The Politics of Life Itself* (Princeton: Princeton University Press, 2007).

8. Jake Paul, YouTube, https://www.youtube.com/channel/UCcgVECVN4OKV6DH1jLkqmcA

9. Dr Disrespect, Twitch, https://www.twitch.tv/drdisrespectlive

10. Brandon LaBelle, *Sonic Agency: Sound and Emergent Forms of Resistance* (London: Goldsmiths Press, 2018), 16.

11. See Joanna Demers, *Anatomy of Thought Fiction* (Zero Books, 2017).

12. Paul Roquet quotes Watsuji Tetsurō from *Climate and Culture*, in *Ambient Media / Japanese Atmospheres of the Self* (Minneapolis: University of Minnesota Press, 2016), 7.

13. Paul Roquet, *Ambient* Media, 7-8.

14. See the new right 'frog-twitter' awards show and 'culture' journal, *Autistic Mercury*, http://www.autisticmercury.com/and-the-nominees-are...html

Chapter 2: Enchantment can be Formalised

1. Jack Kerouac, 'Sea: Sounds of the Pacific Ocean at Big Sur', *Big Sur* (Penguin Books, 1962), 112.

2. See 'Phone Voyants', James A Herrick, *Scientific Mythologies: How Science and Science Fiction Forge New Religious Beliefs* (Downers Grove: InterVarsity Press, 2008), 114.

3. See Sophie Fyfe, Claire Williams, Oscar Mason, and Graham Pickup, 'Apophenia, theory of mind and schizotypy: Perceiving meaning and intentionality in

randomness', *Cortex* 44, no. 10 (2008), 1316-1325.

4. Gilles Deleuze and Felix Guattari, quoted in *Necroeconomics*, https://steemit.com/accelerationism/@altwoke/hlax-hyper-left-accelerationism-the-short-and-dirty-version

5. Bonnet, *Order of Sounds*, 135.

6. Roland Barthes, 'Listening', quoted by Bonnet, *Order of Sounds*, 135.

7. Conscious Collective, *Max loughan CERN could destroy the universe!!, Full Length HQ*, YouTube, 2017, accessed 5/12/2017, https://www.youtube.com/watch?v=OfMl1ptqi3Y

8. Adam Curtis, *HyperNormalisation*, BBC, 2016.

9. The Invisible Committee, *To Our Friends* (South Pasadena: Semiotexte, 2014), 22.

10. Hannah Barton, 'Memes, Manifestations and Magical Thinking', lecture 22/3/2017, Stedelijk Gallery, Amsterdam.

11. Carole M Cusack, *Fiction, Invention and Hyper-reality: From Popular Culture to Religion* (London: Routledge, 2016), 184.

12. See, Patrick Dunn, Postmodern Magic: The Art of Magic in the Information Age

13. (Llewellyn Publications, 2005).

14. ZEROACH, *Mermeticism and the Post-Truth Mystic*, Ensorcel, 2017, accessed 10/11/2017 https://ensorcel.org/mermeticism-and-the-post-truth-mystic/

15. See, William Breeze, 'De Harmonia Mundi', *Arcana V: Music, Magic, Mysticism*, Ed. John Zorn (New York: Art Publishers, 2010).

16. See Silvia Federeci, *Caliban and the Witch: Women, the Body and Primitive Accumulation* (Autonomedia, 2004).

17. Iannis Xenakis, *Formalised Music: Thought and Mathematics in Composition* (New York: Pendragon Press, 1992), 4.

18. See https://www.ccc.de/en/ Chaos Computer Club. A declaration of the independence of Cyberspace manifesto https://www.eff.org/cyberspace-independence.

19. Lisa Blanning, *GEN F: TCF Turns Algorithms into Music*,

Fader, 2014, accessed 13/1/2018, http://www.thefader.com/2014/10/01/gen-f-tcf-interview

20. See Wendy Hui Kyong Chun, *Programmed Visions: Software and Memory* (Cambridge MA: MIT Press, 2011).

21. Caleb Garling, *Smart Software Can Be Tricked into Seeing What Isn't There*, MIT Technology Review, 2014, accessed 9/6/2017 https://www.technologyreview.com/s/533596/smart-software-can-be-tricked-into-seeing-what-isnt-there/

22. Peli Grietzer, *A Theory of Vibe*, 'Glass-Bead' 2017, accessed 22/1/2018, http://www.glass-bead.org/article/a-theory-of-vibe/?lang=enview

23. Nina Power, *Inhumanism, Reason, Blackness, Feminism*, 'Glass-Bead' 2017, accessed 3/3/2018, http://www.glass-bead.org/article/inhumanism-reason-blackness-feminism/?lang=enview

24. Hito Steyerl, *Duty Free Art: Art in the Age of Planetary Civil War* (London and New York: Verso, 2017), 105.

25. See dubious headline, Cherei Hu, *Why Spotify Thinks Its 'Self-Driving Music' Will Benefit Creators*, Billboard, 2018, accessed 21/3/2018, https://www.billboard.com/articles/business/8249695/why-spotify-thinks-self-driving-music-strategy-will-benefit-creators

26. Ana Teixeira Pinto, *Biased Futures Lecture*, Transmediale 2018, Berlin.

27. Bonnet, *Order of Sounds*, 130.

Chapter 3: Revenant Speed: Spirits of the Singularity

1. E M Forster, *The Machine Stops*, accessed 4/2/2018, http://archive.ncsa.illinois.edu/prajlich/forster.html

2. See Eugene Thacker, *Cosmic Pessimism* (University of Minnesota Press, 2015).

3. Eldritch Priest, *To Make a Better Crease,* TheOcculture, 2013, accessed 9/11/2016, http://www.theocculture.net/to-make-a-better-crease/

4. See, Elizabeth Sandifer, *Neoreaction a Basilisk: Essays on* and Around the Alt-Right (Eruditorum Press, 2017).

5. Syffr, *Requiem for Left-Accelerationism*, Medium, 2017, accessed 8/6/2017 https://medium.com/@syffr/requiem-for-left-accelerationism-4048d8bec72e

6. Benjamin Noys, *Apocalypse, Tendency, Crisis*, Mute, 2010, accessed 3/4/2017 http://www.metamute.org/editorial/articles/apocalypse-tendency-crisis

7. Wolfram Klinger, *Silicon Valley's Radical Machine Cult*, Motherboard 2017, accessed 14/12/2017, https://motherboard.vice.com/en_us/article/kz7jem/silicon-valley-digitalism-machine-religion-artificial-intelligence-christianity-singularity-google-facebook-cult

8. N1x, *Cyber-Nihilist Manifesto*, Ensorcel, 2017, accessed 4/1/2018, https://ensorcel.org/author/n1x/

9. N1x, *Cyber-Nihilist Manifesto*.

10. Land describes himself in *Collapse* as, 'a palsied mantis constructed from black jumpers and secondhand Sega circuitry, stalking the crumbling corridors of academe systematically extirpating all humanism.' See *Collapse Vol.1* (Urbanomic, 2006).

11. See Land, *Fanged Noumena,* 'Shamanistic Nietzsche'. And Lord of Null Lines, *Hyper on Experience*, YouTube 2009, accessed 14 January 2017, https://www.youtube.com/watch?v=NwQYGIeppBk

12. Rif on Ed Atkins, *A primer for Cadavers* (London: Fitzcarraldo Editions, 2016).

13. Nick Land, *Fanged Noumena: Collected Writings 1987-2007* (Urbanomic, 2012).

14. Matthew Phillips, *2015: The Neofuturist Aesthetic: Technology and Counterfuture in the Electronic Avant-Garde,* Tiny Mixtapes, 2015, accessed 13/11/2016, http://www.tinymixtapes.com/features/2015-neofuturist-aesthetic

15. Benjamin Noys, *Days of Phuture Past: Accelerationism in the*

Present Moment, lecture from 'Accelerationism – a symposium on tendencies in capitalism' (Berlin, 14 December 2013), 2.

16. Mark Fisher comes to the same conclusions in Chicago Footwork, in *Break it Down: Mark Fisher on DJ Rashads 'DoubleCup',* Electronic Beats, 2013.

17. http://www.e-flux.com/journal/79/94686/1-life-0-blackness-or-on-matter-beyond-the-equation-of-value/

18. Aria Dean, *Notes on Blacceleration,* Eflux, 2017, accessed 3/12/2017, https://www.e-flux.com/journal/87/169402/notes-on-blacceleration/

19. Kodwo Eshun, *More Brilliant than the Sun: Adventures in Sonic Fiction* (Quartet Books, 1998), [A]193.

20. Eleni Ikoniadou in *The Rhythmic Event: Art, Media, And the Sonic,* writes: 'Folding bending and stretching form arises out of a direct link between mathematical models of topology and computer techniques.' (MIT Press, 2014), 36.

21. See, Gean Moreno, 'Notes on the Inorganic, Part 1: Accelerations', *Internet Does Not Exist.*

22. CCRU, 'Swarmmachines', *Ccru Writings 1997-2003* (Time Spiral Press, 2015).

23. Robert Hassan, *Empires of Speed: Time and the Acceleration of Politics and Society* (Brill, 2009), 67.

24. Patricia MacCormac, 'Cosmogenic Acceleration: Futurity and Ethics', *The Internet Does Not Exist,* Ed. Julieta Aranda, Anton Vidokle, Brian Kuan Wood, (Sternberg Press: 2015), 299.

25. See Anna Lowenhaupt Tsing, *The Mushroom at the End of the World: On the Possibility of Life in Capitalist Ruins* (Princeton University Press, 2017).

26. Ray Brassier, 'Prometheanism and Real Abstraction', *Speculative Aesthetics,* Ed. Robin Mackay, Luke Pendrell, James Trafford (Falmouth: Urbanomic, 2014), 74.

27. Michael James, '*The Only Thing I would Impose is Fragmentation' – An Interview with Nick Land,* Archive Fire, 2017, accessed

4/7/2017, https://syntheticzero.net/2017/06/19/the-only-thing-i-would-impose-is-fragmentation-an-interview-with-nick-land/

28. Georg Lukács, quoted by Parralaxoptics, *Faster, Daddy: A Tale of N Accelerationisms,* accessed 7/2/2018, https://parallaxoptics.wordpress.com/2018/02/05/faster-daddy-a-tale-of-n-accelerationisms/

29. Parralaxoptics, *Faster, Daddy.*

30. Parralaxoptics, *Faster, Daddy.*

31. Ngai, *Ugly Feelings*, 20.

32. Carl Freedman, *Art and Idea in the Novels of China Miéville* (Gylphi Limited, 2015), 40.

33. Reinhart Koselleck, 'Crisis', Translated by Michaela W Richter, *Journal of the History of Ideas*, Vol. 67 (2), 2006, pp. 357-400.

34. Peter Stadler, 'Wirtschaftskrise und Revolution bei Marx und Engels. Zur Entwicklung ihres Denkens in den 50er Jahren', *Historische Zeitschrift*, Vol. 199 (1), 1964, pp. 113-114.

35. Eugene Thacker, *In the Dust of This Planet: Horror of Philosophy Vol.1* (Zero Books, 2011), 1.

36. LaBelle, *Sonic Agency*, 21.

37. Read Xenogoth at https://vastabrupt.com/2018/01/16/reaching-beyond-to-the-other/

38. Philip Sherburne, *Fix the Future: Holly Herndon's Collective Vision,* Pitchfork, 2015, accessed 16/7/2016, http://pitchfork.com/features/update/9619-fix-the-future-holly-herndons-collective-vision/

39. Mauricio Vargas, *Interview with Chino Amobi*, Blaaah Magazine, 2016, accessed 13/1/2018, http://www.theblaaahg.com/interview-with-chino-amobi/

40. Kodwo Eshun, Mark Fisher Memorial Lecture, 19/1/2018, Goldsmiths, London.

41. Eshun, Memorial Lecture.

Flooded World Prologue

1. Independently, me and theorist Rebekah Sheldon have intuited the importance of this opening of The Road. A heartfelt recommendation to read her monograph *The Child to Come*, and thus I quote her phrase here.

2. Pedro Neves Marques, 'Look Above the Sky is Falling: Humanity Before and After the End of the World', *Supercommunity*, Ed. Julieta Aranda, Brian Kuan Wood, Anton Vidokle (London and New York: Verso, 2017), 414.

3. Douglas Kahn, *Noise Water Meat: A History of Sound in the Arts* (Cambridge MA: MIT Press, 2001), 110.

Chapter 4: Oil Music

1. John Wiseman, *The Great Energy Transition of the 21st Century: The 2050 Zero-Carbon World Oration*, ResearchGate, accessed 5/1/2018, https://www.researchgate.net/publication/320901928_The_great_energy_transition_of_the_21st_century_The_2050_Zero-Carbon_World_Oration

2. Bogna Konior, *Generic Humanity: interspecies technologies, climate change and non-standard animism*, Academia, accessed 12/4/2018, https://www.academia.edu/35564703/Generic_humanity_interspecies_technologies_climate_change_and_non-standard_animism_2017_

3. See Timothy Morton, *Realist Magic: Objects, Ontology, Causality* (Open Humanities Press, 2013).

4. Carolyn L Kane, 'Plastic Shine: From Prosaic Miracle to Retrograde Sublime', *Supercommunity*, Ed. Julieta Aranda, Brian Kuan Wood, Anton Vidokle (London and New York: Verso, 2017), 157.

5. Kane quotes, Susan Freinkel, 'Our "Toxic" Love-Hate Relationship with Plastics', *Fresh Air*, National Public Radio, 19/4/2011.

6. Kenneth Goldsmith, *Uncreative Writing* (New York: Columbia University Press, 2011), 96.

7. Grafton Tanner, *Babbling Corpse: Vaporwave and the Commodification of Ghosts* (Zero Books, 2016), 12.

8. See Ben Esposito, *Ambient Dark Souls*, accessed 3/1/2018, http://torahhorse.com/Ambient-Dark-Souls

9. The ASMR Geek, Bioshock Ambience – Welcome To Rapture (ASMR, White Noise, Relaxation), YouTube, 2017, accessed 3/1/2018, https://www.youtube.com/watch?v=W8pzvRVtXvE

10. See, Fredric Jameson, *Postmodernism, Or, The Cultural Logic of Late Capitalism* (Durham: Duke University Press, 1991).

11. David Kanaga, *Music, Object, Substance, Organism (GDC 14)*, Vimeo, 2014, accessed 14/12/2017, https://vimeo.com/90271157

12. David Kanaga, 'Ecooperatic Music Game Theory', *The Oxford Handbook of Algorithmic Composition*, Ed. Alex McLean, Roger T Dean (Oxford: Oxford University Press, 2018), 453.

13. Everist Pipkin, *An Interview with Dog Opera manager and Koch Games employee David Kanaga, on Oikospiel, Book I*, Medium, 2017, accessed 14/12/2017, https://medium.com/@everestpipkin/an-interview-with-dog-opera-manager-and-koch-games-employee-david-kanaga-on-oikospiel-book-i-452c10c2f76a

14. Moreno, *Notes on the Inorganic*, 82.

Chapter 5: Chimeric Flesh and the Hyper-Child

1. Timothy Morton, 'Spectral Life', *Posthumous Life: Theorizing Beyond the Posthuman,* Ed. Jami Weinstein, Clare Colebrook (New York: Columbia University Press, 2017).

2. At the time of writing these eight videos Как сделать гомункула (Homunculus) have close to 25 million views. https://www.youtube.com/watch?v=HNLPXzlz6-I

3. See, Oneohtrix Point Never, *Sticky Drama,* YouTube, 2015, accessed 15/9/2016, https://www.youtube.com/watch?v=td-

e4i2BL_Q

4. See, Hiroshi Aoyagi, *Islands of Eight Million Smiles*: *Idol Performance and Symbolic Production in Contemporary Japan* (Harvard: Harvard University Press, 2005).

5. Yuji Sone, 'Hatsune Miku, Virtual Machine-Woman', *Japanese Robot Culture: Performance, Imagination, and Modernity* (Palgrave Macmillan, 2017), 140.

6. Translation from the software: Vocaloid3 Hatsune Miku V3 Bundle, *Expansion Pack*, made by Crypton Future Media.

7. Morton, 'Spectral Life'.

8. William Gillis, *Authoritarians and the Ideology of Love*, Human Iterations, 2017, accessed 3/2/2018, http://humaniterations. net/2017/05/23/authoritarians-and-ideology-of-love/

9. Julia Kristeva, *Powers of Horror: An Essay on Abjection*, Translated by Leon S Roudiez (Colombia University Press, 1982), 3.

10. Vyshali Manivannan, *Attaining the Ninth Square: Cybertextuality, Gamification, and Institutional Memory on 4chan*, Enculturation, 2012, accessed 4/2/2017, http:// enculturation.camden.rutgers.edu/attaining-the-ninth-square

11. Peter Sotos and Jamie Gillis, *Pure Filth* (Feral House, 2012).

12. Scott Wilson, *Oneohtrix Point Never Unpicks the Secrets of Garden of Delete*, FactMagazine, 2015, accessed 5/11/2016, http://www.factmag.com/2015/11/12/oneohtrix-point-never-garden-of-delete-interview/

13. Timothy Morton, *Hyperobjects: Philosophy and Ecology after the End of the World* (Minneapolis: University of Minnesota Press, 2013), 30.

14. VNS Matrix, *Cyberfeminist Manifesto of the 21st Century*, Sterneck 1991, accessed 4/10/2017, http://www.sterneck. net/cyber/vns-matrix/index.php

15. Kristeva, *Powers of Horror*, 69-71.

Chapter 6: Whispered Honesty

1. Patrick Frank, *CRITIQUE*, Lecture: Darmstadt 48th International Festival for New Music, 2016.

2. Corey Savage, *Four Reasons Why The Collapse Will Be The Best Thing to Happen For Men,* Return of Kings, 2016, accessed, 18/1/2017, http://www.returnofkings.com/88671/4-reasons-why-collapse-will-be-the-best-thing-to-happen-for-men

3. Gentle Whispering ASMR, - -ASMR Gentlemen's Suit Fitting Session- -, YouTube, 2013, accessed 7/2/2017, https://www.youtube.com/watch?v=tO9JGISzb9Q

4. Pandora ASMR, *ASMR You've Been Mind Controlled! Dieslepunk Dystopian Role Play,* YouTube, 2017, accessed 21/3/2018, https://www.youtube.com/watch?v=e90Lc1L8h-M

5. Phillip Sherburne, *Fix the Future: Holly Herndon's Collective Vision,* Pitchfork, 2015, accessed 10/12/2016, https://pitchfork.com/features/update/9619-fix-the-future-holly-herndons-collective-vision/

6. Youarelamedot.com, *Dedekind Cut + Yves Tumor's Trump$America,* YouTube, 2017, accessed 5/3/2017, https://www.youtube.com/watch?v=HLu5fuAS2s0

7. Morton, *Hyperobjects,*190.

8. Morton, *Hyperobjects,* 173.

9. Toby Shorin, *Haute Baroque Capitalism* quoting Gean Moreno, *Notes on the Inorganic,* Subpixel Space, 2017, accessed 8/9/2017, https://subpixel.space/entries/haute-baroque-capitalism/

10. Ngai, *Ugly Feelings,* 27.

11. Donna Hahastuneraway, *Simians, Cyborgs, and Women: The Reinvention of Nature* (Routledge, 1990), 291.

12. Metahaven, *Can Jokes Bring Down Governments: Memes, Design and Politics* (Strelka Press, 2013), 27.

Epilogue: An Abandoned Oil Rig Stands in for the Garden of Eden

1. Jaakko Pallasvou, 'AS ANGELS RIG HOOK', SoundCloud, accessed 1/10/2016, https://soundcloud.com/amnesia-scanner/as-angels-rig-hook-1

2. Hito Steyerl, *The Spam of the Earth: Withdrawal from Representation*, Eflux, 2012, accessed 9/3/2017, https://www.e-flux.com/journal/32/68260/the-spam-of-the-earth-withdrawal-from-representation/

3. Friedrich Schiller, *On the Aesthetic Education of Man* (Dover Publications, 2004), 107.

Hearing the Cloud

CULTURE, SOCIETY & POLITICS

Contemporary culture has eliminated the concept and public figure of the intellectual. A cretinous anti-intellectualism presides, cheer-led by hacks in the pay of multinational corporations who reassure their bored readers that there is no need to rouse themselves from their stupor. Zer0 Books knows that another kind of discourse – intellectual without being academic, popular without being populist – is not only possible: it is already flourishing. Zer0 is convinced that in the unthinking, blandly consensual culture in which we live, critical and engaged theoretical reflection is more important than ever before.

If you have enjoyed this book, why not tell other readers by posting a review on your preferred book site.

Recent bestsellers from Zero Books are:

In the Dust of This Planet
Horror of Philosophy vol. 1
Eugene Thacker
In the first of a series of three books on the Horror of Philosophy, *In the Dust of This Planet* offers the genre of horror as a way of thinking about the unthinkable.
Paperback: 978-1-84694-676-9 ebook: 978-1-78099-010-1

Capitalist Realism
Is there no alternative?
Mark Fisher
An analysis of the ways in which capitalism has presented itself as the only realistic political-economic system.
Paperback: 978-1-84694-317-1 ebook: 978-1-78099-734-6

Rebel Rebel
Chris O'Leary
David Bowie: every single song. Everything you want to know, everything you didn't know.
Paperback: 978-1-78099-244-0 ebook: 978-1-78099-713-1

Cartographies of the Absolute
Alberto Toscano, Jeff Kinkle
An aesthetics of the economy for the twenty-first century.
Paperback: 978-1-78099-275-4 ebook: 978-1-78279-973-3

Malign Velocities
Accelerationism and Capitalism
Benjamin Noys
Long listed for the Bread and Roses Prize 2015, *Malign Velocities* argues against the need for speed, tracking acceleration as the symptom of the ongoing crises of capitalism.
Paperback: 978-1-78279-300-7 ebook: 978-1-78279-299-4

Meat Market
Female Flesh under Capitalism
Laurie Penny
A feminist dissection of women's bodies as the fleshy fulcrum of capitalist cannibalism, whereby women are both consumers and consumed.
Paperback: 978-1-84694-521-2 ebook: 978-1-84694-782-7

Poor but Sexy
Culture Clashes in Europe East and West
Agata Pyzik
How the East stayed East and the West stayed West.
Paperback: 978-1-78099-394-2 ebook: 978-1-78099-395-9

Romeo and Juliet in Palestine
Teaching Under Occupation
Tom Sperlinger
Life in the West Bank, the nature of pedagogy and the role of a university under occupation.
Paperback: 978-1-78279-637-4 ebook: 978-1-78279-636-7

Sweetening the Pill
or How We Got Hooked on Hormonal Birth Control
Holly Grigg-Spall
Has contraception liberated or oppressed women? *Sweetening the Pill* breaks the silence on the dark side of hormonal contraception.
Paperback: 978-1-78099-607-3 ebook: 978-1-78099-608-0

Why Are We The Good Guys?
Reclaiming your Mind from the Delusions of Propaganda
David Cromwell
A provocative challenge to the standard ideology that Western power is a benevolent force in the world.
Paperback: 978-1-78099-365-2 ebook: 978-1-78099-366-9

Readers of ebooks can buy or view any of these bestsellers by clicking on the live link in the title. Most titles are published in paperback and as an ebook. Paperbacks are available in traditional bookshops. Both print and ebook formats are available online.
Find more titles and sign up to our readers' newsletter at http://www.johnhuntpublishing.com/culture-and-politics
Follow us on Facebook
at https://www.facebook.com/ZeroBooks
and Twitter at https://twitter.com/Zer0Books